TEACHING BEHAVIOR
TO
INFANTS AND TODDLERS

TEACHING BEHAVIOR
TO
INFANTS AND TODDLERS
A Manual for Caregivers and Parents

By

BERNICE STEWART, ED.D.

and

JULIE S. VARGAS, PH.D.

C H A R L E S C T H O M A S • P U B L I S H E R
Springfield • Illinois • U.S.A.

Published and Distributed Throughout the World by

CHARLES C THOMAS • PUBLISHER
2600 South First Street
Springfield, Illinois 62794-9265

© *1990 by* CHARLES C THOMAS • PUBLISHER

ISBN 0-398-05638-2

Library of Congress Catalog Card Number: 89-35963

With THOMAS BOOKS *careful attention is given to all details of manufacturing
and design. It is the Publisher's desire to present books that are satisfactory as to their
physical qualities and artistic possibilities and appropriate for their particular use.*
THOMAS BOOKS *will be true to those laws of quality that assure a good name
and good will.*

Printed in the United States of America
SC-R-3

Library of Congress Cataloging-in-Publication Data

Stewart, Bernice.
  Teaching behavior to infants and toddlers: a manual for
caregivers and parents / by Bernice Stewart and Julie S. Vargas.
    p.   cm.
  Includes bibliographical references.
  ISBN 0-398-05638-2
  1. Day care centers—United States. 2. Day care centers—
Standards—United States. 3. Discipline of children.
  4. Reinforcement (Psychology)   I. Vargas, Julie S. II. Title.
HV854.S75   1990
372.21—dc20   89-35963
                                                         CIP

*To Amanda Maree Neal, a Grandchild, Eve a Mother, and
All the Babies and Their Caregivers Everywhere*

INTRODUCTION

One of the hardest decisions working parents face is choosing a child care arrangement for their young children. Different centers have different philosophies and procedures, and parents should know about and agree with those in the arrangement they choose.

There is much debate about what comprises quality care. In this book it is defined as "care that ensures the physical health and development of the child, and which provides experiences and interactions for behavioral health." The experiences and interactions that provide for behavioral health are referred to as behavioral care. Although most people are aware of the importance of good physical care during the first critical years, few people are aware of the importance of behavioral care.

Whether parents and caregivers realize it or not, what children do in a center is what that center environment is teaching them to do. Every interaction, or lack of interaction between a caregiver and baby affects the way that baby will behave in the future. Both caregivers and parents would like a center environment in which infants and toddlers thrive physically and also learn the behaviors which make babies so adorable and loving.

The basic tenet of behavioral care is teaching such appropriate behavior, and the contingencies of reinforcement are the means through which behavior is taught and learned. The contingencies of reinforcement are to behavioral care, what developmental appropriateness is to developmental care. How the contingencies of reinforcement are used to teach appropriate behavior, without the use of punishment, not even the frequently recommended timeout, is one of the two main themes of this book. The behavior of the babies in a center is not only a critical indicator of quality routine care, it is also the quality control for teaching appropriate behavior and thus behavioral care.

As the center environment in which caregivers care for their babies is specified by state licensing standards, the second theme concerns the mandated standards, the procedures they generate, and how the actions in the procedures can be selected and sequenced to streamline routine caregiving tasks. The term, care loading, which is defined as "the number of tasks a caregiver performs during a specified time," is introduced and used to analyze how the actions in procedures impact quality care. Looking at a procedure as a set of actions makes it easier not only to measure care loading for each caregiver, but also easier to measure compliance with licensing requirements. If caregivers are to have time to provide behavioral care, routine care loading must be reduced. This does not require cutting down or omitting required tasks. It implies analyzing actions in procedures and organizing them for efficiency.

The center described in the text, "Infant and Toddler Center USA," is an imaginary center. However, it reflects the elements or lack of elements of many centers in the United States as well as those in Canada and Australia. The caregivers and babies who star in the episodes are also imaginary, but again have traces of the caregivers and babies seen in the countries mentioned above. The licensing standards that underlie this imaginary center's operation have been selected from state, territory and military standards. Many were chosen, not because they were superior to others, but because they were pertinent to the episode described or the issue discussed. Although a reference is usually made to state licensing standards, it is done for economy of words. Such a reference to state licensing standards is intended to also include those of the military and the territories.

By using the positive methods for behavioral care described in this book, caregivers can teach their babies all the appropriate behaviors that make infants and toddlers so adorable and loving. Thus the time spent in centers for the children and their caregivers can not only be a pleasurable experience for them both, but can give our youngest citizens a good start in life.

ACKNOWLEDGMENTS

The authors would like to thank the personnel from the state, territory, and military licensing authorities, who promptly and courteously answered all queries, the people from the many child oriented groups and organizations who obligingly sent all information requested. Additional thanks are extended to the Dean's office and the helpful personnel in the Microcomputer Laboratory Allen Hall, West Virginia University.

Dr. Bernice Stewart would also like to thank all those, who during the past five years, so willingly offered support and encouragement. Special thanks to her children Robert, George, Patrick, Bridget, Ruth, and Amanda; sons-in-law Ronald (U.S. Army), and Mark (U.S. Marine Corp); Tina Merritt for her consideration and useful suggestions; Eve and June, child care personnel in Australia; Hilda and Dan; and last but not least Janet and Orson.

Dr. Julie S. Vargas would like to give special thanks to her husband, Ernest.

CONTENTS

TEACHING BEHAVIOR
TO
INFANTS AND TODDLERS

PART ONE
QUALITY CARE AND BEHAVIORAL HEALTH

Chapter One

PLANNING FOR QUALITY CARE

MIKKI, THE DIRECTOR OF INFANT AND TODDLER CENTER USA, CONSIDERS LICENSING STANDARDS AND QUALITY INDICATORS

OBJECTIVES

After you read this chapter you should be able to . . .

1. Briefly list the main responsibilities and duties of the director of an infant or toddler center.
2. Define quality indicators.
3. Describe the main quality indicators of a child care center, and explain why the behavior of the infants is a quality indicator.
4. Define child/staff ratio and explain how it affects the quality of care. Specify the ratio permitted in your state.
5. Identify the main functions of child care licensing authorities and standards.
6. Identify the categories of personnel mentioned in your state licensing standards, and draw up a staff work schedule.
7. Define the following terms and give or identify examples of: (a) primary caregiver; (b) balanced exchange caregiving.
8. Give examples of some different ways of defining infant and toddler and tell why the definition is important.
9. Explain the difference between physical health and behavioral health.

Today's infants and toddlers become our next generation. The quality of care they receive in their early years sets a foundation for both their physical health and for their behavioral health. Most people are aware of the importance of good physical care during the first critical years, but few people are aware of the importance of behavioral care. Yet the moment to moment interaction between caregivers and infants affects all aspects of the babies's behavior. It affects their general outlook on life, the way they interact with others, and what and how much they learn.

5

Their early experiences and opportunities thus establish behavior patterns which help or hinder their chances in life.

The lifestyle revolution of the past decade has increased dramatically the need for quality nonparental care for babies (see Appendix B: DYK 1.1). But what is quality care and who is responsible for making sure that children receive it?

When most of us think of quality care for an infant, we visualize a mother and baby laughing and playing together in a loving relationship. This picture is a good one. It is important for a baby to have close, happy, and loving interactions with caring adults. Of course, loving a baby or tickling her to make her laugh, is not all there is to quality care. But it is a beginning, and an important part as we shall see.

One individual who is responsible for quality care for children is the center director. To get a picture of what quality care involves from a director's viewpoint, we will visit Mikki, the director of Infant and Toddler Center USA.

1.1 NARRATIVE: MIKKI, THE DIRECTOR OF INFANT AND TODDLER CENTER USA, CONSIDERS LICENSING STANDARDS AND QUALITY INDICATORS

Infant and Toddler Center USA is a child care facility licensed for twenty four infants and thirty toddlers. Mikki, now forty years old with two teenage children, has been its director for three years. The center has gained a good reputation. Mikki attributes her success to the way her caregivers care for the babies and toddlers. What they do and how they do it is detailed in the procedures and plans that Mikki described in the Plan of Operation that she submitted to the Licensing Authority with her original application for a license, and the later renewals of her license.

1.1.1 The Plan Of Operation

A plan of operation states *how a center will meet or exceed the licensing requirements for the state or territory in which it will operate.* Mikki's plan went far beyond the standards required for her state. In the first few months of operating her center, Mikki wondered whether she had been too ambitious. But now, the plan was working better than even Mikki had imagined. Her major task as director of Infant and Toddler Center

USA, is to see that her staff follow the Plan of Operation, which includes everything from the design of the facility to staffing. (see Table 1.1)

1.1.2 The Design Of Infant And Toddler Center USA

Mikki designed her center with two, identical ground floor units for infants from four weeks of age to the age of walking independently, and two ground floor identical units for toddlers to two years. The license to operate the facility as an infant/toddler center, in compliance with her state's licensing requirements, is framed and posted on the wall opposite the entry door where it is visible to all who enter the center. Mikki added her own touch to the placement of the document by putting it under a large colored photograph of the infants and staff enjoying outside activities on a sunny Spring day.

Each unit is self-contained and has an open play/feeding space called the activity area, a diapering room, a formula/food preparation room, and a nap/sleeping room. There is an outdoor play area shared by all units, and an isolation room where children who become sick are cared for until their parents can take them from the center. Mikki designed the layout so all areas would be accessible and easily supervised (see Figure 5.3). The center also has a central office, a small laundry room, a staff room, and adequate bathroom facilities for the staff.

Because she wanted the center to be cheerful even on gray days, Mikki had the walls painted a light lemon yellow and placed matching print curtains on the windows. Mikki likes to keep the walls and woodwork looking fresh and bright, and believes that a little colored lead-free paint here and there makes a difference. Mikki is no artist, but she has an eye for detail and knows that a nicely framed picture or two can give life to an otherwise plain area. She has many animal pictures. Some are natural drawings and others are of Disney characters. She likes to change them every so often to suit the season, her mood, the program, or a suggestion or request from the parents or the caregivers. Mikki is partial to pandas and her office walls hold two panda pictures that she got at the Washington Zoo one summer. By shopping around Mikki was able to choose a decor that was cheerful and interesting without being cluttered.

TABLE 1.1 SAMPLE PLAN OF OPERATION (CALIFORNIA, 1988)

Each licensee shall have and maintain on file a current, written, definitive plan of operation.

The plan and related materials shall contain the following:

(1) Statement of purposes, and program methods and goals.

(2) Statement of admission policies and procedures regarding acceptance of children.

(3) A copy of the admission agreement.

(4) Administrative organization, if applicable.

(5) Staffing plan, qualifications and duties, if applicable.

(6) Plan for inservice education of staff if required by regulations governing the specific facility category.

(7) A sketch of the building(s) to be occupied, including a floor plan which describes the capacities of the buildings for the uses intended, room dimensions, and a designation of the rooms to be used for non ambulatory children, if any.

(8) A sketch of the grounds showing buildings, driveways, fences, storage areas, pools, gardens, recreation areas and other space used by the children.

(9) Sample menus and a schedule for one calendar week indicating the time of day that meals and snacks are served.

(10) Transportation arrangements for children who do not have independent arrangements.

(11) Rate setting policy including, but not limited to, policy on refunds.

Any changes in the plan of operation which affect the services to children shall be subject to licensing agency approval and shall be reported as specified in Section 101212.

The facility shall operate in accordance with the terms specified in the plan of operation. (Issue 918)

1.1.3 Staff Selection And Screening

Mikki has spent a lot of time in selecting her staff. A 1974 Child Abuse Prevention and Treatment Act, established the National Center on Child Abuse and Neglect. (see Appendix B: DYK 1.2) The center provides grants to states to help them improve their child abuse and neglect prevention and treatment programs. Such funding helps support state child abuse or neglect registries. Mikki is required to contact the registry in her state to see whether any record of child abuse or neglect concerning the applicant is filed there.

In order for her state to qualify for federal funding for training, Mikki's state licensing standards have recently been revised to match the national Model Child Care Standards (see Appendix B: DYK 1.3). Mikki is now required to initiate a fingerprint check and a check of possible criminal background for all staff. These requirements take time and cost money. Licensing Authorities generally permit applicants to start employment before the process is complete, so Mikki occasionally finishes her checks on caregiver's backgrounds after they are hired.

Mikki is also required to tell the applicant where the required health screening may be obtained, and she arranges training if the applicant does not have a current First Aid Certificate. Mikki must also verify references to make sure that the education, training, and experience that the applicant claims are accurate.

When a person inquires about a job, Mikki schedules a screening interview. In this initial interview, Mikki asks about the person's background and general outlook and philosophy about infant/toddler care. After talking, Mikki escorts the applicant, who is usually female, around the center. She always points out how the center procedures comply with the licensing requirements, and she answers any questions the woman may have. If the person wishes to apply for a position at the center, Mikki then gives her an application form to take home.

Before Mikki hires a person, she tries out the applicant. She asks her to assist in caregiving and pays her for a half a day at the center. Ruth, the program supervisor, assigns the applicant to a specific staff person who models the center procedures. Mikki and Ruth monitor this trial period closely. Mikki knows there is a lot for a new person to learn and does not expect anyone to master it all in half a day. But she does expect an applicant to interact well with the babies and she notes how the babies respond. Ruth checks on how well the applicant follows directions, observes details, and adheres to the steps modeled in the center's established caregiving routines.

After the half day trial, if the applicant shows potential as measured by Mikki and Ruth's observations, Mikki invites the parents of enrolled children to examine the application documents and Mikki's own written report of the applicant's trial performance. Finally an employment interview is scheduled. Parents may attend, and they are encouraged to question and talk with the person seeking employment at the center. Mikki explains in more detail how her center's procedures and program are formed. If all parties are in agreement, the new staff person signs a probationary contract and gives Mikki a receipt stating that she has read and agrees to follow the philosophy, rules, and regulations on which the center is run. Far from discouraging good caregivers, the tough requirements that Mikki imposes have brought her an excellent staff.

1.1.4 The Staff Of Infant And Toddler Center USA

In each of the four units Mikki employs three full time caregivers who work an eight hour shift from 7:00 AM to 3:00 PM. They are relieved by three part time caregivers who work a three and a half hour shift from 2:45 PM to 6:15 PM. Another part time person (Tamie) works from 11:00 AM to 2:30 PM to help relieve the caregivers for their daily lunch breaks. The staff use the last fifteen minutes of each shift to check and complete records.

Mikki also employs a full-time program supervisor named Ruth, who designs the daily program for the four units and directs and supervises the staff. Last, but not least, Bridget, the consultant nurse, comes once every other week. Bridget answers staff and parent questions about infant health and care. She also evaluates and directs the health care and sanitation procedures for the children. Mikki is lucky to have Bridget and Ruth. They are well-trained and experienced, and both have a friendly but no-nonsense way about them. Nothing escapes Bridget's eye, and she is not hesitant to tell Mikki if a procedure needs to be changed. Ruth can quickly define tasks, pinpoint problems, and design procedures to meet the needs of the center. Here, then, is Mikki's staffing plan. (see Table 1.2)

1.1.5 Primary Caregiving And Balanced Exchange Caregiving

Some states have no requirements about which staff members take care of which babies. Other states require that a specific adult be assigned to

TABLE 1.2   MIKKI'S STAFFING PLAN

Unit #1 (Infants)		Unit #2 (Infants)	
FULL TIME STAFF			
Amanda	7:00 AM - 3:00 PM	Jean	7:00 AM - 3:00 PM
Priscilla	7:00 AM - 3:00 PM	Edna Mae	7:00 AM - 3:00 PM
Eve	7:00 AM - 3:00 PM	June	7:00 AM - 3:00 PM
PART TIME STAFF			
Marilyn	2:45 PM - 6:15 PM	Lindsey	2:45 PM - 6:15 PM
Joyce	2:45 PM - 6:15 PM	Hilda	2:45 PM - 6:15 PM
Beverly	2:45 PM - 6:15 PM	Mary Lou	2:45 PM- 6:15 PM

Unit # 3 (Toddlers)		Unit # 4 (Toddlers)	
FULL TIME STAFF			
Justine	7:00 AM - 3:00 PM	Beth	7.00 AM - 3.00 PM
Kris	7:00 AM - 3:00 PM	Niley	7.00 AM - 3.00 PM
Carol	7:00 AM - 3:00 PM	Michelle	7.00 AM - 3.00 PM
PART TIME STAFF			
Victoria	2:45 PM - 6:15 PM	Colleen	2:45 PM - 6:15 PM
Liz	2:45 PM - 6:15 PM	Lilli	2:45 PM - 6:15 PM
Susan	2:45 PM - 6:15 PM	Audree	2:45 PM- 6:15 PM

PROGRAM SUPERVISOR
Ruth: 8 hours per day. Time scheduled between Units #1, #2, #3, and #4

CONSULTANT NURSE
Bridget: 1 hour in each unit every other week

SUBSTITUTE STAFF
On call as needed. Names and numbers posted by the telephone

LUNCH BREAK
Full time Staff, 1/2 hour each: Arranged from 11:00 AM to 2:00 PM
Mikki, Ruth and Tamie (fill in caregivers)

COFFEE BREAKS
As needed or when convenient.

each group of children or that a specific adult be assigned to each infant as that baby's primary caregiver. Mikki's state has no requirements about staff assignment, but Mikki feels that the primary caregiver system benefits both infants and caregivers. The stability of interacting with the same person every day allows special relationships to develop between babies and primary caregivers. Mikki believes that this is the first step in removing the custodial or institutional label that center-based child care has received.

The system works as follows: A baby, for example, Tina, is assigned to a caregiver named Amanda, who welcomes her in the morning and is responsible for her needs throughout the day. Although Amanda is Tina's primary caregiver, other caregivers also interact with the baby. Mikki finds that her center runs more smoothly when caregivers follow what she calls balanced exchange caregiving and which she describes as a temporary exchanging of infants for care so caregiving tasks between caregivers are balanced or more evenly spread out. Balanced exchange caregiving lets caregivers assist each other during rushed times. One of a caregiver's babies may awake from a nap just as a parent of another arrives, a third conspicuously needs a diaper change, and a fourth needs to be fed. Another caregiver may have one or more infants absent that day, or perhaps sleeping. It makes sense for the caregiver with fewer babies to help the one who has several babies needing care.

The infants also benefit socially through the balanced exchanges. While still receiving continuity of care by their primary caregivers they get to know all the staff, and they also learn to interact with other babies besides those in their own primary caregiver's group. Mikki explains to her staff that this helping out is a *balanced exchange* and *not* a shifting of care. Primary caregivers are still responsible for their infants.

1.1.6 Child/Staff Ratio

The ratio of number of children to the number of caregivers in a center is called the child/staff ratio. A child/staff ratio of six to one (6:1) means that for every six infants there is one caregiver directly caring for them. A person doing cleaning or clerical tasks is not counted in the child/staff ratio. The ratio is based only on staff directly caring for the children.

The licensing standards that Mikki follows permits a ratio of five infants to one caregiver (5:1). Mikki read that there is a trend towards lowering child/staff ratios to three infants to one caregiver (3:1). She would have liked to have had only three infants for each caregiver, but when she prepared her budget, she discovered that she needed a ratio of four infants for each caregiver (4:1) to be able to afford the quality of personnel that she wanted. Still her ratio of four to one (4:1) is better than the state licensing requirements. Mikki's center has a ratio of five toddlers to one caregiver (5:1). This is lower than the toddler/staff ratio of seven toddlers to one caregiver that is permitted by the state.

Mikki stays in touch with what is happening in the center by acting as a caregiver for two hours each day. She and the program supervisor help the part time person she hired specifically to relieve the staff for their lunch break. (When Mikki is caring for the babies, her two hours of work count towards the staff part of the child/staff ratio). When a caregiver is absent, Mikki also fills in until one of the regular substitute caregivers arrives.

Mikki likes to tell the story about the time June, one of her caregivers, thought that Friday was Saturday. June did not set her alarm clock and took the phone off the hook so she could have a nice long sleep in. When June did not arrive on time, Mikki assumed she had been caught in traffic and Mikki worked as caregiver in her place. After forty five minutes had gone by and June still had not arrived or called, Mikki tried to call her and of course could not get past the busy signal. When another half hour had elapsed and there was still no word from June, Mikki had Ruth call the center's substitute staff, but no one was immediately available.

About 11:30 June stretched lazily and decided to amble outside and pick up the paper to read with the coffee and warm croissant she was thinking of making for herself. When she saw the date, she gasped. Getting dressed and out in record time, she still arrived at the center five and a half hours late. She told Mikki she had felt as though she were in the Twilight Zone when she saw the day and date on the paper.

1.1.7 Safety And Sanitation Procedures

As director of Infant and Toddler Center USA, Mikki monitors all safety and sanitation procedures. To make sure that the center is always sanitary and fresh, she designed schedules that list the times and days when areas, equipment, and furnishings are to be cleaned (apart from spills that are cleaned immediately). Mikki has a check mark system to indicate the tasks that have been completed. The staff find it easy to work from her typed schedules because they can see who has to do what and when.

Early each day Mikki goes on an inside and outside safety check walk. So that she does not miss potential hazards she has a typed Safety/Hazard Checklist. She attaches the checklist to a stiff piece of cardboard with one of the porcelain panda clips the staff gave her for her birthday. When she scrutinizes her premises for hazards, she likes to record immediately what needs to be removed, replaced, fixed, or adjusted so that the center is always safe and meets the state safety requirements.

1.1.8 Record Keeping

The home-made clipboard holding the safety/hazard checklist is only one of the clipboards that Mikki uses. Unlike a lot of people, she actually enjoys record-keeping tasks. Not only do her records make her feel that she is doing her job well, but they make it easy to give information to the licensing authority personnel that occasionally visit. Mikki has no trouble finding the required information. She can easily locate records on the child/staff ratio, current First Aid Certificates, and inspections.

For state-required records and for those that she has added, Mikki has a color coded system. For example, although Bridget the consultant nurse, directs health care, it is Mikki's responsibility to see that the infants' immunization records are kept up to date, and to remind parents when shots are due. Mikki keeps all the infant immunization records in a red folder, and writes notes on a big monthly wall chart in her office on the days she should send parents reminders. When it comes to the babies' files, Mikki keeps to the traditional blue for boys, but as pink files are not readily available to her she uses yellow files for girls.

In each child's file, Mikki maintains the medical information required by the state, (the pre-admission medical certificate, a copy of the immunization record, an emergency care plan with telephone numbers, a record of illnesses and accidents, and special treatments including medications). In addition to these health records, Mikki also keeps on file a copy of the pre-admission identifying information, the admission agreement, the infant's daily records, as well as detailed records of the baby's behavior and of the meetings she has with his or her parents. (see Chapter Two)

1.1.9 Communicating With Parents

One of Mikki's favorite duties is talking with parents. She likes to listen to the parents tell her about how they are managing to work and care for their babies, too. She loves hearing them exchange stories about the things their babies are doing and saying, and finds it refreshing to hear them talk in a complimentary way about their babies' behaviors. Just this week, for example, she heard the following:

"He waved bye-bye to my mother. She was so happy, tears came to her eyes."

"As soon as she saw the spoon she opened her mouth. We were surprised she recognized it so quickly."

"Almost everyone in the store stopped to talk to her and she smiled and babbled to them all. Her father was so proud."

"When I said, kisses, she moved her lips and tried to kiss me. I didn't know she knew that word."

Mikki holds many discussions with the parents, both individually and in groups. She knows that they are concerned about what they see and hear in the media about the effects of center care on infants. They frequently ask her if it is true that infants cared for in centers become more insecure, withdrawn, or aggressive than babies cared for by their mothers or fathers.

Mikki usually begins her reply by assuring the parents that good center care is in no way harmful to infants. She reassures mothers that research shows their babies in day care form their primary attachments to parents and not to their center caregiver. Because several of her parents are professionals, Mikki gives them a Special Reprint of Zero to Three (September, 1986) which summarizes research on the affects of nonparental care on infants. She then broaches her favorite topic, the behavior of the babies.

Mikki believes that babies should be alert, active, responsive, and happy. There is no such thing as a bad baby. Babies respond to their environment and what they do is what they have learned through interactions with their world. Mikki keeps up a steady battle against comments like the following:

"He is four months old and mean like his granddaddy."

"Jason is a real bully."

"He spits out his vegetables. It's a stage he's going through."

"You may think she's cute for one but she's a tantrum thrower."

"Crying is natural. It is good for a baby's lungs."

"Babies are real tyrants."

Mikki tells the parents that no baby is mean or a bully. If a baby hits or grabs things or spits or throws tantrums, it is because such actions get results that the child has not learned to achieve in better ways.

One function of a center, Mikki believes is to teach those better ways. In her center, she explains to parents that every interaction between a caregiver and a baby is designed to increase the probability that the baby will behave appropriately.

In her office Mikki has a plaque placed where a visitor cannot fail to see it. It says,

"Every interaction, or lack of interaction, between a caregiver and a baby affects the way that baby will behave in the future. Good care thus includes teaching appropriate behavior."

Mikki explains that babies are learning during all of their waking hours. Whether or not parents and caregivers are aware of teaching, their moment to moment interactions with the infants affect every aspect of that baby's development.

1.1.10 Behavioral Health: An Introduction

When she interviews staff or introduces prospective parents to her center, Mikki explains her concern about the lack of awareness of the kinds of interactions needed to teach appropriate behavior. "Many infant centers," Mikki says, "provide good physical care, but *they do not pay enough attention to behavioral care.* For example, most parents tell me they want their babies to be active and happy, so we teach babies to explore their environment and not to cry."

Parents who have not heard Mikki talk about this before usually interrupt with, "But how can you teach a baby not to cry?"

"We do it by prevention and by selection," Mikki explains. "We prevent situations that are likely to encourage crying. For example, instead of waiting until a baby cries because she is hungry or bored, we anticipate her needs. This requires preplanning. (see Chapter Six) Candice, for example, is only six weeks old and she needs to be fed every three hours. Her caregiver plans ahead so she can have Candice's formula ready *before* Candice starts to whimper."

Here Mikki draws in a breath. It is more difficult to explain how to select behaviors to strengthen. "A baby's behavior is constantly changing.

Everything she does, every interaction she has with people, is a learning experience. At the most basic level, we make sure that our caregivers respond in some positive way to all of the behaviors we want to encourage. Instead of leaving alone a baby who is happily playing, for example, we make sure to catch her eye, to go over and play with her, to let her know we approve of what she is doing. You would be amazed at how sensitive babies are and how rapidly they learn."

"Really," Mikki sums up, "the behavior of the infants is one of the most important quality indicators of a center. A quality indicator," Mikki explains, "is something one must check in evaluating whether or not a center is providing quality care. In addition to checking quality indicators for health and safety, parents need to look at the behavior of the children. They should decide whether or not they would like their baby to behave like those already in the center."

Mikki always ends with some version of this statement. She finds that it is not her explanation which convinces parents, but rather their observation of the infants in her center. When the parents see the children sharing and co-operating, and even the tiny infants playing, babbling, and interacting with each other, they want to place their babies in Infant and Toddler Center USA.

1.2 ANALYSIS 1: REGULATION AND BEHAVIORAL HEALTH

The United States has a long tradition of legal protection for its young. Even in Colonial days, poor laws shielded apprenticed or indentured children from cruel or unusual treatment. Woolsey, 1977, summarizes Rothman's account of the history of child care in the United States. It began in New York in 1854 with the opening of a foundling home and day care nursery for the babies of unwed mothers. The mothers acted as wet nurses for affluent families. Out of home care increased during the war years. Under the Lanham act of 1943, the Children's Bureau (see Appendix B: DYK 1.2) approved local and state child care plans for federal funding. The first federal standards for child care were issued, but they were only recommendations and were not mandatory. After the war federal and most state funds were withdrawn. Only two states California and New York kept their state child care departments. Although the Child Welfare League of America (See Appendix B: DYK 1.4) had played a major role in setting standards for quality care during the war years, they did not publish their standards until 1960. During the late sixties, due to the renewed interest of middle class parents in sending young children to nursery schools, center care for young children again came under the spotlight. Most states once again directed their attention to licensing requirements for group care.

1.2.1 Licensing Authorities

The state licensing authorities are directed by departments which have various names, for example, the Department of Health and Social Services, or the Department of Human Resources. The authorities are frequently housed in divisions such as, Child Protective Services, Bureau of Child Development Programs (See Appendix A for a list of licensing authorities and the names of the licensing publications for the military, states, and territories). As well as overseeing the care of children in child care facilities, the licensing authorities compile and publish standards, to which licensed centers must comply. State statutes or laws, for the safety and protection of children, provide the legal base for the content of the standards, and in fact many are similar to the statutes on which they are based. The content of most statutes and standards reflects the influence of the accreditation criteria for center programs sponsored by the National Association of Early Childhood Education (NAEYC). (see Appendix B: DYK 1.5) Recent revisions of state standards have also been influenced by the Model Child Care Standards Act. Increasingly, Advisory Committees, composed of child care professionals, center personnel and parents, assist in the revision of their state standards. It is usual for the proposed standards to be published, in draft form, for a public comment period before being adopted as rules.

1.2.2 Licensing Standards
(Also Called Regulations, Rules Or Requirements)

The licensing standards published by the licensing authorities run from slender pamphlets to half inch thick handbooks with titles and content that vary from state to state. Some states call their child care facility specifications rules or regulations. Others refer to them as requirements or standards, while some states use terms such as procedures, principles, or refer to the chapter in the state code.

The term minimum used with licensing standards has caused some misunderstanding. Many people, in talking about regulations, comment that "only minimum standards are required anyway." They seem to believe that the quality level of the licensing requirements is low. But the standards published by the licensing authorities are minimum only in the sense that licensees must meet at least those requirements for the protection of the safety, health, and supervision of the children. Minimum standards do not necessarily lack vigor. In fact, many states have rigorous regulations for many aspects of care.

To expand minimum licensing standards some states have designed ways to encourage centers to go beyond what is required. New Jersey (1989) in its licensing standards uses shall to denote a provision that a center must meet to qualify for a license and should to denote "a recommendation that reflects goals towards which a center is encouraged to work." (p. 11) North Carolina (1988) has two levels of licensing. One, the A license, is issued to centers that meet minimum requirements. The other, the AA license is optional and is issued to centers who meet specified higher voluntary standards. Tennessee (1987) has licensing standards that specify both requirements and recommendations. The requirements must be met before an agency receives an annual license, or their intent demonstrated before a temporary license is issued, while "recommendations are intended to provide guidance to those who wish to go beyond minimum licensing requirements by providing for the child's total needs while in group care." (p. 7) Louisiana (1984) apart from publishing minimum standards issues a "Guidelines and Enrichment Booklet." It contains suggestions above those in the standards that centers may implement if they choose.

1.2.3 Differences In State Standards As Potential Indicators Of Quality Problems

Although minimum standards can be rigorous, some regulations are minimal as well as minimum. As late as 1988, Idaho, which has only recently established mandatory licensing for centers, specified a general limit of no more than twelve children per caregiver without a breakdown for infants and toddlers! But there are at least four cities in Idaho (Coeur d'Alene, Boise, Pocatello, and Chubbuck) that have ordinances that established more stringent standards than those specified by the state. Similarly, regulations vary from state to state. The differences include all aspects of facility regulation; caregiving policies and procedures, staff training, the physical environment, and the definitions of terms used.

The U.S. Dept. of Labor (1988) says that the differences among the states in regulating child care facilities is considered a potential indicator of quality problems.

Variation In Definition Of Infant And Toddler

State definitions of infant and toddler illustrate the variation in licensing standards. Oklahoma (1987) defines an infant as a child under nine months, and New York (1988) defines an infant as a child from eight weeks to three years, while in Alabama (1988) and Oregon (1988), an infant and toddler are defined by whether or not a baby is walking; an infant becomes a toddler when he or she starts to walk. Sometimes the terms infant and toddler are used together, for example, Kentucky (1988) uses infant/toddler to mean a child under two years, and Arkansas (1986) uses infant/toddler to refer to children between six weeks to thirty six months. Arkansas, however, specifies child/staff ratio in chronological age, and has a lower child/staff ratio for younger infants/toddlers than it does for older. Montana (1989) does not use the term toddler; a child under twenty four months of age is an infant and one over that age is a preschooler. New Jersey (1989) Iowa (1988) and North Carolina (1988), avoid both the term infant and toddler by using straight chronological age and refer to programs for children of specific ages. Some states, for example, Tennessee (1987) provide overlapping definitions to allow for more flexible grouping. One state Pennsylvania (1988) includes the term developmental level to refer to the approximate age ranges specified in the definition of infant and toddler. An infant is a child approximately 0 to 18 months, and a toddler is a child approximately 18 to 36 months. The regulations specify that "any child in these approximate age ranges may be placed in another developmental level if determined by the facility staff and the parents to be more appropriate for the child's developmental progress." (p. 8). The military also has its own definition. (see Appendix B: DYK 1.6) The U.S. Marine Corp (1983), the U.S. Navy (1983), the U.S. Air Force (1983), and the U.S. Army (Draft 1988) consider an infant to be a child under eighteen months. In the manner of the state of Arkansas the United States Navy (Draft, 1989) also specifies a lower child/staff ratio for younger infants and toddlers than it does for older ones.

Since licensing standards for infants and toddlers are written for particular age groups of babies, it is important to know which babies are covered by which regulations. A baby who is called an infant in one state could be considered a toddler in another, or even a preschooler as in the case of Montana (1989). A center licensed only for infants must adhere to standards which may require a lower infant/staff ratio than a center for toddlers.

1.2.4 Going Beyond Regulation

In the narrative section of this chapter we looked at a licensed center. We saw how Mikki, the center director, met her state's licensing standards with regard to center layout, the staffing requirement, child/staff ratios, safety and sanitation, record keeping, and communicating with parents. Mikki, however, went beyond the regulations needed for retaining her license. She required her staff to attend not only to the safety and physical development of the infants, but to work with their behavior.

To provide quality care, a center must, of course, comply with state licensing requirements, but just meeting licensing standards does not guarantee quality care. The National Academy of Early Childhood Programs offers an accreditation for center programs. (see Appendix B: DYK 1.7) As we have already said, this accreditation system has influenced the content of state standards, and there has been a general trend towards concern with behavior. Early in this century, standards emphasized *physical* health and safety. A few states, for example, Wyoming (1985) and Nevada (1989) still take that approach. The director of an infant center in Wyoming must be a registered nurse, and the director of an infant center in Nevada is required to be a registered nurse or a licensed practical nurse. Increasingly, due mainly to the efforts of NAEYC, the regulations have started mentioning the social and emotional development of the child. Most standards now require training in child development for center directors and for staff. Most states also require a planned program of developmentally appropriate activities for the children, and some kind of parental participation.

Specifying An Environment For Behavioral Health

A baby's well-being depends upon its social environment as well as its physical environment. Just as parents would not be happy with an unsafe or unhealthy physical environment, they would not want a social environment which threatened the behavioral well-being of their baby. While in most respects, the National Academy of Early Childhood Programs presents valuable components, it has not been precise enough in specifying the kinds of interactions needed for the behavioral care of infants and toddlers. Possibly for this reason behavioral health is addressed in some state standards in only the most general terms.

Caregivers are usually told to "promote the child's positive self-image" or to "foster a sense of independence", as though everyone would know how to accomplish these goals. Imagine a caregiver with four babies. The caregiver wishes to work on building "positive self-esteem." What exactly is she to *do?*

One could look in vain through most state standards for any specific suggestions. In contrast, no state standards leave the area of sanitation to a few general statements such as, "It is important to provide a sanitary environment for the child." In contrast, they specify, in great detail, specific procedures for everything from how to sanitize diaper changing tables to temperatures allowed in refrigerators used to store food.

State standards approach the subject of behavior in their discussions of discipline. Most states list methods of discipline which are NOT allowed. (see Chapter Eight) Some suggest how to handle existing problems, but they fail to address procedures for preventing the inappropriate behavior in the first place. To draw a parallel, imagine a document which encouraged sanitation and safety, but gave no guidelines except what NOT to do when a child gets sick or injured.

Fortunately, state sanitation and safety regulations follow the principle that it is better to establish an environment in which babies will not get sick or hurt in the first place. They work on preventing problems by establishing a healthy and safe environment. But licensing authorities are only beginning to address the kind of environment which provides for *behavioral* health.

Why, when behavioral health is so important, do state standards neglect to specify details to help caregivers provide it? Partly, it is because the principles governing how behavior evolves have not yet become widely understood by the public. Also it takes time for procedures that benefit children to appear in state standards. For example, before 1970, at least sixteen states failed to include regulations for discipline, even though the affect of harsh methods on a child's social and emotional health was well documented. Such lags are not unusual. They occur even in areas of biological health. It took a long time for such basic sanitation procedures as hand washing to enter the regulations, too. Prior to 1970, few standards required caregivers to wash their hands after changing a diaper, even though it was well known that disease could be spread by dirty hands.

1.2.5 Quality Care

In this book we define quality care as care that ensures the physical health and development of the child, AND which provides experiences and interactions for behavioral health. Quality care goes beyond the licensing standards in the area of behavior. Caregivers must provide those kinds of interactions which produce happy, inquisitive, and responsive children.

1.3 ANALYSIS 2: QUALITY CARE AND QUALITY INDICATORS

Factors which are critical for the health, development, and well-being of children are called quality indicators. A cheerful color scheme may impress a visitor, but the child/staff ratio is a better quality indicator of the care the infants and toddlers are receiving in that center than the way it is decorated. Center directors, like Mikki, and parents who are evaluating centers, use quality indicators to help them concentrate on the most important aspects of center care.

Many lists of quality indicators have been proposed (see Table 1.3). Some are just common sense, like a safe environment (electrical outlets covered, gates at tops and bottoms of stairs, etc.) Other quality indicators originated in research results. For example, several studies have shown group size to be related to social adjustment of infants, and group size is specifically mentioned in many lists of quality indicators. (see Chapter Five)

While agents, such as state licensing authorities, base their quality indicators on various interpretations of research results, parents judge centers more by the warmth, frequency and kind of interaction between the child and caregiver and whether or not the center's values are consistent with their own (*Working Mother Magazine*, 1988). Parents thus come close to the position taken in this book, which emphasizes child-staff interactions. But they have not quite reached the true test of a center's quality with respect to behavior; namely the behavior of the children themselves. Yes, it is important that a center has a "planned program of developmentally appropriate activities." But a program that looks good on paper must have some desirable affect on the infants and toddlers who are supposedly benefiting from it. Yes, it is important that a center provide "staff child development training." But courses and workshops for staff are only tools and are useless if the infants and

TABLE 1.3   A TYPICAL LIST OF QUALITY INDICATORS

The Report of the Secretary's Task Force (U.S. Dept. of Labor, 1988) cites these Quality Indicators:

1.   The presence of absence of a planned program of developmentally appropriate activities.

2.   The degree of parental involvement with the program, including the amount of parental access to observe the child.

3.   The training and knowledge of the staff about child development.

4.   The ratio of children to providers.

5.   The size of the groups in which children receive care.

6.   The nutritional value of the meals provided.

7.   The safety of the physical environment.

8.   Other policies and practices affecting the health of the children such as staff hygiene and the handling of medications.

<u>One item the Task Force does not include which we would add is:</u>

9.   **The behavior of the infants or toddlers.** (Are the children active, friendly, happy, and behaving the way you would want YOUR children to behave?)

toddlers do not benefit from what the staff are learning. One must look at the behavior of the infants and toddlers themselves: Are they happy, active, cooperative, alert, and inquisitive? Do they respond readily to language and delight in showing what they have learned? Are they, in sum, behaving the way you would want *your* child to behave? Along with physical development, health, and safety, behavior is THE most important quality indicator of center care.

1.3.1: The Behavioral Component Of Quality Care

The first two years are active learning years. The behaviors that babies learn, and how they learn them, during this time form the foundations for all future learning: Not only do they learn academic behaviors such as the names of things, they learn patterns of communicating with others and what the world is like—whether it is an interesting and rewarding place or a boring and frustrating one. The importance of building behavioral health cannot be over-emphasized. In fact, there is considerable evidence that the kinds of interactions occurring between infants and their caregivers affect much more than the behavior of a child. As one doctor puts it, "infants develop poorly, even die, when they are provided food and physical necessities but are denied intimate contact with caregivers." The author, Leonard Sagan (1988) pleads for the preservation of the family. But it is possible for infant care centers to provide the kind of interactions that children need for Sagan's goal of growing up "in circumstances that foster self-reliance and optimism rather than submission and hopelessness." Exactly how to provide these "circumstances" is the subject of this book. The point here is that the kinds of interactions which produce behavioral health are a major part of quality care.

1.4: SUMMARY

We opened this chapter with a description of an infant and mother close together, playing happily. Such a picture represents much of what this chapter has emphasized. Note that mother and infant are *interacting*. The mother is talking to her child and responding to what he does. She is not involved in her own preoccupations, with her baby propped up nearby in a chair or swing. The mother is doing more than just providing physical care of changing or feeding her baby. She is, in fact, working with behavior, and her baby is learning about his world through the interaction she is providing.

Center directors are responsible for the way centers operate. They must adhere to state licensing standards. But quality care must usually go beyond what is specified in the standards. In particular, to provide quality care, a center must teach infants the kinds of behaviors that will give them equality of opportunity in their world. It is not enough to provide an environment for physical health and well-being. The environment must also be designed so that caregivers can provide for the behavioral health of the children in their care.

Chapter Two

COMMUNICATING WITH PROSPECTIVE PARENTS

ROBERT AND ALISON, NEW PARENTS, LEARN ABOUT PRE–ADMISSION VISITS AND ADMISSION AGREEMENTS

OBJECTIVES

After you read this chapter you should be able to . . .

1. Describe the purpose of interview (conference) visits (as opposed to informal drop-in visits) and list topics on which parents and center need to agree before an infant or toddler is enrolled in a center.
2. Identify examples of written information that a center is required to record before admitting an infant or toddler.
3. Describe several reasons for a written admission agreement, and include an example of a potential misunderstanding between parent and center it could prevent.
4. List your own examples of appropriate and inappropriate behaviors in infants and toddlers.
5. Explain why, in judging what is being taught by center staff, one must look at the behavior of the children.
6. Explain the differences between providing physical care and providing behavioral care of an infant or toddler, and the difference between a babysitting, and a teaching approach to child care.

One of the hardest decisions working parents face is choosing a child care arrangement for their young children. Parents have the option of arranging care in their own home, care with a relative, family type small group care, or center based care. Once the arrangement has been chosen, parents usually either interview potential in-home child care applicants, or talk with friends and contact resource and referral services about the availability and quality of services offered by local child care providers. (see Appendix B: DYK 2.1)

Before parents place a child in an infant care center, they are advised to visit several centers. From the parents' point of view, these visits give an opportunity to compare centers. From the center's point of view, such

27

visits provide an opportunity to explain the center's philosophy and to make sure that parents agree with it and will cooperate with procedures. The center program supervisor must also make sure that introductory visits do not interrupt daily caregiving routines. Centers vary widely in their arrangements for observation visits. Some centers require parents to schedule a specific time to visit, and provide a person to show the parents around. Others have what is called an open door policy, that is, visitors may drop in any time. In this chapter we will look at one system for pre-admission visits and for the written agreements which should be reached before an infant is accepted into a center.

2.1 NARRATIVE: ROBERT AND ALISON, NEW PARENTS, LEARN ABOUT PRE–ADMISSION VISITS AND ADMISSION AGREEMENTS

Robert and Alison are in their early thirties and have enjoyed the benefits of well-paid and satisfying careers for the past ten years. Alison is a senior stewardess for a major airline and Robert is an artist who works from his home studio as a graphic illustrator. The two are professionally and financially secure and are excited about the baby they are expecting to adopt within the next few weeks. Medical tests have shown that their baby is a girl. They are going to name her Theodora, and plan to call her Teddi.

Alison works a total of twelve days a month and wishes to continue with her work. So she applied for, and was granted, two months unpaid maternity leave. (see Appendix B: DYK 2.2) During her maternity leave Alison will care for and get to know Teddi. Alison and Robert are confident that they can provide the right environment for Teddi and that Robert can be responsible for her while Alison is on flights out of town.

Robert and Alison both went to private boarding schools and enjoyed the experience. They spent a lot of time away from their parents and yet kept a close relationship with them. So they are not as skittish as most new parents about placing their expected infant in a child care center. They both agree, however, that the center must meet the high standards of care that they want for their baby.

When they first called Infant and Toddler Center USA to arrange a visit to see the center and get information about the fees and program, they spoke with Mikki, the director. She told them that the center had an open door policy for prospective parents, and she encouraged them to observe at the center.

"You must remember, however," she explained, "that our staff's first job is to take care of the infants, so caregivers are not usually available to answer questions. If you like what you see and are seriously interested in our center for possible placement for your baby, after your initial observation visit, you may schedule a second visit called an interview or conference visit."

When they hung up the phone, Robert said, "She sure sounds official. We can't just stop by for a look. We have to have an Initial Observation Visit.

"I like the fact that she lets you visit any time." Alison said. "It sounds as though she has nothing to hide. And she is serious about the babies. I can imagine some parents I know cornering one of the staff for hours."

Robert smiled. He knew just which one of their friends Alison meant. The two decided to make their initial observation visit to Infant and Toddler Center USA the next day.

2.1.1 The Initial Observation Visit

Infant and Toddler Center USA was located in a three story brick building in a section of town that was part business, part residential. The center occupied the ground floor. Robert and Alison parked the car and followed the concrete path that twisted around to what looked like the main entrance.

"Should we knock or just walk in?" Robert asked.

"I think we'd better knock." Alison replied.

A short, but trim, well-groomed woman with gray flecked hair answered the door. She was dressed in a muted heather blue sweater and skirt which Alison judged were expensive but not new.

"Hello," the woman said, "I'm the director, Mikki. Please come in." They stepped inside and found themselves in an entry hall, close to a door marked office. Mikki asked them to write their names and the purpose of their visit in a visitor's book that she picked up from her desk. She then led the couple into Unit #1, and introduced them to the staff. Before she left them, she reminded them not to take too much time from the babies by chatting too long to their caregivers. She smiled as she told them that before they left she would give them some pamphlets that described the center's policies.

Clearly the decor was animals. Animal pictures were hung on the walls and animals decorated the fabric of the drapes and matching cushions that were placed about the floor. Alison even spotted panda stickers on the clipboards hanging on one wall. The overall effect was, however, one of order. The walls were not crammed full of decorations the way they were in some of the centers Alison and Robert had visited.

"Nice and cheerful," Robert was whispering to her, "look at the baby in green. I hope our Teddi turns out like her."

Alison looked. A beautiful little baby, dressed all in green, was sitting against a big cushion turning a fluffy toy over with great concentration. Another alert-looking baby was lying on his side studying the rabbits on a page of a big cotton stand-up book. Nearby, a caregiver was playing peek-a-boo with a laughing baby she had just burped.

Alison and Robert, somewhat in awe, could hardly take their eyes off the babies. Alison, who was starting to feel motherly, would have liked to have held the beautiful baby in green. But she thought that it was better not to be too pushy. Also the babies all seemed to be enjoying what they were doing and she was not sure how Mikki would react to her picking them up. In hushed tones they exchanged comments and agreed that they were impressed with what they had seen. They thanked the caregivers, and as they left the room they smiled and waved to the babies. When the babies smiled and waved back they felt a rush of joy, and visualizing their own Teddi waving to them, they walked happily back to the director's office.

Mikki welcomed the couple to her office, and when they were seated comfortably she handed them two pamphlets. One, published by the state was called *Reporting Child Abuse and Neglect*, and the other, designed by Mikki, was called *Infant and Toddler Center USA: Information for Parents.* Mikki told them they would find the answers to most of their questions in the pamphlets. She asked them to sign for them, explaining that the licensing authority required her to keep receipts on file, showing that parents had received the information. She also told them that, if they wished, they could borrow a copy of the state's booklet on *Licensing Standards for Infant and Toddler Centers.* Robert and Alison gladly took all the literature that Mikki offered them.

Over the next few days, they carefully sifted through all of the information they had received from the centers they had visited. Both could not stop thinking about the adorable, happy babies they had seen at Infant and Toddler Center USA. They decided that they wanted to find out more about how the center cared for the babies, and so made an appointment for an interview or conference visit.

2.1.2 The Interview Or Conference Visit

It was a sunny day when they arrived for their interview. Mikki greeted them at the door of the center and showed them into her office. She said that she had set aside time to answer any questions they may have after reading the center literature she had previously given. Then she would go over the forms that had to be filled in before a baby was admitted to the center. After that Ruth, the program supervisor, would stay with them while they again observed the caregivers caring for the babies. She would also tell them more about the center's program and philosophy. Then, if they and the center were in agreement, a place would be reserved for Teddi.

Services A Center Has The Option To Provide

Robert spoke readily and told Mikki that he and Alison had been pleased to note that the center had a firm policy on the exclusion of sick babies (see Chapter Three), and were curious to know how the parents arranged care for their sick infants.

Mikki said, "Some use a home nursing aide service, others ask relatives to help, and a few use centers that are licensed to care for mildly ill children." (see Appendix B: DYK 2.3)

"I don't think we'll have a problem, as I can always arrange my time to care for Teddi, if she is ill. But it is good to check on the options." Robert said.

Alison said, "We noticed that the licensing standards require centers to have a nondiscriminatory admission policy which also refers to handicapped infants. We did not see any infants here who obviously had special needs."

"Our center layout and program are not designed to provide those services. To be licensed to care for handicapped infants a center has to make environmental modifications to meet the special needs of the babies, have specially trained staff, and a lower child/staff ratio. As we do not advertise that we provide care for handicapped infants, we are not discriminating, if we do not admit infants who need specialized care." Mikki explained.

Robert said, "I have one more question. Your center, in contrast to the others we visited does not provide transportation. Is there a specific reason you do not?"

"When I first opened the center, it was a matter of cost. Then I found that the parents managed well enough without the service. Now, I would be reluctant to offer transportation for the babies." Mikki paused and pointed to the state licensing regulations, "Do you know that each baby must be given a Health Inspection, each morning, before being transported? At least three caregivers plus the driver, would have to be in the van to meet the supervisory, safety and health regulations."

"We did not know about *that.*" Robert and Alison said in unison. Mikki laughed, and said, "We also do not have drop in or night care."

"That suits us." Alison said. "For health reasons we would prefer to have Teddi in a center that did not provide drop in care, and we have no need of night care."

"Well, that takes care of that." Mikki said. "Shall we move on to the paper work?" She already had four documents laid out in a row on her desk. She nodded her head towards them and said, "There's a lot of paperwork in running a center."

Identifying Information And Authorization Form

"This first form is required by our state, and must be completed before a baby is enrolled," she told them as she picked up a copy and gave it to Robert and Alison. "It is for personal and emergency information. One copy is kept in each infant's file, and one copy is posted near the telephone." Robert and Alison dutifully noted the blanks for their names, addresses, and other information usually needed for identification and authorization purposes.

Optional Form: Our Baby

As she picked up the next form, Mikki smiled at the couple. She handed the page to Robert and Alison. It was blank, except for the heading Our Baby. "We encourage parents to tell us about their babies and their feelings about their baby. It introduces the baby to the caregiver and also helps remind them about the responsibilities of child care."

Robert responded quickly, "You mean they don't take their job seriously?" Mikki glanced at him intently and said, "Perhaps I should have said it another way. Our caregivers generally love their work. In fact it is their fondness for the babies that keep many of them in child care." She laughed as she said, "It's certainly not the pay." (see Appendix B:

DYK 2.4) Then using a more sober tone she continued, "Caregiving requires compliance with many regulations which sometimes can seem burdensome to a busy caregiver. It helps caregivers appreciate the need for all of the regulations when they read what parents have written about their babies, if you see what I mean."

Robert grunted agreement, but he still felt uneasy. He still had not got over the shock of thinking for even a minute of anyone not enjoying all of the routines involved in taking care of *his* baby.

Plan Of Payment

"And this is a **Plan of Payment.**" Mikki continued, "In here you will find 'All you wanted to know about fees, but were afraid to ask.'" Mikki chuckled at her own joke.

Robert wondered whether she always used the same phrase.

"Seriously," she continued, "this form will tell you all about our fees; payment dates, hourly, monthly and overtime rates. It includes the hours and days of operation and the policy on late or delinquent fees."

Admission Agreement

"And finally, we have the most important document—the Admission Agreement." She paused as she handed them a form several pages long. (see Figure 2.1).

"This form," Mikki explained, "is the most important. It specifies all of the caregiving routines for your baby. For example, on page one you will see details about clothing, diapers, plastic pants, and so on. Our parents like to know who is expected to provide diapers and other baby supplies. This form also satisfies our state's licensing requirements for informing parents.

The couple looked at the first page. Robert started to turn the next page, but Alison motioned for him to wait. She hadn't realized how many options there were for simple tasks. All the lists of supplies gave her a twinge of excitement, like that she felt when passing department store windows displaying baby things.

"The Admission Agreement," Mikki continued, "is really a detailed individualized *Plan of Care* for your infant. Note that we ask parents to help us provide quality care."

Robert looked up. Mikki recognized the look.

"That doesn't mean that you will be cleaning the center and taking out the trash," Mikki smiled and assured him. "But we ask cooperation of

FIGURE 2.1: PART OF A COMPLETED ADMISSION AGREEMENT
(ROUTINE CARE)

This agreement helps us reach an understanding with you on the details of care for your infant. We will fill it in with you prior to your baby's first day at the center.

Part 1: PHYSICAL AND SANITARY ASPECTS OF CARE

CLOTHING CHANGES

SUPPLIED BY: PARENT ✓   **LABELED BY:**   CENTER: PARENT ✓

STORED BY: CENTER ✓   **WHERE?:** *Infants cubby hole*

LAUNDERED BY: PARENT: *Returned to parent daily, unrinsed, and stored in plastic bags, in an area separate from infant's clean belongings/clothing*

DIAPERING

DIAPER TYPE: **DIAPER SERVICE: HOME LAUNDERED: DISPOSABLE ... BRAND**

SUPPLIED BY: CENTER: PARENT ✓   **LABELED BY:**   CENTER:PARENT

STORED IN: CENTER SUPPLIES: INFANT'S INDIVIDUAL LABELED STORAGE

LAUNDERED BY: SERVICE: PARENT: NONE (disposable)

PINS USED: YES: NO **IF YES, TYPE:**

SUPPLIED BY: CENTER: PARENT   INDIVIDUAL USE ONLY

STORED IN: CENTER SUPPLIES: INFANT'S INDIVIDUAL LABELED STORAGE

PLASTIC PANTS: YES: NO **IF YES, TYPE:**   PULL ON: SNAP: OTHER

SUPPLIED BY: PARENT: **LABELED BY:**   CENTER: PARENT

STORED IN: CENTER SUPPLIES: INFANT'S INDIVIDUAL LABELED STORAGE

LAUNDERED BY: PARENT: *Returned to parent daily, unrinsed, and stored in plastic bags, In an area separate from infant's clean belongings/clothing*

HYGIENE ARTICLES FOR DIAPER CHANGES: DISPOSABLE WIPES: WASHABLE CLOTHS ✓

SUPPLIED BY: CENTER: PARENT   **LABELED BY:**   CENTER:PARENT

STORED IN: CENTER SUPPLIES: INFANT'S INDIVIDUAL LABELED STORAGE

LAUNDERED BY: CENTER: PARENT: NONE (disposable)

SPECIAL PRODUCTS: FOR EXAMPLE, LOTIONS, CREAMS, **MUST** BE SUPPLIED BY PARENTS AND AUTHORIZED BY A PHYSICIAN WITH PHYSICIAN'S INSTRUCTIONS

DIAPER CHANGING SURFACE: (Changing Table)

COVERING: WATERPROOF: PAPER ROLL (used once and discarded) ✓

SANITATION: AFTER EACH USE: BLEACH SOLUTION IN SPRAY BOTTLE ✓

            DISPOSABLE PAPER PRODUCTS (used once and discarded) ✓

DIAPERING PROCEDURE

POSTED: COPY GIVEN TO PARENTS: DISCUSSED WITH PARENTS

parents. For example, we set up morning arrivals and end of day departures so that not all babies arrive or leave at the same time. Once we have set a mutually convenient time, you will be asked to bring your baby every day at that time. Parents also cooperate with our procedures on...." Mikki looked over and pointed as she read, "daily health inspections, administration and storage of medications, keeping of records, and the care of the infant's belongings.

"So that there are no misunderstandings about what we ask and what we offer, we fill in the Admission Agreement with the parents just prior to admitting their baby. We ask parents to sign a copy of that document to indicate that they agree with what it describes."

"Oh, one more thing," Mikki added, "we follow traditional medical practices. Some centers around here will take babies that have not been vaccinated, but we do not. We require a medical statement from a licensed physician for all entering babies, and parents must agree to have their infant immunized at the appropriate age. We had a bit of a problem with one couple two years ago. They said they would not enroll their infants at a center unless all of the parents adhered to immunizations and traditional medical practices. In fact, they suggested I add the section about it in the Admission Agreement."

Alison was flipping pages looking for the section. Mikki waited until she found it, before she continued. "The Admission Agreement is for your benefit and protection, and that of your baby. Of course, it is useful to us, too, in running the center. If you think of anything we have left out, please feel free to make suggestions."

Alison noted that she was beginning to talk as though they had already decided on Infant and Toddler Center USA. She smiled at Mikki's self-assurance.

"... best suggestions have come from parents." Mikki was saying. "Teddi's caregiver will also get a copy of this form as a basis for primary care. It also helps the center to have all authorizations, notifications and procedures clarified and formally agreed upon."

"We looked at the authorizations required on the other form you showed us." Alison said. "But what are the notifications we should know about."

"Well," Mikki replied. "If your baby Teddi is enrolled at this center you must notify us if she comes in contact with a person who has a communicable disease, when you designate another person to pick her up, when you will be arriving late or picking her up early, and of course when you intend to withdraw her from our care. We on the other hand must notify you immediately if your baby becomes ill, and when she comes in contact with a communicable disease here. We also have to notify you that our center is licensed, as well as about a variety of things ranging from medication administration on your authorization, to unusual occurrences or unusual behavior on the part of your baby."

"There are many details to remember." Robert said.

"Here," Mikki said, "you can take a blank Admission Agreement home so you can study and discuss them at your leisure. I'll keep the sample filled-out one."

As they swapped forms Mikki said, "I nearly forgot to tell you that before Teddi is admitted to the center, you will be asked to tell us what appropriate behaviors you would like us to encourage and what inappropriate behaviors you would like us to discourage. You might want to give some thought to what you would like your baby to do and what you would not like your baby to do." Mikki noted that they looked a little puzzled and gently said, "But don't worry about that now. Ruth will tell you more about it when she talks with you."

After asking if the couple had any questions, Mikki suggested that they visit the unit where Teddi would be placed. She stood up and led the couple out into Unit #1.

2.1.3 Ruth The Program Supervisor Explains The Center's Philosophy Of Behavioral Care

Mikki introduced Robert and Alison to a tall and very slender young woman with lovely thick dark brown hair.

"This is Ruth, the program supervisor," she said.

Ruth shook hands firmly but a bit shyly. She quickly introduced Robert and Alison to the caregivers and infants, and then led the couple to the side of the room.

"Would you like me to explain, or would you like to ask questions?" Ruth began.

"Oh questions, for me," Alison answered, glancing for agreement from Robert.

Robert nodded. "We have a lot of questions to ask."

Alison began. "We don't understand the behavior part. We see that a center takes care of babies. But what is this about appropriate behavior?"

Ruth answered readily.

"It is a relatively new development in infant care," she explained. "We have known for a long time that infants need more than just physical care to grow up healthy. They need to explore their physical environment to develop motor-perceptual skills. Every movement they make," (here Ruth reached like a baby towards a toy sitting on a shelf) teaches them how to coordinate what they see with their muscle movement. In addition to learning how to interact with their physical environment, babies learn how to interact with other people." Ruth turned to Alison. "That's where the appropriate and inappropriate behavior comes in. We teach our staff to teach the infants to behave appropriately."

Robert looked thoughtful and asked, "But how do you know what is appropriate and inappropriate for such tiny infants?"

"Really, that is the easiest part," Ruth replied, "For example, look at Gregory, over there. He's the little one being fed by Eve, the caregiver in the bean bag chair. What is Gregory doing that you would like your baby to do? What would you not want your baby to do?"

Gregory was drinking contentedly from a bottle. He looked over in the observer's direction when Ruth gestured, without losing hold of the nipple. Sitting near and leaning against Eve, her caregiver, bottle in hand, was a larger baby (Lorraine 10 months) also drinking. A third baby (Woodrow, 6 months) was sitting in a swing, sleepily looking at the other infants. Eve was talking to Gregory. They heard her tell Gregory that she was going to put him on the floor for a few minutes while she changed Woodrow and settled him in his crib for a nap. She then took the bottle out of Gregory's mouth, burped him, and placed him stomach down, on a padded quilt that was in front of a wall mirror. Gregory lifted up his head and looked in the mirror at his reflection, and cooed.

Robert remembered being told how, when *he* was a baby, he would scream when his bottle was taken away from him. "Gregory is certainly very patient," he remarked.

Alison answered the original question more directly. "Gregory is cooing and looking in the mirror. That would be appropriate behavior. He could have cried when his bottle was taken away and instead he began to play."

"Exactly," said Ruth.

Meanwhile Eve, his caregiver, had walked into the diapering room to wash her hands. She smiled and called a few words back to Gregory and Woodrow. She then walked quickly back to the swing and unstrapped

Woodrow. As she carried him to a changing table, she danced in time to the music that was playing softly.

Robert asked, "But why did the caregiver—what's her name—interrupt Gregory's feeding? He wasn't finished."

"A very good question." Ruth nodded, "Gregory had taken more than half his bottle. You could see he was almost through, because he was looking around. He doesn't do that when he is really hungry. Don't forget, Eve has three others to care for. She saw that Woodrow was getting sleepy, and she did not want him to fall asleep in the swing, or to go to sleep without having on a clean double diaper. She'll get back to Gregory. Anyway she has taught Gregory to be patient."

Robert protested. "But I thought personality was inborn. I mean, aren't some babies naturally good-natured and some not."

"No one really knows how much is inborn. What we do know, though, is that babies learn to be fussy or to be patient. In fact, every interaction between adult and infant is a learning experience for both child and adult. Just as babies learn how the physical environment works by moving and seeing what happens, they learn about how the social environment works by their interactions with caregivers. Suppose that Eve had waited until Woodrow fussed or cried before taking him from the swing. Woodrow would have found out that one way to get moved from the swing was to cry. In fact, in some centers, fussing or crying is about the only way that babies can get anyone to take care of them. Without realizing it, the caregivers are teaching their babies to cry."

Alison shuddered. She recalled a center they had visited in which most babies had been crying.

Ruth continued, "It is easy for a caregiver to ignore a baby when he is playing quietly and only be roused into action when he cries or fusses. But in our center we emphasize how important it is to interact with the babies while they are content. We try to catch their eye when they are stacking rings, or talk back when they babble, or pick them up and dance with them when they have waited for their turn to get ready for a walk outside."

Ruth had been talking animatedly. Now she slowed down. "You cannot teach a baby appropriate behaviors by ignoring crying. You must build all of the things that happy, inquisitive, and friendly babies do. In fact, I spend most of my time working with the caregivers on building behaviors we and the parents want, so that we almost never get crying."

Robert asked, "What about a baby that comes already crying a lot?"

Ruth raised one eyebrow. "Oh, we've had those." She glanced at Eve who smiled back. "It takes a while. But we eventually teach them to be happy, too."

Alison had caught Ruth's glance. "Was one of Eve's babies a crier?"

"Um Hm. But you can't tell which one now."

"Which one was it?"

But Ruth would not say. She just replied, "The baby's not a crier any longer."

2.1.4 An Example Of A Center Procedure: Staggered Nap/sleeping

Ruth continued, "We work hard to arrange what we do so that we prevent crying, rather than letting it happen and then trying to stop it. Our procedure of staggered nap/sleeping is an example. Ruth now directed Robert and Alison's attention to a nap/sleeping reminder, placed on a wall, near the one-way vision mirror, outside of the nap/sleeping room. The board showed the names of the babies who were sleeping, the name of their caregiver, and the time that the babies were put in their cribs to nap. (see Figure 2.2) Robert and Alison could see that Eve's fourth infant, Gavin had been sleeping for thirty minutes.

Alison had a question. "Don't the babies in the nap room disturb each other?"

"No." Ruth answered, "Remember, the infants are only put in their cribs when they are tired and they soon, sometimes immediately, go to sleep. And we keep a close watch to catch them as soon as they wake up."

"So they won't cry?" Alison asked playfully.

Ruth laughed. "You've got it." She paused, "One thing I should mention is that we stagger the naps as much as possible. We do not want all of the infants to sleep at the same time. Licensing regulations say that babies must be allowed to sleep on their own schedules. Usually the babies' own schedules differ anyway, so it works out easily enough that each caregiver has her babies sleeping at different times. We call it staggered nap/sleeping. It streamlines the caregiving tasks so that a caregiver isn't faced with two or three tired babies that need to be changed and put down for their naps all at one time . . . and all wake up about the same time. In addition, staggered napping makes it easier to work individually with the babies. A caregiver has more time to interact with her babies, when three are awake rather than four."

Ruth told the couple that the licensing regulations also required that

FIGURE 2.2: A SAMPLE NAP/SLEEPING REMINDER

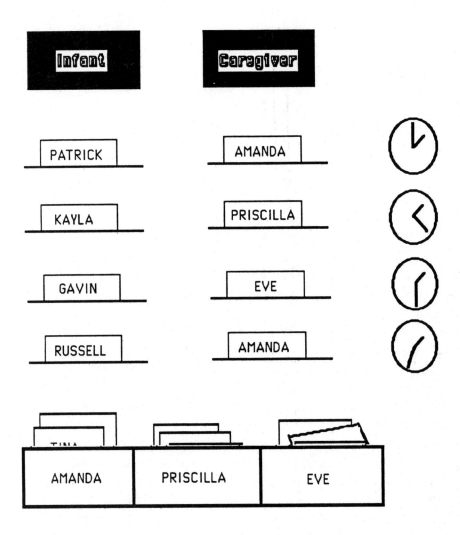

When a baby is ready for a nap, a caregiver puts that baby's name card in the card holder and positions the hands of the clock to mark the time the baby started his or her nap. The name cards let supervisors know instantly whose babies are in the nap room. The clocks also reminds caregivers of the approximate time they can expect a baby to wake up.

infants be supervised continuously, even when they are sleeping. She led the parents away from the door of the nap/sleeping room, and continued talking.

"Even though the nap/sleeping room is a separate room, we can see the infants from outside the room. We do so through the one way vision mirror. Also, from various places in the activity room we can see the infants' reflections in the mirror placed on the far wall of the nap/sleeping room. Look."

Alison and Robert looked where Ruth was pointing. They could, indeed, see the reflections of all of the babies in the room.

Robert looked at his watch, and Ruth picked up the cue.

"Do you have any other questions?" she asked leading the couple towards the front door.

Robert and Alison paused, and then both agreed they had sufficient information.

"One last thing," Ruth said, reaching above the cubby holes, "did Mikki give you one of these?" She offered Alison an Admission Agreement.

Alison double checked through the forms she was holding.

"Yes we have one," she said. "I don't know whether or not Mikki mentioned it yet, but here we outline our center's philosophy and list appropriate and inappropriate behaviors. Mikki and the parents go over the Admission Agreement together just before the baby is admitted, and the parents sign the agreement. They must also mark behaviors they want encouraged and those they want discouraged."

"What kinds of behaviors do parents want encouraged and discouraged?" asked Alison.

"A lot of parents tell us they want their baby to wave them bye-bye rather than cry, to be still and help while being changed and dressed, to go happily down for a nap, to look at books without tearing the pages. One parent had an ex-baseball-player father who taught the baby to throw a ball. Unfortunately, he taught too well, and the infant threw everything he got his hands on. The parents asked us to help with that problem, so we taught the baby to hand over things nicely. The inappropriate throwing disappeared in three days. Most parents, of course, want their babies to babble, sing, play with toys, hug, kiss, . . . "

Robert interrupted Ruth by saying, "In short they don't want brats."

"Let's put it this way." Ruth continued, "They want to enjoy their babies."

"Sounds good to me." Alison said.

"Behavior is too often neglected. We want our parents to know we consider it just as important as other aspects of infant care," Ruth told them. "The checklist, in the Admission Agreement makes it clear to the parents that we are teaching appropriate behaviors and not just babysitting."

There was a pause, and Ruth reached for the door handle. She shook hands with the prospective parents and showed them out, expressing her hopes to see them again after they had received their adopted baby.

Outside, Robert and Alison were full of talk. The had thought about Teddi being well cared for in the sense of being fed, changed, played with, talked to, loved and so on. They had not thought at all about a center teaching her to behave. But that was what would happen when her caregivers fed, played and talked to her. That was an intriguing but frightening idea.

2.2 ANALYSIS 1:
COMMUNICATING WITH PROSPECTIVE PARENTS THROUGH CENTER VISITS AND ADMISSION AGREEMENTS

Increasing numbers of parents seek child care for very young children. Before the 1980's, many mothers worked to get extra spending money. But today, most mothers who work do so to provide basic support for their families. Both the single and the married mother, as well as the father, depend upon child care services in order to continue work, or to have an adequate family income.

What parents are required to do prior to entering a child in a licensed center varies from state to state. Many states, but not all, require the interview or conference visit described in this chapter. But all states, territories, and the military require centers to obtain identifying information and authorizations prior to (or at the time of) admission.

2.2.1 Pre-admission Identifying Information And Authorizations

Some states, such as Maine (1987) and Delaware (1988) specify what information is to be gathered before enrolling or admitting an infant, but leave the center choose the way the information is recorded. Sometimes, as in Indiana (1985) the authorizations and identifying information is record along with the plan of care in an Intake Record. But more commonly states provide a document whose name varies with the state, for example, Utah (1987) has a form called a Child Day Care Register,

North Carolina (1988) has a Child's Application for Day Care, Iowa (1988) has an Intake Information sheet, and Alabama (1988) has a Child's Pre-admission Record. Many states provide one or more forms for pre-admission information and require them to be filed in a record for each infant. In case of emergency, center staff would need to locate such information quickly, so most states require that it be posted near the telephone.

At Infant and Toddler Center USA, the *Identifying Information* and *Authorizations* for each infant are recorded on a form named for its contents. A copy is posted by the telephone in the director's office, and a copy is posted by the telephone in the activity area of the infant's unit. The *medical history, behavior patterns* and *developmental milestones* are kept in the baby's file and any *restrictive conditions* or *special needs* are described in the Admission Agreement which details the *Plan of Care*, a portion of which we have already seen. The infant's caregiver is also given a copy of the Admission Agreement and it is clipped on a clipboard behind each *Infant's Daily Record*. The clipboards are hung above the infant's storage cubby hole. (see Chapter Three) What is done at Infant and Toddler Center USA is, of course, only one way of recording and handling pre-admission enrollment information.

2.2.2 Admission Agreements

Several states require centers to have written agreements signed by parents prior to admitting an infant. The agreements range from those that require authorizations such as emergency medical care and medication administration to details about routine care. Alabama (1988) and Virginia (1988) list items that are to be included in an agreement with the parents, but do not name the type of document that is to be used. California (1988) provides specifications for an Admission Agreement, and in the 1989 regulations specify details for an Infant Needs and Services Plan. (see Table 2.1)

Although written agreements can be considered a safeguard for infant, parent, and center, states do not require an admission agreement to be as detailed as the one illustrated in the narrative of this chapter. For parents and center alike, the Admission Agreement underscores the seriousness of the decision of center care placement. (see Appendix B: DYK 2.5) Most infants cared for by centers, spend a major portion of their waking hours during their first two years of life in the center. Center experiences

TABLE 2.1: SAMPLE REQUIREMENTS FOR INFANT NEEDS AND SERVICE PLAN (CALIFORNIA 1988/89)

(a) Prior to the infant's first day at the center, the infant care center director or assistant director shall complete a needs and services plan.

    (1) Such plan shall be completed with the assistance of the infant's parent at the personal interview specified in Section 101319.1

    (2) The parent's or guardian's participation in the preparation of the plan shall be verified by the parent's or guardian's signature on the plan.

(b) The needs and services plan shall be in writing and shall include the following:

    (1) The individual feeding plan.

    (2) The individual toilet training plan if applicable.

    (3) Any services needed by the child which are different from those provided by the center's normal program. Such items shall include but are not limited to if appropriate to the infant, the following:

        (A) Any special exercises for the physically handicapped.

    (4) A plan for subsequent personal interviews with the parent or guardian.

(c) Parents/guardians shall be provided with a copy of the Needs and Services Plan and any subsequent updates. (Issue 398)

thus have a major impact on their development. By requiring parents to go over the critical aspects of child care and to sign an agreement, a center shows that it takes its responsibility for the infant seriously. It is not sufficiently informative for a center director to explain center procedures in a meeting. Such meetings are usually brief, and there is no guarantee that the director will remember everything that he or she should mention, nor that the parents will remember what was said when they get home. Then, too, parents need time to reflect upon policies. A written agreement solves all of these problems. It serves as a checklist for initial meetings, so that the director is more likely to cover everything that needs to be said and gives parents time to consider all aspects of the care the center provides.

At Infant and Toddler Center USA, the Admission Agreement is used not only to establish an initial agreement between parents and center, it is also used by the staff. We have already mentioned that the primary caregiver for each infant receives a copy of the infant's Admission Agreement for use as a Plan of Care. As the infant develops and his or her requirements change, the document is updated.

One other function of Admission Agreements should be mentioned. In addition to helping establish understanding between center and parents, an Admission Agreement forces a director to think about the center and its philosophy. In writing the document, center personnel must take time to reflect on goals for the center, many of which can get overlooked in the day to day bustle. An Admission Agreement is thus likely to remind center staff and parents alike that care consists of more than changing diapers and feeding infants. The physical and behavioral development of the child must be considered.

2.3 ANALYSIS 2: TEACHING AND BEHAVIORAL HEALTH

Behavioral health consists of all of those behaviors which are characteristic of happy, confident, loving, and loved individuals. A behaviorally healthy infant reacts in an appropriate way to its environment.

2.3.1 Appropriate And Inappropriate Behavior

Not everybody always agrees on what behavior is appropriate in a particular situation. One parent may approve of a child grabbing a toy back from a child who has grabbed it from her, for example, while another parent would prefer his baby to find another toy to play with. But although there are some differences, most parents and caregivers agree on the basics: Babbling is usually better than crying. Sharing is better than grabbing. Taking an interest in one's environment is generally healthier than sitting passively. Responding in a friendly way to others is better than cowering. And it is healthy for babies to respond readily to language, answering questions such as, "Where is you nose?" or following simple directions such as "Wave bye-bye." People agree on most of what constitutes appropriate and inappropriate behaviors.

In judging appropriateness, the context of behavior must be taken into account. For example, while we may think of pushing others as bad, in some circumstances it may be appropriate. The pusher might be helping another child climb into a chair. The meaning of the push depends upon the situation in which it occurs. Appropriate behavior, then, means behavior which is suitable in the circumstances under which it occurs.

As we have seen, the notion of behavioral health is implied in state licensing standards. Most regulations acknowledge the fact that infants are learning social and emotional behaviors during their interactions with caregivers. The standards thus imply that infant care involves teaching appropriate behavior, and not just physical care and supervision.

2.3.2 The Difference Between Supervision And Teaching

Supervision of an infant generally means that the infant must be within sight and hearing at all times. That does not necessarily mean within reach. The Minnesota (1989, p. 4) standards say that "supervision occurs when a program staff person is within sight and hearing of a child at all times so that the program staff person can intervene to protect the health and safety of the child." Some states require a caregiver to be in the nap/sleeping room with the infants, but others do not. In our example of Infant and Toddler Center USA, there was no caregiver stationed in the nap/sleeping room. Supervision was achieved by the positioning of the caregivers and by the use of mirrors.

Clearly keeping an eye on the babies is different from teaching them. Teaching requires more than sitting back and watching infants or toddlers in free play, interrupting situations only when problems arise. Teaching involves responding to the infants' behavior, interacting with individual babies when all is going well. Even small gestures are important. The wink that Ruth gave baby Gregory, who played patiently even though his feeding had been interrupted, showed approval. The wink taught appropriate behavior if it helped Gregory wait more patiently in the future.

For toddlers, teaching involves not only the structured activities with art, music, and language, but also the moment to moment interactions between staff and toddlers which influence behavior. Caregivers may conspicuously attempt to teach social behavior when they give rules about sharing and taking turns, or not grabbing or hitting. But they teach more effectively each time they acknowledge appropriate behaviors. Like infants, toddlers are sensitive to attention as well as praise, and they need to gain that attention when they are behaving well. The way that caregivers handle inappropriate behavior is also critical for behavioral health. (see Chapter Eight)

Because state licensing standards specify the teaching of social behaviors only in general terms, parents cannot assume that a center actively promotes behavioral health. Thus the role of the center in teaching the infants and toddlers appropriate behavior—and what constitutes appropriate behavior—is one of the areas in which parents and centers need to agree. This can be made clear in the Admission Agreement. (see Figure 2.3)

2.3.3 Teaching Versus Babysitting

Some educators argue against teaching youngsters. They are not protesting against the kind of teaching mentioned here which is goes on in every interaction between infant and caregiver. What they fear is the kind of teaching that most of us associate with formal schooling. They fear that caregivers will set tasks for babies which some babies may not enjoy. They fear the effect on a youngster of hearing WRONG, when he or she does something incorrectly. They fear that babies will be punished by disapproval, and worry about the effect on the baby's self concept. These are all valid fears. Forcing a child to engage in an activity, or punishing a child for failing an academic task will not only fail to teach the desirable skill, it will undermine self-confidence and contribute to a dislike of education.

To fail to teach because teaching can be done badly, however, is to injure the child too. A baby who is never encouraged to name things, for example, will not learn words that other children will know. This child will be at a handicap in later life (at age three or four). She will not only have more difficulty learning in preschool or first grade, but will suffer all of the humiliation that accompanies failure.

The issue is not whether or not children should be taught, but *how* they are taught. Clearly no one would object to a game of pointing to parts of the body when an infant clearly enjoys it. Similarly, both those

FIGURE 2.3 THE BEHAVIORAL DEVELOPMENTAL PART
OF AN ADMISSION AGREEMENT

Philosophy:

In Infant Center USA we are concerned not only with your baby's physical health, but with his or her behavioral health. We provide an environment which develops physical skills and which teaches your baby to interact with others in appropriate ways. As part of our program we encourage the following kinds of behaviors. Please check those that you feel are particularly important for your baby, so we can attend to them first.

Area

Appropriate Behaviors

☑ Interacting with strangers

Smiling for a stranger,
Going willingly to a person who is
holding out arms to take the baby

☑ Playing by himself or herself

Playing contentedly with toys for
an appropriate time (usually 5-10
minutes for a baby under 1)

☑ Responsiveness to others

Smiles and babbles to other
infants nearby, watches others.

☑ Self-confidence

Tries new things readily. Explores
his or her environment.

☑ Waiting his or her turn

Watches caregiver getting another
infant ready for a walk without
fussing.

☑ Expressing desires when asked

Bounces up and down when
asked, "Do you want to go for a
walk?"
Opens mouth for yes or turns away
for no when asked "Do you want
more banana?"

for and against teaching infants would agree that forcing a child to point to his nose (making him cry in the process) is damaging to that child's development. Everyone wants children to learn, but to do so enjoyably and without penalty for the mistakes that are bound to occur. (see Chapter Nine)

This book is pro-teaching in the sense that it encourages caregivers to attend to their day-to-day-interactions with an eye to how those interactions affect the behavior of their infants. Infants and toddlers need to learn many things. Quality care includes and attends to the individual interactions from which babies learn those behaviors that result in competent and happy children.

2.4 SUMMARY:

Different centers have different philosophies and procedures. Parents should understand and agree with, the procedures that will affect their child before that infant or toddler enters a center. Parents can of course, take their child to another center, but every change disrupts the continuity of care for the infant. Also, with the scarcity of child care facilities in many areas, parents may find that they cannot immediately place their infant in a new center. When centers carefully explain their procedures and approaches at the outset, they can help parents decide whether or not their idea of child care fits with the approach of the parents.

In this chapter we looked at three methods for encouraging a good match between parent and center philosophies: (1) initial observation visits (2) pre-admission conferences or interviews, and (3) admission agreements.

In addition to providing physical care and supervision, a center influences social behavior. Children learn to interact with others by the kinds of contact they have with caregivers. They learn such basics as how to get what they want—either by gesturing and asking, or by whining and demanding. Whether or not parents and caregivers realize it, every interaction between caregiver and child affects that child's behavior. Behavior never remains static. It constantly evolves. Parents must consider what kinds of behavior patterns their children will learn in a child care setting. They must consider behaviors which are appropriate and inappropriate for the setting in which they occur. To find what children are learning in a center, parents must look at what center personnel are intentionally and unintentionally teaching.

PART TWO
WORKING WITHIN RULES,
REGULATIONS, REQUIREMENTS,
AND STANDARDS FOR LICENSING

Chapter Three

MORNING ARRIVAL PROCEDURES:
A REALISTIC VIEW OF CAREGIVING

CLAIRE, A MOTHER, AND AMANDA,
A CAREGIVER, SHOW WHAT IS REQUIRED
WHEN CLAIRE ARRIVES WITH HER BABY PATRICK

OBJECTIVES

After you have read this chapter you should be able to . . .

1. List procedures that occur during the infant and parent morning arrival.
2. Describe the format of an Infant Daily Record and a Sign In/Sign Out sheet.
3. Describe the layout and contents of a diapering area for infants.
4. List signs of illness that require exclusion from a child care center.
5. Describe how licensing standards for daily health inspections and medication administration and storage differ from state to state.
6. List regulations for feeding and food preparation.
7. Explain why some recent regulations (for example, authorization procedures for the release of children, and touch policies) are necessary.

Across our nation caregivers, in infant and toddler care facilities, are nurturing the majority of our nation's youngest citizens. When you consider this important job, you would think that they would be well paid. Unfortunately they are not. Caregivers are underpaid and many lack health benefits and retirement plans. Currently a large pool of women with varying education are willing to work for low wages, and can be hired in caregiver positions. Because licensed facilities must meet regulations on health, sanitation, and the safety and protection of infants and toddlers, the tasks required by caregivers are considerable. In spite of low status and pay, caregivers must work hard to carry out the enormous responsibility of nurturing and tending the babies placed in their care.

In this chapter to introduce the work of a caregiver, we will look at the

Morning Arrival Procedures at Infant and Toddler Center USA. This is a well run center, but not an ideally laid out center. Like many centers, it was organized within the constraints of available and affordable space, and of the cost of redesigning the existing structure into a facility that meets the specifications of the licensing requirements. Few centers have ideal designs and caregivers usually have to work within less than ideal conditions. The facilities of Infant and Toddler Center USA, and how the center's trained caregivers, comply with the licensing standards, were deliberately depicted to show this.

3.1 NARRATIVE: CLAIRE, A MOTHER, AND AMANDA, A CAREGIVER, SHOW WHAT IS REQUIRED WHEN CLAIRE ARRIVES WITH HER BABY PATRICK

Claire is twenty-seven years old and is the mother of an eight month old son Patrick. She works as a fashion photographer. While she works Patrick is cared for at Infant and Toddler Center USA. Most week days for the past seven months, at roughly 7.10 AM, she and Patrick have entered Unit #1 of the center. They are usually the first parent and infant to arrive. Claire carries Patrick in one arm and her pocket book and a bag full of Patrick's things in the other. As she rounds the corner to the front door, she wonders whether her assistant will be on time for the shooting session she is to do today. She has a knit wear catalogue to complete, and if her assistant is even ten minutes late to set up the lighting . . . Oh well, she'll handle that problem if it occurs. The door of the center interrupts her thoughts.

As Claire opens the door, Patrick hears the music that is played for the morning arrival. He bounces up and down in his mother's arms, and Claire almost drops his things as she brings her arm around to hold him.

3.1.1: The Infant Daily Record

Claire stops in front of a shelf by the door. The shelf rests across the top of a row of twelve cubby holes. (see Figure 3.1) Deftly slipping Patrick's bag off her arm, she puts it temporarily in the cubby hole labeled Patrick. The compartment is large, and easily holds the bulky bag. Claire places her pocket book on the shelf near a stack of forms.

"Hold on, there, Long Ranger," she laughingly tells her bouncing son, "I've still got to make my notes in your record."

FIGURE 3.1: INFANT CUBBY HOLES AND DAILY RECORD CLIPBOARDS

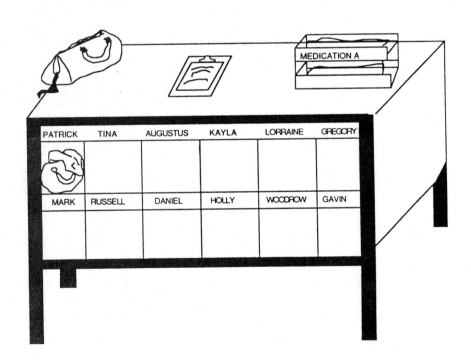

Above the cubby holes hang twelve clip boards, grouped in sets of four corresponding to each caregiver. Claire takes down the clip board labeled Patrick under Patrick's caregiver's name, Amanda. She moves Patrick in a position facing over her shoulder, which makes it easier for her to write. She gives him a few jounces in time to the music and Patrick responds with a giggle.

Putting the clipboard on top of the shelf, Claire picks up the attached pen and, with her free hand, begins to fill in the Infant Daily Record form. (see Figure 3.2) She writes hard to make sure that the carbon she will get will be legible. The original, she knows, is filed in the center records.

Claire looks at the Health section.

"How's your health, Patrick my boy?" she asks as she writes teething in the space under Parent's Statement. Patrick responds by patting her on her head.

"Easy, baby." Claire says recalling the time she had spent getting her hair the way she wanted it. She fills in the Medication section and writes 6:00 AM, the time she last applied Patrick's medication.

"Here, Patrick," she says putting Patrick down so she can look up the prescription number of the medicine, "Play with these," she gives Patrick her keys. Claire moves to the Feeding section and writes in the times Patrick started and completed his last bottle and the amount of formula he drank. While Patrick jangles the keys, she writes the time she last changed Patrick, checking Wet to show that she changed a wet diaper.

In the Sleeping section Claire records: 5:00 AM, sighing briefly at the early time Patrick awakened.

One more section: TODAY ONLY. Claire remembers that this is the day her mother, Naomi, takes Patrick to the Infant and Grandparent class at the Community College. So she writes, "Grandmother, Mrs. Hughes, will pick up Patrick at 11:00 AM." She pauses for a second and thinks about what could go wrong. The regular staff know that her mother is authorized to pick up Patrick. But what if there were a substitute today? Her mother doesn't approve of Patrick going to a center for care. She had tried to persuade Claire to place Patrick with a provider of family type care who cared for one or two infants in her home. (see Appendix B: DYK 3.1) So Claire knows that Naomi would be impatient, if she were made to wait while the authorization was checked before Patrick was released to her. To avoid any problems Claire prints, "See Patrick's file for authorization and identification." Then she adds, "Change

Patrick into the blue and white track suit before Mrs. Hughes arrives. Thanks." At least her mother won't be able to say that the center doesn't keep Patrick neat and clean.

Claire calls out, "We're here," just as Amanda steps out of the kitchen to greet her and Patrick.

3.1.2 The Daily Health Inspection

Patrick smiles and puts out his arms when he sees Amanda, dropping the keys in the process. Amanda picks him up, gives him a big hug and dances with him towards the *diapering room*. Patrick looks at her fondly, and they both smile and wave to Claire as they circle by. Claire checks her watch. It is 7:12 AM. Good. No hurry yet, she thinks as she picks up her keys. Amanda lays Patrick on the changing table. He looks up at her expectantly. He knows Amanda always says a rhyme as she does his Daily Health Inspection. (see Table 3.1)

Amanda has a large repertoire of rhymes. Today, as she checks Patrick for signs of ill health, bruises, swellings, bumps, scratches and other marks, she chants,

"Two little eyes twinkling at me.

Two little ears like shells by the sea.

Two lovely cheeks as pink as a rose.

That's Patrick Charles as everyone knows."

Patrick giggles as Amanda tickles the parts of his body.

"Patrick is cutting another tooth. You might want to look at it." Claire tells Amanda.

Amanda touches Patrick's lips. "Open up, Patrick. We've got to see your gum . . . Oh, it does look tender."

"I brought some more medicine for it," Claire says, "It is something new that seems to work."

3.1.3 Diapering

Since Patrick is wet, Amanda starts to change him. She puts Patrick's wet diaper in a plastic lined receptacle labeled, Soiled Cloth Diapers Only . . . Diaper Service. (See Figure 3.3) Claire watches as Amanda takes a pre-dampened cloth from a shelf above the changing table and wipes Patrick's bottom, talking to him all the while. Keeping one hand on the baby, Amanda reaches over and puts the soiled cloth in a four gallon

TABLE 3.1: SAMPLE SIGNS/SYMPTOMS OF ILLNESS FOR EXCLUSION FROM A CHILD CARE CENTER (OREGON, 1988)

(a)   A center shall not admit or retain in care, except, with the written approval of the local health officer, a child who:

  (A) Is diagnosed as having or being a carrier of a day care-restricted disease as defined by the Health Division rules;

       or

  (B) Has one of the following symptoms, or combinations of symptoms, or illness:

    1. Fever over 101.5 $^\circ$ F

    2. Diarrhea (more than 1 abnormally loose stool per day)

    3. Vomiting

    4. Nausea

    5. Severe cough

    6. Unusual yellow color to skin or eye

    7. Skin or eye lesions or rashes that are severe, weeping, or pus filled;

    8. Stiff neck and headache with one or more of the symptoms listed above;

    9. Difficult breathing or wheezing; or

    10. Complaints of severe pain

(b)   A child who shows the above signs of illness, shall be isolated and the parent(s)notified and asked to remove the child from the center as soon as possible.

(c)   If a child has mild cold symptoms which do not impair his/her functioning, the child may remain in the center and the parents notified when they pick up their child. (p. 22)

FIGURE 3.2: INFANT DAILY RECORD

FOR_____   Date:_____

<u>Caregiver:</u>_____   <u>Time Baby Arrived</u>: _____   <u>Departed:</u>
_____

===

<u>HEALTH</u>

Medication:

<u>Parent Statement:</u>   <u>Time</u>:   <u>Type</u>:   <u>Amount:</u>   <u>Prescription#:</u>

_____

<u>Daily Health Inspection:</u>

===

<u>FEEDING:</u>

Time Started: Time Completed: Type :   Amount: Comment:

_____

_____

_____

_____

Supplements:_____

===

<u>DIAPERING:</u>

<u>TIME</u>   <u>Check</u>   <u>Wet</u>   <u>BM</u>   <u>TIME</u>   <u>Check</u>   <u>Wet</u>   <u>BM</u>

_____

_____

_____

===

<u>NAP/SLEEPING</u>   Pacifier :   Blanket :   Toy :

Time Down: Time Down: Time Down: Time Down:

Time Up: Time Up: Time Up: Time Up

===

<u>ACTIVITIES:</u>   Indoor: Outdoor:

===

<u>TODAY ONLY</u>:

plastic pail labeled, Soiled Cloths... Bleach Solution. The pail, which has an attached lid, is mounted on the wall within Amanda's reach, but out of splashing distance from the babies. Amanda then pats Patrick dry with a paper towel. She opens a Soiled Paper Products receptacle with a foot pedal and drops the towel in. She turns to Claire and asks, "Did you notice this new receptacle? It's great. I wish all of them had foot pedals."

Claire smiles.

"I know, it's weird to get excited about a waste container. But you'd be surprised how much of a difference it makes over a day's time."

"I'm sure it does. Every aid helps," Claire agrees, "In fact, I made myself one of those diaper pin holders you have and it does make a difference." Claire gestures to a six inch carpet square that is glued above the shelf, from which Amanda is taking a diaper pin. "No more panic about a lost safety pin."

"No," Amanda laughs, "it solved our disappearing diaper pin crisis. We all used to lose pins when diapering. You wouldn't think it would be possible to misplace a pin. But you'd be ready to pin a baby's diaper and the pin would be gone. Just gone. Of course, the first time you'd be sure that the baby swallowed it, even though you were watching her all the time. Then later you'd find pins in your pockets or even under the clean diaper pile."

Another staff member, Eve, overhears and adds, "Remember the time I placed a pin in my shoulder pad and forgot where I'd put it. Ruth saw it. I was so embarrassed! What if an infant had grabbed it?"

As Amanda pins the clean diaper she looks once more at Patrick's body, limbs, head, and face. She sees nothing unusual and so redresses him.

With a final, "There you go, my fellow," Amanda picks up Patrick and takes him to a barrier protected crawling space in the open play/feeding room that is called the *activity area*. She places him on his stomach in front of an unbreakable wall mirror. Claire understands the signal. Patrick has passed Amanda's health inspection and has been accepted into the center. Claire can now unpack Patrick's things and she goes back to the cubby holes to do so. Amanda meanwhile moves to the diapering room. Claire can hear her spraying the changing table surface with a disinfectant and tearing off a paper towel to wipe it dry.

It is 7:17 AM. Claire has Patrick's things unpacked and goes into the diapering room to tell Amanda that she is almost ready to leave. Amanda is at the sink between the two changing tables. She can see Patrick

FIGURE 3.3: DIAPERING ROOM

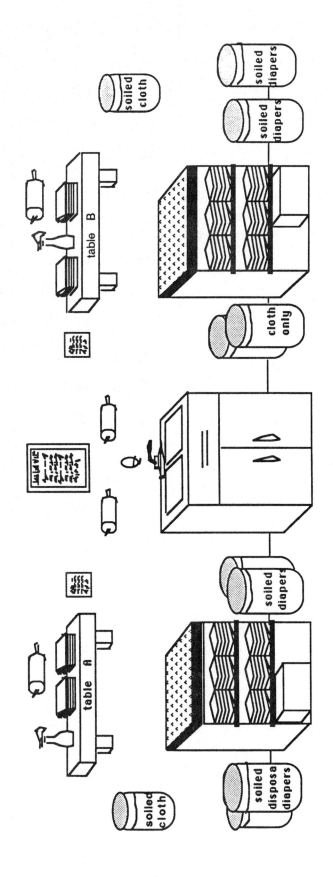

through the diapering room window which lets the caregivers watch their babies as they wash their hands. Amanda uses soap and hot running water, and rubs her hands together vigorously. Claire asked her about that once. She replied that Bridget, the center's consultant nurse, told her it was friction that removes the bacteria, not just the soap. Amanda dries her hands with a paper towel and drops it into the soiled paper products receptacle, opening it with a flourish of her foot. She looks at the open gate of the diapering room and thinks that as the babies have started to arrive, it is time to close and latch it.

Patrick is talking to his image in the mirror. Amanda goes towards him. She bends down and leans over the barrier that is around the crawling space. She catches Patrick's eye in the mirror and sings,

"Patrick, Patrick, Patrick,

Come and have your hands washed.

Patrick, Patrick, Patrick."

Patrick rolls over and crawls swiftly to Amanda. He sits, holds out his hands to her and says, "Up." Claire beams.

Amanda says, "You little darling. Yes, Patrick I will pick you up and wash your hands ready for breakfast."

Amanda washes Patrick's hands and dries them with a paper towel. Patrick looks at his hands and Amanda says another of her rhymes,

"Four little fingers and a thumb are on each.

Washed and ready to hold a spoon or a peach."

She then hands Patrick to his mother so Claire can give her baby one last hug before leaving him for the day.

3.1.4 Authorization And Storage Of Medication

"Oh, I almost forgot," Claire says and hands Amanda the physician's medication authorization. It is written on a standard form provided by the state child care Licensing Authority. It is dated and signed by Claire and Patrick's pediatrician.

Amanda reads the physician's directions. Then while Claire is holding Patrick and saying goodbye, she picks up his Infant Daily Record and in the medication section she writes, Check Current Medication File. (see Figure 3.4) Ruth, the program supervisor, demands that staff use the physician's original directions rather than a paraphrased version.

Claire looks at the clock. It is 7:25 AM. She is happy to be able to hold Patrick while his caregiver takes care of the medical procedures.

FIGURE 3.4: CURRENT MEDICATION FILE AND CARD

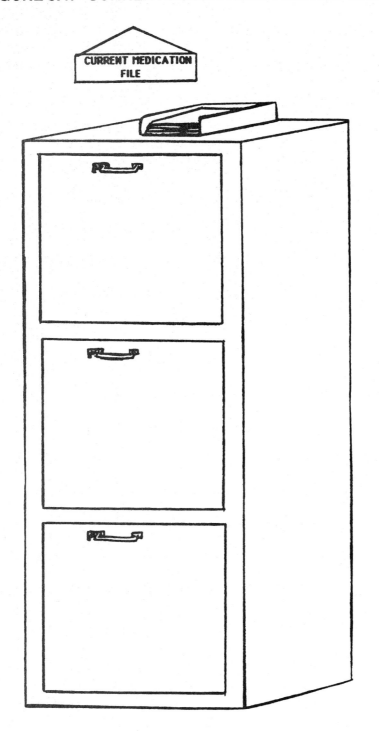

"What's Amanda doing, Patrick?" Patrick and she watch as Amanda hurries to the filing cabinet near the telephone and takes out a file labeled Current Medication. She puts Patrick's medication authorization and directions in the file and removes a sturdy card from the back of the file. The card has Current Medication File printed on it in large letters. She hooks it by the attached string loop to a hook on the wall above the filing cabinet. Amanda places the Current Medication file on top of the filing cabinet beneath the sign. Claire knows that the purpose of the card is to alert the program supervisor, who monitors medication administration, that someone is having medication today. She then comes back to Claire for Patrick's medication and carries it to a small cabinet high on the wall labeled, Medication Internal Use: Not Refrigerated. Amanda takes the key from the hook beside the cabinet, unlocks it, puts Patrick's medication inside, relocks the cabinet and replaces the key. Claire is impressed with the safety precautions and reminds herself to get a lock for her medicine cabinet at home.

3.1.5 Departing And Signing In

Time to leave. Claire gives Patrick one last squeeze and says, "Kiss Mommy bye bye." Patrick opens his mouth to give her his version of a kiss, then puts out his arms to go to Amanda. At first it gave Claire a pang to see Patrick so willingly go to Amanda, but now she is thankful. It is one indication that Patrick is happy at the center, and she can concentrate on her work during the day without worrying about her baby. Then, too, she knows that at the end of the day Patrick will be expecting *her.* She is comforted by thoughts of how he greets her with outstretched arms and his little yelp of pleasure.

Claire picks up the clipboard holding the *Sign In/Sign Out Sheet* from the shelf on top of the cubby holes. The sheet lists the names of the twelve enrolled infants and their caregivers. (see Figure 3.5) She checks her watch and writes 7:30 AM and her signature besides Patrick's name.

Claire then takes a blank *medication authorization form* from the stack on the top of the cubby holes, in case she needs one for Patrick's next doctor's visit. She puts the form in her pocket book, picks up Patrick's empty bag and hurries out the door.

Once outside, Claire looks back and sees Amanda and Patrick waving to her from the window. She starts the car and as she backs out, she glances one last time at the center window. Patrick and Amanda are

FIGURE 3.5: A FILLED-IN SIGN IN/SIGN OUT SHEET
(UNIT#___)

DATE: _____

BABY	TIME SIGN IN	SIGNATURE	TIME SIGN OUT	SIGNATURE
Patrick	7.30AM	Claire Hunt	5.45 PM	Claire Hunt
Lorraine	7:45AM	Anne Furch	5.10 PM	Anne Furch
Augustus	7.55AM	Adam Blake	6.05PM	Adam Blake
Tina	8.0 am	Stefan James	6.0 Pm	Stefan James
Gregory	8.05 Am	Maggie Hanna	5.55 pm	Maggie Hanna
Mark	8.0 am	Nancy Osche	6.15 PM	Nancy Osche
Kayla	8.22am	Carol Danski	5.20 Pм	Carol Danski
Russell	8.25am	Margaret Jane	6.30PM	Margaret Jane
Daniel	8.35	Patricia Chen	5.3PM	Patricia Chen
Harrison	8.40 am	Orson Martons	6.30 Pm	Orson Martons
Holly	9.00AM	Victor Donald	6.15PM	Victor Donald
Tavin	9.05AM	Ronald Barr	5.30 pm	Ronald Barr

CAREGIVERS:

NAME	TIME SIGN IN	SIGNATURE	TIME SIGN OUT	SIGNATURE
Amanda	6.48am	Amanda Lynley	3:00 pm	Amanda Lynley
Priscilla	6.45am	Priscilla White	3.00PM	Priscilla White
Eve	6.55am	Eve Wallington	3:00 PM	Eve Wallington
Marilyn	2.45 Pм	Marilyn Martin	6.00Pm	Marilyn Martin
Joyce	2.45Pm	Joyce Janzen	6.45 Pm	Joyce Janzen
Beverley	2.45 PM	Beverley Muscadine	6.45 Pm	Beverley Muscadine

bobbing up and down dancing in time to the morning arrival music. She feels a momentary twinge of regret that she is not there with her baby, but is reassured by knowing that he is safe and enjoys the time he spends with the other babies and caregivers.

3.1.6 Food Preparation And Feeding

Back in the center, Amanda and Patrick dance until the end of the song. Amanda knows she will have to hurry if she is to have Patrick fed and playing in a crawling space by the time Tina arrives at 7:45 AM. Still carrying Patrick, she bends down to unlatch the gate that is in front of the food preparation room doorway. It is tight and hard to manipulate. "Something will have to be done about this." Amanda mutters to herself. Then, not wanting to squander time, she swiftly steps over the gate. She is glad it is low enough for her to step over, but high enough to keep crawling or walking infants from toppling over. (see Chapter Five)

Patrick likes to go into the food preparation room in the morning. He turns and stretches his neck to see what food Priscilla, another of Amanda's co-workers, is serving up. Priscilla is the first caregiver to arrive at the center each morning and generally arrives a little before 7:00 AM. She is always busy at this time unpacking the dishwasher, preparing the formula for the day, and measuring out the food for breakfast and lunch. Although she has a lot to do, within the forty minutes before her first baby Augustus arrives, she takes time to exchange Hi's with Patrick.

Priscilla hands Amanda Patrick's breakfast. It is served in two sterilized glass baby food jars. Patrick is hungry and looks at Priscilla questioningly. "See Patrick," she says, "one jar contains cereal mixed with your yummy formula and the other contains freshly mashed bananas." Patrick bounces in Amanda arms, "Yes, this is yours," Amanda tells him, "see your name on the jars." Mikki likes the caregivers to use baby food jars to measure and serve the soft baby style food. "One reason," she says, "you know how much each jar contains and so can measure the babies food intake more accurately." Mikki also likes to use them because they are abundantly available, easy to store and sanitize, and, as she frequently says, "It is a shame to throw such functional things away." Priscilla likes to write on the clear glass. The black waterproof ink she uses to label the jars with the baby's name stands out, and as she likes to remind everyone they can also be thrown away after being used by an ill infant . . . or if dish washing becomes too much of a chore."

Amanda places Patrick's food on top of the toy storage shelves in the activity area. She moves a high chair close by, straps Patrick in with the safety straps, and adjusts the tray. "Only one more thing to do Patrick, and then you can eat," she says. She takes a plastic bib from the cloth bag attached to the back of the high chair and puts it on Patrick.

Patrick says, "Na na na." Amanda smiles, "You can smell the bananas, can't you Patrick?" She pulls up a chair and sits down. Patrick opens his mouth as Amanda picks up the spoon. Amanda talks to Patrick as she feeds him. Between mouthfuls Patrick says, "Na na na," and Amanda repeats, "Bananas. Patrick likes bananas."

Amanda sees that Priscilla's first infant, Augustus, and his father Adam have entered the center. She looks at the clock. It is 7:40 AM. She also notes that Eve has completed her first infant's Daily Health Inspection and is redressing her. She asks Eve to watch Patrick for a minute, making sure that she replies. Ruth, the program supervisor, makes a point of these replies: "Your infants must be continually supervised," she always says. "Never assume another caregiver will watch your infants. And if you ask another person to keep an eye on them for a moment, make sure that person has heard. Listen for her reply."

Amanda goes to the food preparation room, rinses Patrick's empty food jars, and places them in the dishwasher. She waves to Patrick through the large window in the wall that separates it from the activity area. The morning arrival tape is playing and Amanda can see Patrick moving in time to the music. She only has a short time before her next infant, Tina, arrives. So she hurries back to Patrick, removes his bib, releases the tray, undoes the safety straps, and picks him up. Taking Patrick with her she again quickly steps over the gate to the diapering room and walks towards the sink. "Patrick you keep me in good shape," she says as she bends down, opens the cupboard under the sink, and puts Patrick's used bib in a receptacle labeled Used Sheets, Blankets, Bibs.

"I know you want to dance Patrick, Paddy-Pat," she says using her pet name for him. "So we'll do a little jig while we tidy up." Amanda and Patrick sway to the music as she dampens a paper towel, wipes off the high chair tray, puts the paper towel in the used Paper Products Receptacle, and then washes and dries Patrick hands.

"That little dance should keep you going for awhile," she tells Patrick as she carries him to the activity area and places him in a barrier protected crawling space. Amanda sits him beside a small plastic basket of toys she had ready and props a large cushion behind him in case he topples backward.

3.1.7 Planning Ahead

It is 7:44 AM. Amanda goes back to the cubby holes. She must note Patrick's health inspection, diaper change, and feeding on his *Infant Daily Record* before she forgets the details. She would like to be able to fill in her records as each event occurs, but as she knows only too well that seldom happens. But she likes her records to be accurate and her writing to be readable and time has to be made for this. She still feels a flush of embarrassment as she recalls the panic she created when as a novice caregiver she muddled up her records. The parents of a two month old baby were more than surprised to read on the infant daily record that their little one had eaten spinach, carrots, and chicken, while the parents of a lively ten month old wanted to know why their daughter had only been fed small amounts of formula. "Mistakes like that must not be repeated," Amanda says to herself as she double checks Patrick's name before she fills in his record.

Amanda can see through the window that Tina and her father, Stefan, are getting out of the car. Amanda returns to the diapering area and, with an eye on Patrick, washes and dries her hands to be ready to greet Tina. She must complete Tina's Daily Health Inspection and have her playing on the floor with Patrick before Mark, her third infant, arrives at 8:00 AM. She is thankful that Stefan gives Tina her breakfast and she hopes Tina won't need changing immediately. Next Mark, and after that, Russell arrives. She knows that Priscilla has their food ready and labeled. Anyhow, she calculates, she has almost an hour to get ready for Russell. That should give her time to get the other three babies settled and to try out the clapping game she thought up while watching TV the night before. "One thing, for sure," she thinks. "In this job you are never bored!"

3.2 ANALYSIS 1: WORKING WITHIN LICENSING STANDARDS

In the narrative you have just read, you can see that caregivers are busy. Amanda, as she cares for her first infant Patrick, continually checks the time and plans ahead for the arrival of her other infants. It may seem that she spends a lot of time washing her hands, wiping off surfaces, and depositing waste or dirty products in special labeled containers. These procedures are not set by the whim of the center director. They are mandated by the licensing minimum standards. Details for health care, storing the babies' clothing, handling of medications, diapering, feeding, recording information, as well as when the caregiver is to wash her hands and those of the baby are specified in the standards.

3.2.1: A Closer Look At Health And Safety Precautions

The safety and health of infants and toddlers is of prime concern to their parents and caregivers. The Centers for Disease Control has called child care facilities, a major hotbed for the spread of infection. Any time children are brought together a child with a contagious illness can infect one or more of the others. It is particularly important, therefore to guard against the spread of illness by specifying regulations and monitoring compliance.

Daily Health Inspections: Wide Variation

An examination of the licensing standards regulating Daily Health Inspections over the last three decades reveals a surprising fact. Several states, which in earlier versions specified that Daily Health Inspections must take place *upon arrival or before the child joins the group,* leave out that requirement in later versions. Instead, they make less specific statements such as, "staff shall observe each child daily," "no child who appears ill shall be admitted" or, "If a child suffers an illness during the day he shall be isolated." On the other hand many states have expanded their regulations and include signs or symptoms to observe, a written plan specifying the Daily Health Inspection procedure, and required staff training in performing the procedure. California, for many years, has had precise regulations about the daily admittance of a child to a center. Parents cannot simply leave a child off, with a call that he or she is there: They must sign in the child *after* center personnel have checked that the child is free of illness.

As well as the health of the babies, the health of the caregivers should also be monitored. One state, New Hampshire (Draft, 1988) specifies that the director (or the director's designee) shall observe each staff member, daily upon arrival and throughout the day, for symptoms of illness. Staff members showing signs of illness must be isolated from the children and must not prepare or handle food.

Hand Washing: Time Consuming But Necessary

The Arkansas standards of 1969 printed in large bold print the following: **Workers must wash their hands with soap after each diaper change regardless of how many babies are to be changed.** (U.S. Dept. Of Health, 1971) At that time few states addressed hand washing. Today it would be most unusual for a state not to specify when caregivers wash their own hands and the hands of the children in their care. Without a doubt, caregivers who are feeding and changing several infants throughout the day must frequently wash their hands. Usually caregivers check or change each baby's diaper every hour, and may be required to wash their hands *after* each change or before *and* after each change. Visualize a caregiver caring for *four* infants for *eight* hours a day who is required to wash her hands *after* each diapering, with diapers checked or changed hourly. In such an instance the caregiver, for diapering alone, would wash her hands thirty-two times. At two minutes for proper washing, thirty two after diapering hand washes would occupy at least sixty-four minutes of the day. And that is only for the washing of the caregiver's hands after diapering and does not include the time spent in washing the infants' hands. Remember, hand washing is also done before and sometimes *after* feeding, administering medication or supplements, removing caregiver protective clothing, as well as after wiping noses, spit ups, and dribbles. There is an increasing tendency for center staff to use food service type gloves when diapering. But as the hands can be contaminated when removing the gloves, hand washing is also required. As it is now recognized that hand washing is an effective way to decrease the spread of disease, frequency and thoroughness are necessary, and time must be given to this health precaution.

Medication: Many Rigorous Safety Regulations

Some states have regulations for prescription and non-prescription medication, while others make no distinction between them and use the term medication to cover both types. Typically state licensing standards require centers to obtain authorization or instructions from a licensed physician or a parent before administering medication to children. Some provide forms on which the authorizations and/or instructions are to be written. Some let centers use whatever form they choose and others accept the prescription label as the physician's order.

Generally, licensing regulations specify that medication must be kept in the original labeled container and stored out of the reach of children in locked and labeled storage. Usually medication for internal use and medication for external use have to be stored separately. Medication that requires storage in the refrigerator must be stored away from food. Some states require refrigerated storage to be locked. Others permit storage of refrigerated medicines in a closed, leakproof, and labeled receptacle.

Many states require centers to take precautions to avoid duplicating administering medicine. These range from having one person responsible for medication to having a bulletin board or chart that displays the time for medication and a notation when it has been administered. Centers are also usually required to have a written plan for procedures for recording medication, for reporting to parents and for filing and keeping the medication record on hand for a specified time.

A trend, evident in recent revisions of licensing standards, is the medication administration option given to providers. For example, California (1989) has medication standards for centers where the licensee chooses to handle medication, and New Mexico (1987) regulations state that facilities have the right to refuse to give any medications. In the United States Navy centers many commands and directors prefer not to administer medication to children. Instead they request that a parent come to the center and give his/her child the medication. The United States Army (Draft, 1988) regulations allow caregivers to administer medication in full day care programs and in sick child care settings. However, they require a physician or parents to administer the first dosage, and the child must be on oral medication for forty-eight hours before dosage is administered by the Child Development Services personnel. This goes along with the increasing number of states that license centers to provide Get Well Care or care for the Mildly Ill. This care for temporary illness can be a primary service of a center, or an optional component of a regular child care facility.

As indicated in the narrative, medication *is* administered at Infant and Toddler Center USA. Each infant's caregiver is responsible for administering the dosage and recording it in the Infant's Daily Record. Authorization for *all* medication is required from the infant's licensed physician and parent, and is written on a form supplied by the licensing authority. The forms are stored on top of the infants' cubby holes, so they are always available to parents. Parents, as we saw Claire do, take a new form whenever they give a filled-in one to the caregivers. The medication is kept under locked storage. The current authorization forms are kept, not in each infant's file, but in a single file, on top of a filing cabinet. A card above the medication file reminds all the staff that "Someone is having medication today." It also alerts the program supervisor, who oversees and monitors the medication procedure, that medication is stored and is being administered at the center that day.

Authorization And Identification For The Release Of Children: A Reflection Of The Times

As well as taking precautions to guard the physical health and safety of children, providers must guard their personal safety. Most child care safety regulations specify that custodial parents must authorize, in writing, the center release of their child to another person. This is generally done prior to the enrollment of the child, when parents are required to name a person(s) the center can contact in an emergency. The techniques used today would surprise workers of a decade or so ago. An increasing number of centers require the authorized person to present a photo identification for verification as well as a signature, each time the child is released from the center. Unforeseen emergencies occur and a parent may have to contact the center by phone to authorize the release of their child. Today, this type of release is not taken lightly. For example, the Arizona (1988) licensing standards require centers to develop procedures to verify phone authorizations made by custodial parents. The Delaware (1988) standards require centers to develop a procedure to follow when an unauthorized person or one showing signs of drug or alcohol use, requests release of a child.

Touch Policy: *United States Army Child Development Services (CDS): Protection For Children And Their Caregivers*

Standards for the care of infants and toddlers generally require caregivers to nurture, hold, cuddle, or rock the babies they care for. Most caregivers find it easy to love and caress young children, but today's caregivers need to know that an innocent pat or tickle could be construed as an inappropriate action. The United States Army (Draft, 1988), with the assistance of the considerable resources available to the personnel of its Child Development Services (CDS), has designed a policy that describes appropriate and inappropriate touches. (see Table 3.2) State licensing authorities will undoubtably incorporate a similar policy in future revisions of their licensing standards.

TABLE 3.2: TOUCH POLICY UNITED STATES ARMY CHILD DEVELOPMENT SERVICES (CDS)

The CDS touch policy will address appropriate versus inappropriate touches.

(1) Appropriate touching involves: (a) Recognition of the importance of physical contact to child nurturing and guidance. (b) Adult respect for personal privacy and personal space of children. (c) Responses affecting the safety and the well being of the child e.g., holding hand of the child when crossing the street; holding child gently but firmly during a temper tantrum. d) Direct service personnel modeling appropriate touching.

(2) Examples of appropriate touching include hugs, lap sitting, reassuring touches on the shoulder, and nap time back rubs for a tense child.

(3) Inappropriate touching: (a) Involves coercion or other forms of exploitation of the child's lack of knowledge. (b) Involves satisfaction of the adult's needs at the expense of the child. (c) Violates a cultural taboo against sexual contact between children and adults. (d) Attempts to change child behavior with adult physical force, often applied in anger. (e) Reinforces concept with child of striking out to respond to a problem.

(4) Examples of inappropriate touching include forced goodbye kisses, corporal punishment, slapping, striking or pinching, prolonged tickling, fondling or molestation. (a) Because boundaries for appropriate and inappropriate touch have often been unconscious and undefined, CDS management personnel must discuss touch of this issue with CDS direct services personnel to ensure a correct understanding.

(United States Army Draft, 1988 p. 2-25)

ANALYSIS 2: THE PLIGHT OF THE NATION'S CAREGIVER

In the late 1980's child care advocates formed a national alliance for promoting federal legislation. The alliance, known as the Alliance for Better Child Care (see Appendix B: DYK 3.2) concentrated on regulations and training. Although a requirement for states to develop a plan for raising the salaries, and addressing other compensation for child care workers was included, an issue it warranted was not made about the low wages and lack of benefits of those who care for the nation's young. Cherlin (1988) notes that trends in the late 1980's tended to favor the middle class: Although, in 1987, the Federal government funded child development food and education (Head Start), and job training programs intended to break the welfare cycle, over half (3.5 billion of the $6 billion dollar total) went to assist middle class parents through the dependent care tax credit. The poor pay almost a quarter of their family incomes for child care, while the non-poor pay only a tenth. One could argue that the middle class could pay for more of child care costs.

Comparative Worth Of Caregivers

Improvements such as more comprehensive regulations for the care of children in child care facilities, monetary assistance to parents to pay for their children's care, and training for child care providers and staff, are necessary. But these actions will be futile without improvements in the comparative worth of caregivers. It is a national scandal that those responsible for our nations youngest citizens are so poorly compensated compared with non-skilled workers. In Seattle, for example, a person who waves a flag for traffic on the ferry docks makes three or four times as much in pay and benefits as a child care worker! Improving the pay and benefits, and thus the status of child care workers, should also alleviate the high turnover rate of child care workers. That in turn would improve the stability of personnel, so that children receive continuity of care. (see Appendix B: DYK 3.3)

The Impact Of Upscale Child Care Centers

Entrepreneurs have invested in the $12 billion child care industry. (see Appendix B: DYK 3.4) Many have located their centers in affluent neighborhoods, and designed their services to provide high quality, high priced child care for two income families in the $70,000 and up income bracket (New York Times, 1988).

Concerns have been voiced that the growth of upscale child care will create a two tier system, one for the rich and one for the poor. In answer to this, entrepreneurs say that the demand for high quality care will raise standards for all children and increase salaries for child care workers. To attract the best teachers and prevent the high rate of staff turnover that plagues the child care service, upscale child care providers frequently pay as much as 30% above the usual child care worker salaries. (see

Appendix B: DYK 3.5) How does the increased salary of the child care workers affect the profit that entrepreneur providers would expect? One attraction of the child care industry, to investors, is that stable profits can be made without a continual outlay of capital. But as labor can amount to 60% to 80% of the total budget, and high rent districts eat up more, entrepreneurs may have to settle for an 8% profit rather than the 15% they favor. What may we ask . . . if quality care for babies and salaries and benefits for child care workers are improved . . . is the matter with that?

3.4: SUMMARY

In this chapter we looked at a caregiver's morning arrival tasks in an organized and smoothly running center. We saw how busy Amanda was caring for Patrick, one of her four babies. So many regulations govern what caregivers must do, that it may seem impossible to follow them all when caring for several infants. But regulations, such as those shown in this chapter, protect babies cared for in child care facilities, and cannot be ignored. Caregivers *are* busy. Yet with careful design, planning, and parent cooperation, they can accomplish all of the tasks required, and still have time for "teaching" appropriate behaviors while they nurture and care for their babies.

In chapters Four and Five we will look at how the caregiving tasks can be analyzed and how procedures can be designed to help caregivers expeditiously handle the routines required by licensing standards.

Chapter Four

REDUCING ROUTINE CARE LOADING THROUGH PARENT PARTICIPATION

RUTH, THE PROGRAM SUPERVISOR, RECALLS REDESIGNING THE MORNING ARRIVAL PROCEDURES

OBJECTIVES

After you have read this chapter you should be able to . . .

1. Describe the tasks required of caregivers for the morning arrival of infants.
2. Define Care Loading and describe how Arrival Spacing evens out care loading, and improves the quality of care of infants during morning arrivals.
3. Describe factors which must be taken into account when designing an arrival spacing plan.
4. Give an example of how each of the following affect care loading: (1) child/staff ratio (2) licensing standards (3) the design of center procedures (4) parent participation
5. Identify problems in the sequencing of procedures in a real or described center, and design an improved sequence.
6. Tell whether a procedure would or would not meet your state's licensing requirements.
7. List the responsibilities of a program supervisor and state three reasons for him or her to follow a flexible schedule.
8. Write a plan for communication between a center and parents, and identify situations which call for a written memo.

Parents are generally concerned about the welfare and happiness of their babies and usually cooperate with their caregivers. As a matter of course they comply with requests to bring in extra clothing or diaper pins, and frequently donate tapes, toys or books to the center. But parents are not used to being asked to play a more active roll in the center care of their children. In this chapter we will visit with Ruth, the program supervisor of Infant and Toddler Center USA, and learn how by asking the parents to help, she changed a chaotic morning arrival time into a pleasant experience for all.

4.1 NARRATIVE: RUTH, THE PROGRAM SUPERVISOR, RECALLS REDESIGNING THE MORNING ARRIVAL PROCEDURES

Ruth woke up in a reflective mood. The apartment was quiet. Her fourteen year old son and twelve year old daughter had already gone to school. She lay in bed staring at the ceiling, appreciating the schedule she had set up at Infant and Toddler Center USA that let her sleep in two days a week. In fact, she was very happy with her job. She had been supervisor of the four units at the center now for over six months and had made some changes that had worked out well. Ruth stretched, luxuriating in the satin sheets she bought herself for her thirty-sixth birthday a few days ago. Yes, she thought contentedly, the schedule was definitely a success.

Ruth planned her schedule so she would be at the four center units at different hours each day. Days like today she arrives at 10:30 AM, and leaves at 6:30 PM. On most days she arrives at the center at 7:00 AM, and leaves at 3:00 PM, and every so often she arrives at 9:00 AM and leaves at 5:00 PM. So that the staff know when she will be around, Ruth posts in advance her center arrivals and departures.

The schedule wasn't designed just for her personal convenience. She designed it originally so she would be at the center sometimes at the beginning of the day and sometimes at the end of the day. This flexibility lets her model a range of center procedures for staff, see the parents and babies at both arrival and departures times, and be available to help solve problems that occur anytime during the center operation.

Ruth got out of bed recalling the problem that confronted her on her very first day at the center. It was in March and was a cold rainy day. She had arrived early, surprising the caregivers at 6:45 AM. Amanda and Priscilla were already there and Eve arrived a few minutes later. Priscilla was preparing the infant's food and Amanda had just made a big pot of coffee. Eve had brought in some apricot and cheese pastries from her favorite bakery, and they all chatted as they ate the pastries and drank several cups of the chocolate flavored coffee.

At precisely 7:10 AM, Amanda's first baby, Patrick, had arrived. Amanda had completed his Daily Health Inspection, changed his diaper, and had just began to feed him when her second baby, Tina, arrived. Amanda had exclaimed, "Oh, no. Tina is so early."

Priscilla offered to go on feeding Patrick to allow Amanda to greet and attend to Tina. The Daily Health Inspection with Tina had not gone so quickly, since her father, Stefan, was talkative and had wanted the staff to give him their opinion on a new toy he had bought. Then at 8:15 AM, pandemonium had broken loose. Three of Priscilla's babies had arrived at the same time, followed rapidly by two of Eve's and the last two of Amanda's. Ruth pitched in to help but still the whole picture was one of chaos: Caregivers were rushing around to greet each new arrival. Greetings and health inspections were rushed. Parents were trying to give special instructions. Babies were lined up in swings or playpens waiting their turn to be fed or changed. It had taken the harassed caregivers most of the morning to catch up with the care of all their infants. By then the staff were ready to flop down with obvious weariness. "No wonder they start off the day pampering themselves with Danish pastries and chocolate flavored coffee." Ruth had said to herself as she sunk into the big bean bag chair to try to recover from the unexpected pandemonium she had just witnessed. Priscilla caught her eye and must have read her thoughts:

"What a way to start your first day here," she said.

Ruth had asked. "It's not usually like this, is it?"

"No. Usually our babies don't arrive all at once." Priscilla had replied.

But as the days went on, Ruth noted that they usually did. The parents gave approximate times they planned to arrive and some were frequently early, others frequently late. Most mornings this resulted in many arriving at the same time or within a few minutes of each other. Ruth observed that even on more normal days, staff became tense as they rushed to complete the mandatory Daily Health Inspections, feed hungry infants, listen to parents, change diapers, rearrange equipment and materials, and record information. It took only one extra task, such as an infant that required medication or a change of clothing, to throw off timing, so that the changing table would be tied up or several infants would be waiting for care.

Ruth had reflected on what Priscilla had said, "Usually our babies don't arrive all at once", and on the fact that although Priscilla had put her finger on the problem, no one had taken the next step of solving it. She was hired in part to solve such problems and it made her feel good to know she had been needed. It had became clear to Ruth that with several babies arriving nearly at the same time, a caregiver had too many tasks to do in too short a time. She decided to do something about it.

4.1.1 Arrival Spacing

At first Ruth had considered reassigning the infants, so that those that usually arrived together would be assigned to different caregivers. But Ruth had observed that the caregivers had developed special relationships with their assigned babies and clearly would not want to switch. Another possibility she considered was to request a third changing table, but there really wasn't space and she had to consider cost. Mikki had already warned her that the center's budget was limited. So she decided to ask the parents to help space out their morning arrival times.

Ruth called her plan arrival spacing. Arrival spacing she defined as the scheduling of infants' arrivals to provide enough time for each caregiver to get one infant admitted and settled before another of the caregiver's infants arrived.

Ruth had introduced arrival spacing in Unit #1. She had sounded out the parents on their preferred arrival times and had drawn up the schedule shown in Table 4.1. The three caregivers Amanda, Priscilla, and Eve, had at least fifteen minutes between the arrival of each of their infants. Amanda had a thirty-five minute interval between Patrick and Tina. Her other two infants, Mark and Russell, arrived fifteen minutes apart. Priscilla's infants, Augustus, Kayla, Daniel, and Holly, all arrived at twenty minute intervals. Eve had the most time between arrivals. Her first two infants, Lorraine and Gregory, arrived twenty minutes apart. Then forty minutes later Woodrow arrived, with a twenty minute interval between Woodrow and Gavin.

Ruth was very pleased with the parent reaction. Two of the mothers, to help space out the arrivals, had even arranged with their employers to arrive at work fifteen minutes later, and leave fifteen minutes later. (see Appendix B: DYK 4.1) Only one father, Victor, had balked at committing himself to a fixed time. But Ruth had arranged to be in the unit every day for a week after starting arrival spacing, and had finally convinced him not to arrive before 8:40 AM. That way his daughter, Holly, would be Priscilla's last baby to arrive, and after that time it would be less upsetting if she arrived late.

Except for a few moments of waiting for changing tables while two Daily Health Inspections were in progress, the spacing worked exactly as

TABLE 4.1: ARRIVAL SPACING PLAN INFANT AND TODDLER CENTER USA UNIT #1

CHANGING TABLE A

Caregiver: **Amanda**

INFANT	TIME
Patrick	7.10
Tina	7.45
Mark	8.0
Russell	8.15

Caregiver: **Eve**

INFANT	TIME
Lorraine	7.30
Woodrow	8.30
Gavin	8.50

CHANGING TABLE B

Caregiver: **Priscilla**

INFANT	TIME
Augustus	7.40
Kayla	8.0
Daniel	8.20
Holly	8.40

Caregiver: **Eve**

INFANT	TIME
Gregory	7.50

planned. Both the staff and parents were amazed at the difference these simple changes made in the morning routine. The morning arrival was still a busy time, but it was no longer hectic. Mikki was so happy about the way the parents were helping that she made and sent them all smiley face thank you cards. The parents, in turn, had the gourmet bakery across town deliver a cheese cake that they knew the staff enjoyed.

4.1.2 Care Loading

Yes, Ruth thinks as she goes down to eat breakfast, her arrival spacing plan fulfilled what she considers a major part of her job as a program supervisor: reducing care loading for staff, while increasing the level of care for the infants.

Ruth describes care loading as the number of tasks a caregiver performs during a specified time. The care loading during the morning arrival procedures when a caregiver's infants arrived at nearly the same time was much too high. By spacing out the arrivals Ruth had evened out care loading.

Ruth found that parents could help decrease routine care loading simply by being asked to cooperate. In addition to scheduling their infants' arrival times, Ruth asked parents to change the way they recorded information and instructions, and to adhere to center policies about morning greetings and Daily Health Inspections, filing medication authorizations, storing medication, and talking with caregivers. The first was easy.

Recording Daily Information

After instituting her arrival spacing plan, Ruth had observed the morning arrivals with an eye to further reducing care loading. She noticed that staff and parents were writing the information required by the licensing regulations onto four different forms. Parents recorded infant arrival times on one form called Sign In/Sign Out, and requested daily changes on a second form called *Today Only.* The staff, meanwhile recorded diaper changes and other routine caregiving notations onto a third form, the *Daily Record,* and put health and medical entries onto a fourth *Center Health and Medication Record.* Caregivers needed to consult all four different forms to keep track of each infant. Ruth combined three of the forms (the Today Only form, the old Daily Record, and the Center Health and Medication Record) onto one form she called the *Infant Daily Record.* She clipped each baby's Infant Daily Records on clipboards which she hung on hooks above the cubbyholes. On that one form, parents wrote their arrival time, notes, and health instructions for that day, and on the same form caregivers made their records about the child (see Figure 3.2). Ruth kept the old Sign In/Sign Out form as an attendance log for both parents and staff. It stated the time the child was officially admitted into the center and the time the child was officially discharged. Ruth asked the staff to use the Sign In/Sign Out sheet to sign in and out, too, instead of an attendance form they had formerly used. From the new Sign In/Sign Out sheet Ruth could now quickly check the infant/staff ratio in effect in the center, and that information was now also readily accessible to licensing authority personnel. (see Figure 3.5)

In addition to combining three forms into one, (and eliminating the staff attendance form), Ruth changed the time that parents signed in their babies. The licensing standards specified that parents were to sign in their infant *after* the baby's Daily Health Inspection was completed and the baby had been accepted into the center. Ruth observed that on the old *Sign In/Sign Out* sheet the parents wrote the time they arrived at the center, instead of the time the baby was officially accepted into the center. So when she designed the new recording system Ruth provided a space for the parents to fill in their arrival time on the Infant Daily Record, and a space for the parents to fill in the time that the infant was officially admitted on the *Sign In/Sign Out* sheet. Now there were only two working forms in the center: The Infant Daily Record, (see Figure 3.2) and the Sign In/Sign Out sheet. (see Figure 3.5)

Ruth had no trouble in getting Mikki's approval to try the new forms, and the parents and staff switched to them without any problems. Ruth had to work a bit harder, however, with the next changes she made in the morning arrival procedures.

Morning Greetings

As Ruth observed the arrivals she noticed that the staff tended to greet the infants and parents as soon as they entered the center, and that all staff tended to join in greeting each infant and parent. Often several caregivers would be talking to one parent, distracting him or her from filling in the Infant Daily Record and interfering with the direct supervision of the other babies in the center. The staff gathered around new arrivals which also distracted both parents and caregivers from following other licensing requirements. For example, parents would place medication that should be locked up or refrigerated into their infant's cubby hole, or parents would hand a medication authorization form or a physician's instruction slip to the caregivers when they were giving Daily Health Inspections, or at other times when they could not immediately file it. Caregivers would then put the papers in the most convenient place, usually on the shelf above the changing table or on top of the clean diapers underneath the changing table. Later, the caregivers would have to check several places to find where they put the medication paperwork.

Ruth suggested that the parents fill in their morning entries on the Infant Daily Record as soon as they entered the center and *before* the staff greeted them. This, she reasoned, would reduce the chatty greeting time and so speed the parents' recording of the information. She felt that more time would be saved, more distraction eliminated, and the required supervision of the babies maintained, if the staff greeted only the parents of their assigned infants. So she asked the caregivers to limit their morning conversation with the other parents to a brief Hello. She was worried, however, that the parents might think that the staff were aloof or unfriendly because they did not rush to meet the infants or chat to parents about topics unrelated to the care of their infants. She also wanted the staff to feel comfortable about reminding parents that they had other caregiving duties to perform. So she wrote a guideline for parents called *Talking to Center Staff* and a memo for staff called *Talking to Parents of Enrolled Infants.* (see Table 4.2).

Everyone agreed that the parents filling in their entries in their Infant's Daily Record before the staff greeted them was a good idea. The parents said they were now not only able to complete their notations faster, but were able to attend to what they were writing and so make more accurate notes. The caregivers found that this time they usually spent chatting to the parents could be well spent in caregiving tasks. They also had the parent's written comments about their baby's health before they started the infant's Daily Health Inspection.

Compliance With Daily Health Inspection Regulations

The design of the new forms took care of the parents prematurely signing in their infants. But Ruth realized that she *still* had changes to make. The parents tended to unpack their baby's bag, and store clothing and medication, while the Daily Health Inspections were in progress. These actions not only increased care loading for the staff, but as they assumed the baby was accepted into the center, they showed disregard for the intent of the Daily Health Inspection. So to help the parents comply with the regulations and follow the new action sequence she typed a guideline for parents called *Sequence Changes in the Morning Arrival Procedures.* (see Table 4.3) Then to emphasize the importance of following the sequence, as well as giving a copy of it to all the staff and parents, she framed the Guideline and posted it in a prominent position on the wall near the cubby holes.

As she did when she initiated the other sequence changes, Ruth scheduled her time to go through the actions in the procedures one by one with both the parents and the staff. The parents learned to wait until *after* the Daily Health Inspection (when the infant was accepted into the center for the day) before unpacking their infants' bags and giving the staff any medications, authorizations, and or physician's instruction slips.

TABLE 4.2: A SAMPLE GUIDELINES FOR PARENTS AND
MEMO TO STAFF

GUIDELINES FOR PARENTS: <u>TALKING TO CENTER STAFF</u>
From the Program Supervisor

POLICY: Parents of enrolled infants at <u>Infant and Toddler Center USA</u> shall be encouraged to talk about their infant and the center program with the center staff.

CLARIFICATION (1:) We like to talk to you. But we are bound by licensing regulations that are designed to protect your infant. So talk time has to be arranged so we can:

      a. Maintain an staff/infant ratio of 1:4, and a staff/toddler ratio of 1:5

      b. Supervise infants and toddlers at all times.

CLARIFICATION (2): Staff plan their time, during arrival and departure time, so they can get and give information about your infant. This permits <u>brief </u>discussion.

CLARIFICATION (3): Parent and Staff Conferences may be scheduled by appointment for longer discussions. During conferences the staff person is <u>not</u> counted in the staff/child ratio, so she is free to talk to you.

CLARIFICATION (4): The Program Supervisor works directly with center staff in the care of your infant, so she is not always free to talk with you. If by chance she has time she will talk with you on a drop-in basis. Do not count on this, as we have a practice of Infant First and time cannot be taken away from infant care for discussion.

The Program Supervisor may be contacted on (a) A time posted phone-in basis **
(b) A call back basis (c) A by chance basis (d) Appointment ** The phone in times change daily and are posted near the Sign In Sign Out sheet.

CLARIFICATION (5): The Director is usually available and may be contacted on:
(a) A phone-in basis (b) A call back basis (c) A drop-in basis (d) Appointment

REASSURANCE: We always answer the phone and someone is always available to take your message and give you information about your baby. We cannot guarantee that your infant's caregiver can always leave the babies in her care and speak to you. But every effort will be made to facilitate parent and center   communication and contact.

Table 4.2 (Continued)

MEMO TO STAFF: TALKING TO PARENTS OF ENROLLED INFANTS

From the Program Supervisor

POLICY: Parents of enrolled infants may visit the center at any time to:

a. Spend time with their infant

b. Observe the center program

Parents can do both <u>without</u> disrupting the infant/staff ratio and the care of the infants.

CLARIFICATION (1) Infant and Parent Arrivals and Departures are scheduled.

The time and program is planned so the caregiver's task includes giving information to and getting information from the parent. This permits <u>brief</u> discussion.

CLARIFICATION (2): Visits to the Center are not scheduled. The caregiver's task is to provide care for the infants. It is <u>not</u> to socialize with or entertain the parents.

CLARIFICATION (3): Parent and Caregiver Conferences are scheduled.

The caregiver is not counted in the infant/staff ratio and has <u>no</u> care giving assignment. The caregiver's task is to communicate with the parent. This permits a <u>long</u> discussion.

PROCEDURE: During infant and parent arrivals and departures, visits or unscheduled talks , when your main task is caring for the infants assigned to you:

Follow A Practice of Infant First . Be pleasant and polite while continuing your caregiving tasks. If need be excuse yourself from the parent to avoid:

a. Turning your back on the infants

b. Letting any of your infants wait for care

REMEMBER: Parents will be the first to appreciate a Practice of Infant First

Parents were asked to make sure that any medication was put in locked storage, and to sign in their babies *after* they said their farewells and were leaving the center.

Ruth also asked the parents to take their infant's empty bag as they left the center each morning. It was no trouble for them to take the empty bags to their cars, and it eliminated the clutter around the infants' cubby holes.

After a week of monitoring the redesigned procedure, and when the routines seemed to be going well, Ruth introduced the procedures in Unit #2 and then in Unit #3 and Unit #4. When all was running smoothly she went back to her usual schedule, arriving early some days and arriving late some days, like today.

TABLE 4.3 A SAMPLE <u>POSTED</u> GUIDELINE FOR PARENTS

GUIDELINES FOR PARENTS: SEQUENCE CHANGES IN THE MORNING
ARRIVAL PROCEDURE: From the Program Supervisor

INFANTS AND PARENTS

1. Enter the center
2. Place your infant's <u>unpacked</u> bag in his/her cubby hole
3. Fill in the morning entries on your <u>Infant's Daily Record:</u> **Record time arrived**
4. Greet your infant's caregiver
5. Give your infant to his/her caregiver and state <u>pertinent</u> information
6. **<u>Infant's Daily Health Inspection</u>**
7. Is your infant accepted into the center?
   YES   **NO**... Say good bye and leave the center
8. Unpack your infant's bag
9. Is your infant taking/using medication?
   YES   **NO**...Go to step 13
10. Give the medication authorization and written instructions to your infant's caregiver   **AND WHEN FILED**
11. Give the medication to your infant's caregiver
12. <u>Check</u> that the medication is placed in locked storage
13. Say good bye
14. <u>Sign In</u> your infant: **Record time leaving center**. Use legal signature
15. Take the infant's empty bag and a replacement medication form if need
16. Leave the center and have a happy day. We will take good care of your baby.

4.1.3 An Example Of How Ruth Used Daily Records To Monitor The Morning Arrival Procedures

While she is driving to work, Ruth thinks of the changes she has made that helped streamline the caregiving routines mandated by the licensing authority of her state. She thinks of the infants and their caregivers and visualizes them individually and in groups. She sees them in settings and episodes that give pleasure to what she does, or excite her about the challenges that her work brings.

She enters Unit #1, Infant and Toddler Center USA at exactly 10:00 AM. She carefully washes her hands, and greets the infants and staff. As usual, she looks at the *Sign In/Sign Out* sheet, and checks the clip boards holding the *Infant Daily Records.* In particular she looks at the time that Tina's father, Stefan, arrived (noted on the *Infant Daily Record*) and at the time he left the center (noted on the Sign In/Sign Out sheet).

"Hm. 7:42 to 8:15," She mutters to herself, "Over half an hour." Ruth was delighted when she first noted the extra monitoring aid that her new recording system provided. She discovered, one morning, that by checking the parents notation of their arrival time on their Infants Daily Record form and their sign in notation on the parent and staff Sign In/Sign Out sheet she had a specific record of the time spent by each parent and corresponding staff person for the baby's morning arrival procedure. (see Table 4.4)

Ruth notices that the *Medication Card* is not above the filling cabinet, and that the *Medication File* is not on top of it. (see Figure 3.4) "No medications today. Good." She says to Kayla who is lying in a playpen looking at a book. Ruth glances at her watch. She has ten minutes to spare before she has to call back Daniel's mother about some music tapes the parent is lending the center to use in the toddler units.

"Come on Kayla let's bogey to the music." She says as she bends down to pick up the baby.

Priscilla and Eve look at each other and smile. They know that Ruth never leaves without playing or dancing with some of the babies. As she dances with Kayla they see that Gavin is moving in time to the music and trying to catch Ruth's eye. He likes to dances and wants her to know that he is waiting for his turn. They also know that Ruth has seen him. She never misses things like that, and she'll signal him and let him know that he will have a turn before she goes.

TABLE 4.4 TIME IN MINUTES: INFANT ARRIVAL TO
SIGNING IN

INFANT	CAREGIVER	PARENT	TIME ARRIVED taken from Infant Daily R. (Date)	SIGN IN taken from Sign In/Out (Date)	TOTAL TIME
Patrick	Amanda	Claire	7.10	7.22	12 mins.
Lorraine	Eve	Anne	7.30	7.41	11 mins
Augustus	Priscilla	Adam	7.40	7.53	13 mins
Tina	Amanda	Stefan	7.42	8.15	27 mins
Gregory	Eve	Maggie	7.50	8.03	13 mins
Mark	Amanda	Janet	8.0	8.10	10 mins
Kayla	Priscilla	Carol	8.10	8.22	12 mins
Russell	Amanda	Margaret	8.15	8.25	10 mins
Daniel	Priscilla	Patricia	8.30	8.38	8 mins
Woodrow	Eve	Orson	8.30	8.40	10 mins
Holly	Priscilla	Victor	8.45	8.57	12 mins
Gavin	Eve	Ronald	8.50	9.02	12 mins

4.2 Analysis 1: Factors That Affect Care Loading

Care loading is defined as the number of tasks a caregiver performs during a specified time. It can be increased or decreased depending upon several factors listed below, not in order of their effect, but in an order that is convenient for discussion:

  a. Child/staff Ratio
  b. Licensing Regulations that Govern Routine Tasks
  c. The Design of Routine Procedures
  d. The Behavior of the Infant
  e. The Behavior/Training of the Caregivers
  f. Parent Participation
  g. The Center Facilities

In this analysis we shall examine child/staff ratio, licensing regulations that govern routine tasks, the design of routine procedures, and parent participation. The behavior of the infant and the behavior of the caregiver while continually referred to throughout the book will also be briefly discussed here. The center facilities although mentioned in this chapter are covered in detail in Chapter Five.

4.2.1 Child/Staff Ratio

Care loading is reduced when the child/staff ratio is reduced. For example, a caregiver who is caring for three infants has fewer diapers to change, fewer bottles to prepare, and spends less time washing her hands than one who is caring for five infants. But the economics of operating a center imposes a limit to the reduction that centers can make in their infant/staff ratios. As was shown in Chapter Three, if the wages paid to center workers were not so low, many centers could not operate with the ratios they *now* maintain. Hiring more workers is thus not generally a feasible way to reduce care loading in most centers. However, even with a given number of staff, there are ways to even out or reduce care loading. (see Balanced Exchanged Caregiving in Chapter One and Staggered Nap/sleeping in Chapter Two)

4.2.2 Licensing Regulations That Govern Routine Tasks

The licensing standards for health and safety, under which centers operate, have been set up to protect children. Necessary as the mandated regulations are, they increase routine care loading. On the other hand, regulations that fail to specify a necessary requirement do little to reduce care loading. For example, a regulation such as *infants upon arrival and before joining the group shall be observed for signs of illness,* requires a number of time-consuming steps. When a caregiver is complying with these requirements, that caregiver is not available to meet the needs of the other infants in his or her care. In contrast, a less specific regulation such as *infants shall be observed daily for signs of illness,* allows the caregiver to choose the time to observe the infants for signs of illness. The time chosen is frequently after the morning arrival rush is complete and after the parents have left the center. It may seem that eliminating the morning health check, upon arrival, will reduce care loading. But if a child who is sick is admitted, it will increase the amount of work placed upon caregivers later during the day. Not only does a sick baby require more care than a healthy one, but parents must be contacted, and the baby must be isolated and supervised until his or her parents arrive. Someone must be within sight and reach of the sick child. If one of the full time caregivers takes on that role what happens to the rest of her babies? In most centers the other caregivers must care for them along with their own babies, which of course increases *their* care loading. On top of all this, by not administering a health check, a center risks placing other babies in jeopardy of infection. Health inspections may seem to increase care loading, but they are necessary for the health of the children, and may actually reduce care loading in the long run.

4.2.3 The Design Of Routine Procedures

The challenge for the person who is responsible for selecting center routine procedures is to *choose or design procedures that reduce care loading for the staff and at the same time increase the level of care for the babies.* One may ask how this challenging task can be put into operation.

Complying With Licensing Standards

Procedures first of all *must* meet or exceed licensing standards. Reducing care loading does not require cutting down on, or omitting, caregiver tasks. Rather it implies analysing actions and organizing them for efficiency. Centers can adhere to state licensing standards in many ways. In the narrative we saw how Ruth made changes in the morning arrival procedures to ensure compliance with the Daily Health Inspection regulations. We also saw that although centers are required to keep Infant Daily Records the precise format of *how* information is to be recorded is rarely specified. This flexibility let Ruth change the format of the record forms used at the center, so the caregivers could check and record most information in one place instead of spending valuable time running around to locate and check four different forms.

Changing The Sequence Of The Actions In A Procedure

Looking at a procedure as a set of actions makes it easier not only to change what is done, but also easier to measure compliance. (see Chapter Five) Ruth, in her memo, *Sequence Changes in the Morning Arrival Procedures* made it clear for both the caregivers and the parents that the morning arrival procedure consisted of a definite set of actions. (see

Table 4.3) She was able to demonstrate not only that the sequence of the actions in a procedure could be changed, but that changes could eliminate confusion and save time. For example, requiring the parents to give their infant's medication to the caregiver *after* the medication authorization and instructions were filed, saved the time that caregivers later spent looking for the paperwork and storing the medication.

Streamlining To Reduce The Number Of Actions In A Procedure.

As well as making changes in the sequence of what is done, changes can also be made by **streamlining** the procedures to reduce the number of actions needed. Sometimes changing a sequence also reduces the number of actions required of caregivers. Scheduling one time for parents to talk to caregivers, instead of interrupting them at several points during the morning arrival, cuts down on the number of different actions required of caregivers. We saw in Chapter Three, how conveniences such as receptacles for soiled diapers which open with a simple foot movement (rather than requiring opening with the hands) reduce the actions required in the diapering procedure. Other examples will be discussed in Chapter Five.

Changing The Times Activities Are Scheduled

Schedules set times for activities such as going outside to play, going for a walk, and indoor quiet and active play times. It makes sense not to take babies on a walk when it is close to their feeding times. Upon return, apart from the possible diaper changes, care loading is increased if several babies need to be fed at the same time. To avoid the resulting chaos, plan walks after, not before feeding times. Likewise, it makes sense not to arrange active play for tired babies, but rather to schedule such activities when babies will be well rested.

In the narrative, Ruth observed that many infants had to wait for care when several parents arrived at the same time. Ruth could not allow the caregivers to omit the mandatory Daily Health Inspection, so she arranged a schedule for the parents that spaced out arrivals. This not only reduced care loading but also eliminated the problem of waiting parents, and infants in need of routine care.

Quality

The design of routine tasks must also take into account the concept of quality care. Obviously babies who have long waits before they are changed or fed are not receiving quality care. When caregivers are rushing around, babies miss out on the incidental teaching of verbal behavior that can take place when babies are being fed and changed. Ruth was concerned with increasing the level of care for the babies. How does she know whether or not she has reached her goal? Apart from the traditional factors listed as indicators of quality care in Chapter One, Ruth closely observes the factor that is emphasized at Infant Center and Toddler Center USA. That is the behavior of the baby.

4.2.4 The Behavior Of The Baby

We read in Chapter Two that Infant and Toddler Center USA has a philosophy of teaching appropriate behavior to infants. We will see in Chapter Six, when Ruth demonstrates how to settle in a new baby, that the teaching of appropriate behavior begins as soon as a baby enters the center. It is obvious that smiling happy babies are *easier* and more enjoyable to care for than crying, grumpy babies. By using Ruth's concept of care loading and by counting the number of tasks a caregiver performs during a specified time we can more clearly define what we mean by *easier.*

Visualize a caregiver at Infant and Toddler Center USA, feeding solid food to a seven month old contented baby who has learned appropriate feeding behaviors. The interaction between the baby and the caregiver is positive. The baby readily opens her mouth as soon as she sees the spoon. The caregiver talks to the baby, teaching her the names of foods, and other objects in her environment. Between mouthfuls the baby babbles back. The interaction is enjoyable for both baby and caregiver.

Now visualize a caregiver in another center, *trying* to feed solid food to an irritable baby who has not learned appropriate feeding behaviors. The whole experience becomes stressful for both caregiver and child. The baby may pull her face away, hit at the spoon, knock the food over, spit, or just clench her lips and refuse to open her mouth. If food is spilled, the caregiver must spend time cleaning up the baby, herself, and whatever else was soiled. Incidental learning (at least of the positive kind) does not occur.

4.2.5 The Behavior Of The Caregiver

As we have seen routine procedures can be streamlined by changing the sequence of the actions. If care loading is to be reduced by this method, caregivers must be able to *recall and adhere to the action sequence.* As caregivers have more than one infant to care for, in order to use the streamlined procedures effectively, they must be able to *organize time and plan ahead.* The task of organizing time and planning ahead is dependent upon the caregiver's skill to *recognize patterns in their babies feeding, napping and changing requirements.*

The three examples of caregiver behaviors stated above are related to the routine care of the babies. Efficient routine care is of prime concern, not only for the babies' physical well being and comfort but also for the babies' behavioral health. It is only when routine care can be carried out expeditiously that caregivers will have time for the play and interaction with individual babies which is so important for their development.

Just as we can state the behaviors caregivers need to provide quality routine care, we can also state behaviors that caregivers need to provide quality behavioral care. Caregivers who learn these behaviors, do not waste time dealing with such unpleasant episodes as the difficult feeding one described above. Instead they spend quality time with their babies, providing not only physical care but also behavioral care. (see Chapters Six and Seven)

4.2.6 Parent Participation

Parent training became popular during the seventies and has boomed during the eighties. Today, across the nation, there are numerous training programs, geared to help parents understand their children, and play an active and effective role in their care and welfare. (see Appendix B: DYK 4.2)

Most states have licensing standards that require center directors and their caregiving staff to encourage parents to participate in center activities and programs. In many states, parents must be told about this licensing requirement and be notified in writing about center meetings and events. The changes that Ruth made in the morning arrival procedures were dependent upon the help and cooperation of the parents. Parent participation, in the center based care of their infants and toddlers, is often overlooked and is an important factor that helps reduce care loading.

Involving Parents In Infant And Toddler Care Routines

At Infant and Toddler Center USA, Ruth enlisted the cooperation of parents in the spacing of the arrivals of the infants, the filling in the Infant Daily Record, greeting of the caregivers, unpacking the infant's belongings, filing medication authorizations, storing medication and signing in of their infants *after* the Daily Health Inspection was completed.

Parents will often help out with procedures at the beginning or end of the day, as long as what they are required to do does not take too long. After all, they are working people, and are usually hurrying to work, or anxious to get back home after a tiring day. They are willing to do things, such as the ones described in this chapter, that do not infringe upon their time, but help the caregivers caring for their infants.

All parents can assist with some aspect of center operations. Most are willing to give a hand if asked. A system, like the one Ruth used, is usually effective. Too frequently parents are neither asked nor reminded of procedures which help center operations. At Infant and Toddler Center USA, parents were asked to help, reminded of what they were asked to do, shown the need for their aid, and thanked for their assistance.

Involving Parents In Center Advisory Boards

Many centers set up a **Center Parent Advisory Board** to involve parents in center activities. The board usually has monthly meetings and coordinates activities involving parents so that everyone knows what is happening at the center.

Parents frequently assist with fund raising and many like to play an active part in the screening and selection of staff. At times some parents are available to help as aides, helping out at busy times during the day. More often parents volunteer for special projects, such as accompanying children on a field trip, helping the center acquire or build equipment or even helping to paint or decorate.

Involving Parents In Community Child Care Concerns

Parents can also be involved on a larger scale than working in a single center. Some states have **District Advisory Committees** through which parents and citizens become involved with the needs assessment for a district or local community. These committees plan for the future. For example, they project trends to get an estimate of how many families will need day care in two, five, or ten years. They also estimate how much parents will be able to pay for child care, and try to influence policy at the city or state level. These committees frequently become involved with training and staff development as well as with the evaluation of center teachers. Often they publish a newsletter to publicize the need for quality care for infants.

When state licensing standards are being reviewed and revised **State Advisory Committees** are formed. They usually consist of child care professionals, providers, and a small number of parent representatives. During the review process, drafts of the proposed regulations are available, and advertised public hearings are held. Not all parents can be on the Advisory Committee, but parents can obtain copies of the drafts of the proposed standards and attend the scheduled public hearings. Feedback about the language and contents of the drafts is encouraged and suggestions are taken seriously, providing a good opportunity for zealous parents to help form and change the rules which govern the care of their children. Questions, suggestions, and recommendations about standards are not limited to the review process. For example, the North Carolina (1988), licensing requirements include Petitions for Rule Making, which state the procedure to be used. A petition can be made by any person who wishes to request the adoption, amendment or repeal of a rule.

Parents not only serve as a resource for a center or a community, they also have a right to be involved with the policies and procedures that involve their infants. There are several national advocacy groups to which parents may belong. These groups provide information and support for those who want to participate and help make needed changes in child care related legislation. (see Appendix B: DYK 3.4 and DYK 4.3)

4.3 ANALYSIS 2:
COMMUNICATING WITH PARENTS OF ENROLLED INFANTS

Many child care specialists advocate active participation of parents in the centers where their children are placed. As well as for the reasons stated above, they believe parents are good monitoring and evaluating agents who can help to ensure that quality care is provided. Whether parents cooperate or not with center personnel, however, depends in large part on the communication system used.

4.3.1 A Plan For Communication

Most states require licensed centers to have a Plan for Communication between the center and parents. Centers usually require parents to agree in writing to procedures by which the center gives information to and obtains information from parents. The procedures, as well as providing for day to day communication, often includes a method of handling parental complaints and matters related to the child's personal safety. (see Chapter Three) Some regulations specify that centers must arrange to communicate with parents in the parent's own language or mode of communication, for example, in sign language for deaf parents, or in their native language for non English speaking parents.

Generally centers have to maintain individual written daily records for each infant. These must be made available to the parents. A duplicate can be made and given to them. As well as maintaining daily records, periodic conferences have to be scheduled. Frequently a center is required to designate a qualified staff person, such as the head teacher or the program supervisor, to be responsible for providing written and oral reports for parents.

Staff need not always communicate in person. They may use the telephone. A center must have a listed number and a telephone that is not coin operated and that is available at all times for incoming and outgoing calls. The availability requirements usually means that staff must limit telephoning to business calls. Some recent revisions of licensing standards require a telephone to be installed in *all* rooms occupied by infants and toddlers, and specify that the phone must be kept on the hook during napping times. Some states suggest that caregivers write notes to give to parents when they pick up their babies, or post information on a bulletin board, or distribute newsletters to parents.

The system of communication between staff and parents at Infant and Toddler Center USA would exceed most state requirements. The Infant Daily Records are posted, duplicated, and a copy is given to the parents each day. The parents also make notations on these daily records when they arrive each morning with their infants, and so are encouraged to give information as well as obtain it from the caregivers. When Ruth asked the parents to help with the morning arrival procedures, she used three methods to communicate with them. She explained in person, she posted a notice, and she provided memos and guidelines. Although parents, at Infant and Toddler Center USA, are discouraged from talking to the staff when the staff are caring for their infants, they are clearly told how to arrange alternative talking times. Ruth's guidelines to the parents Talking to Center Staff (see Table 4.1) leaves little room for misunderstanding. The guidelines show that the center has many options for parents to contact and talk to the caregivers of their babies.

Speaking In Terms Of Fact Not Opinion

When talking to parents, either on a day to day basis or in a more formal setting such as a scheduled conference, caregivers can improve communication with parents by the way in which they phrase what they say. Ruth's memos show that she communicates with parents in a precise and factual way. Not only do facts represent what actually happened better than opinion, they also allow parents to draw their own conclusions.

Records about routine care, such as how many ounces of formula a baby drank and the times the baby went down and got up from a nap, help caregivers focus on facts. Using the facts to communicate with parents, lessens debate. For example, the narrative showed how records revealed a problem with an overly talkative parent during the high peak caregiving time of morning arrivals. Showing the caregivers and the parents the recorded times of the parents arrival at the center and departure after the babies have been officially admitted, pinpoints the time taken. On the other side of the coin, recorded information can also uncover a problem of rushed arrival procedures when parents and caregivers have too little time to communicate.

Using facts from records also decreases the probability of caregivers presenting inaccurate information. Vague or opinionated remarks about a baby, such as "Sarah is very insecure," often create misunderstandings and cause unwarranted worrying by parents. By describing what Sarah does, namely her exact behaviors, a caregiver presents the facts. It sounds much different to a parent to hear, "Sarah carries her bear with her all the time," than to be told that their daughter is "insecure". Parents tend to believe what caregivers tell them, even though few caregivers have had behavioral training. To avoid misunderstandings, therefore, caregivers should avoid psychologizing. Give the facts, and let parents draw their own conclusions.

In addition to negative comments, positive comments are more effective when they are specific. "Mark is so cute" is rewarding to hear, but it is even better to know that "Mark waved bye-bye to everyone who left today." Being "cute" does not tell much about the baby's behavior. Waving bye-bye, in contrast, gives parents information about the progress of their child.

4.4 SUMMARY

Although centers must work within licensing standards, those standards allow some leeway for redesigning procedures. Parents will usually cooperate in streamlining routine care procedures if asked to do so. No one expects parents to volunteer as extra caregivers, but they can help center functioning in many other ways. In this chapter, we have seen how Ruth, the program supervisor coined the term care loading, instituted arrival spacing, and changed the sequencing of morning arrival procedures. These simple adjustments, made possible by parental participation, changed the morning arrivals from chaotic and stressful events into busy but pleasant times for both caregivers and infants.

Chapter Five

MORE ABOUT REDUCING
ROUTINE CARE LOADING

BRIDGET, THE CONSULTANT NURSE,
TALKS WITH RUTH ABOUT ACTIONS IN A PROCEDURE,
AND HOW CENTER FACILITIES AFFECT CARE LOADING

OBJECTIVES

After you have read this chapter you should be able to:

1. Define task/time plotting and state its uses.
2. Identify actions in a procedure.
3. List several factors that affect the selection of an action in a procedure.
4. Give an example to show how parent preference and authority bias can affect the selection of actions in a procedure.
5. Outline a strategy for analyzing actions in a procedure.
6. Give an example of how the following affect care loading: (1) center layout (2) equipment and materials
7. Define the term diapering arrangement as used in this book.
8. Rank different diapering arrangements according to the care loading involved in each.
9. Outline a diapering procedure to match a diapering arrangement.
10. Describe the duties of a consultant nurse.

In Chapter Four we saw that although licensing standards specify areas of regulation for routine care procedures, they do not specify the format of the procedures. The center personnel who oversee regulation compliance have some leeway in designing or choosing procedures to match the mandated regulations. Ruth, the program supervisor of Infant and Toddler Center USA, wants to design procedures to reduce care loading for the staff and, at the same time increase the level of care for the babies. This is a challenging and worthwhile task. To find out more about what this task involves we will follow Ruth the program supervisor, and the consultant nurse Bridget as they talk about several factors that must be considered in the design of center procedures.

5.1 NARRATIVE: BRIDGET, THE CONSULTANT NURSE, TALKS WITH RUTH ABOUT ACTIONS IN A PROCEDURE, AND HOW CENTER FACILITIES AFFECT CARE LOADING

Bridget is twenty-eight years old and is a registered nurse who specializes in maternal and infant care. She is a consultant nurse to several infant care centers that hire her in compliance with licensing standards that require centers to employ or consult with a licensed or registered nurse. Every two weeks, for the past four months, she has visited the four units of Infant and Toddler Center USA. She is paid by Mikki, on an hourly basis. Her visits usually last one hour, but as she arranges her appointments to allow for flexibility, extra time can be scheduled if needed.

Bridget loves her work and looks forward to her center visits. She likes talking to the caregivers, seeing the infants, and meeting their parents. She is good at evaluating health care, sanitation and safety procedures, and knows how to examine and select infant health care literature and products to match the needs of a particular center. Bridget enjoys conducting on the job training and participating in center inservice programs. She is well prepared to give the staff and parents useful suggestions and constructive feedback about how they care for infants and toddlers.

Bridget smiles as she walks into Unit #1. As usual, the infants look and sound happy and the staff are busy interacting with them. It is obvious that the infants are well cared for and that the staff enjoy caring for them.

During her first visit to Infant and Toddler Center USA, Bridget's trained eye quickly noted several features that told her the center did more than comply with the licensing standards that it was required to follow. In her notebook she had written her first impressions of Mikki's center and staff in Unit #1. (see Table 5.1)

When she had completed her observations, Bridget knew that time had been set aside for her to talk with Ruth about the program, procedures, and general organization of the center. On first impression, Ruth appeared preoccupied with her work and didn't seem interested in talking. So Bridget was glad when Mikki suggested that she and Ruth go to the Deli in the next block and get acquainted. There, she said, they could talk about the center while they had lunch and sipped the excellent cappuccino, a Deli speciality which she recommended. As Mikki walked with them to the door she added, "Take your time and have a nice long lunch. It's a

TABLE 5.1: A PAGE FROM BRIDGET'S NOTEBOOK RECORDING HER FIRST IMPRESSION OF INFANT AND TODDLER CENTER USA (UNIT #1)

Infant and Toddler Center USA Unit #1: **Observation Visit**

First Impression:

    a. Contented   happy   playful   friendly   talkative infants

    b. Staff that talked to the infants rather than each other

    c. Planning

    d. Interesting recording and communication system

    e. Postings nicely displayed

Ask for copy of:

    a.   Infant daily record

    b.   Sign in/sign out sheet

    c.   Arrival spacing plan ... why didn't I think of this!

    d.   Memos to staff and guidelines for parents

    e.   Admission agreement   (detailed) ... love it

Possible Problems

    a. Gates ... stepping over ... suggest changing to half doors ..

    too high to to step over ..

    b. Cloths in bleach solution ... why not wipes? ... (Ask and suggest)

good way to begin a working relationship and I know when you two get started you will have a lot to talk about." Bridget smiled at Mikki and said to herself, "I hope she's right."

Much to Bridget's surprise, by the time they arrived at the Deli, Ruth was very chatty and she did not seem at all intimidating. Later, when she and Ruth became friends, Ruth told her that several observers at the center had felt that though she was never rude, that she seemed a little aloof.

"Caregiving," Ruth continued, "is a great responsibility. It doesn't hurt to show observers that it requires our continual attention. Anyway, I always get involved when I am working with the infants and caregivers."

5.1.1 Directing Observation:
Record Checking And Task/time Plotting

Bridget's eyes crinkle into a smile as she recalls what Ruth told her about what she as a program supervisor did:

"Part of my job is to design, model, and monitor procedures that reduce care loading for the staff and at the same time increase the *level of care* for the infants."

Bridget replied, "You have a good reputation at your center. The staff all feel that when you observe, you are always designing and evaluating *procedures*, not finding fault with them. At some centers, the staff shudder when the program supervisor comes around."

Ruth smiled and said, "I try to streamline what the caregiver *must* do. Often problems can be solved by changing the procedures, rather than by pushing the caregivers to work harder." She had illustrated her point by describing briefly her own first morning at the center, and how after further observation, she had subsequently coined the terms care loading and arrival spacing and had re-sequenced the morning arrival procedures. (see Chapter 4)

Bridget chuckles to herself as she remembers how animated Ruth was when she described how she had accidentally discovered that by comparing the parents' arrival time on the *Infants' Daily Records* with the parents' sign in time on the *Sign In/Sign Out* sheet that she had a record of how long it took for each baby's morning arrival procedures to be completed (see Table 4.4). Bridget, who also liked to check records, had caught some of Ruth's excitement. She had listened intently as Ruth described how this discovery led her to look more closely at the *Infant Daily Records*. She began examining them to check the infants' feeding, napping, and playing patterns, and to see how these were affecting the care loading for each caregiver. She found that she was able to see the care loading more clearly if she isolated a specific time, for example, 10:00 AM to 12:00 AM, and then copied the four Infant Daily Records for a specific caregiver, for that time on a chart. She called this combining of Infant Daily Record information task/time plotting. This as Ruth had said, "Simply means putting the Infant Daily Records of a specific caregiver, for a specific day or a part of a specific day, on a chart to analyze *care loading*" (see Figure 5.1).

Bridget had been pleased that she was able to add, "And it would also show possible problem times and indicate times where changes could be or needed to be made."

FIGURE 5.1 TASK/TIME PLOTTING ACTUAL RECORDS FOR A
CAREGIVER AND HER THREE INFANTS

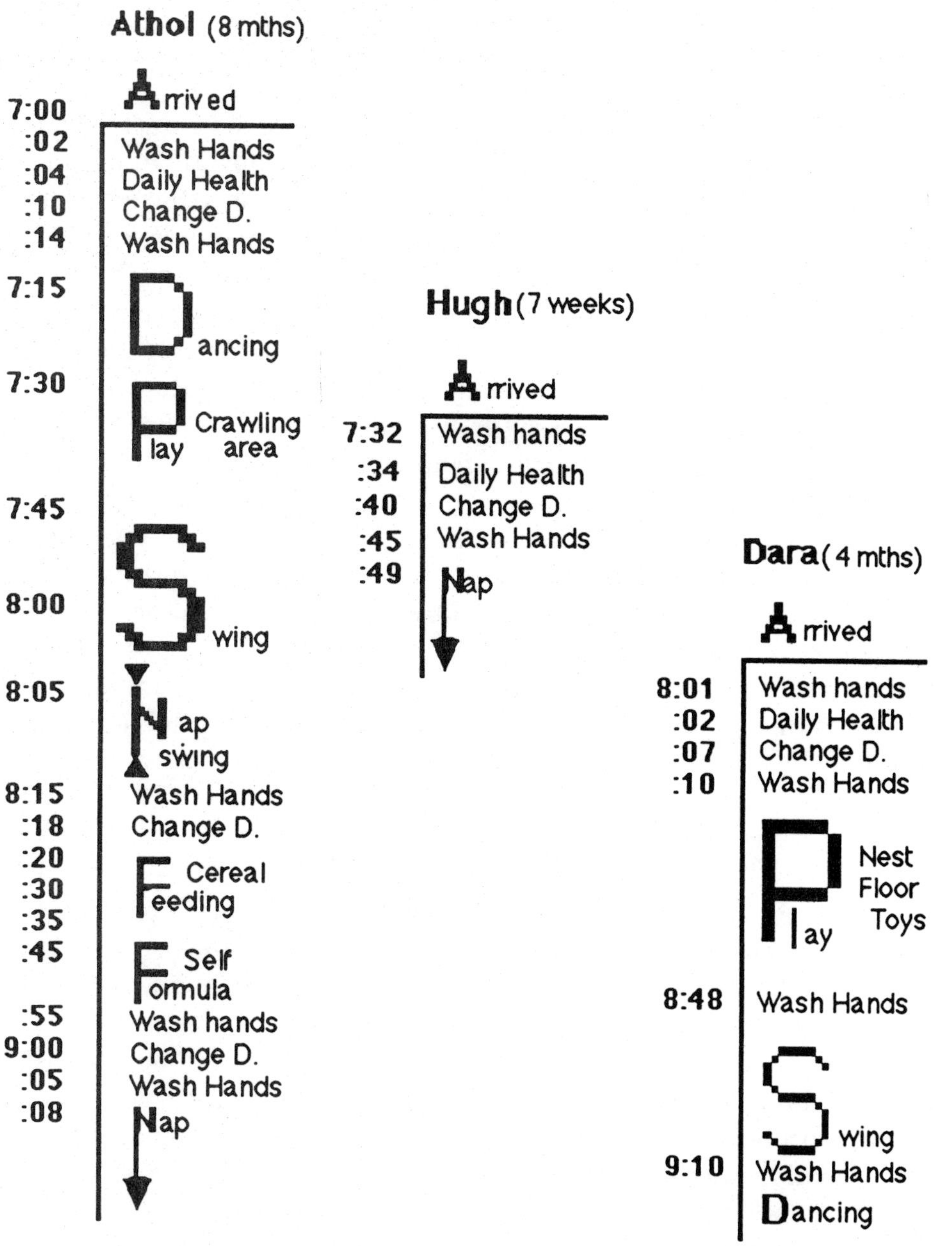

Athol (8 mths)

7:00	**A**rrived
:02	Wash Hands
:04	Daily Health
:10	Change D.
:14	Wash Hands
7:15	**D**ancing
7:30	
	Play Crawling area
7:45	
	Swing
8:00	
8:05	**N**ap swing
8:15	Wash Hands
:18	Change D.
:20	**F**eeding Cereal
:30	
:35	
:45	**F**ormula Self
:55	Wash hands
9:00	Change D.
:05	Wash Hands
:08	**N**ap

Hugh (7 weeks)

	Arrived
7:32	Wash hands
:34	Daily Health
:40	Change D.
:45	Wash Hands
:49	**N**ap

Dara (4 mths)

	Arrived
8:01	Wash hands
:02	Daily Health
:07	Change D.
:10	Wash Hands
	Play Nest Floor Toys
8:48	Wash Hands
	Swing
9:10	Wash Hands
	Dancing

Caregiver washed her hands 11 times

"Exactly" said Ruth delighted with her response, "and to get a better idea of how busy a caregiver has been, one would need to . . . ?" She paused and looked encouragingly at Bridget.

"To examine the procedures and see what exactly the caregivers are doing. Feeding, for example, requires many actions. It is not just one thing as it may appear as written on a record." Bridget said.

"Yes. Are you sure you haven't done this?" Ruth asked. Bridget laughed and shook her head and Ruth continued, "Some people call all the parts of a procedure steps, but I prefer to call them actions. After you have task/time plotted the records of a caregiver and her infants, you identify the actions in a procedure, to analyze or measure care loading."

"I like the word action too." Bridget said, "It's more active." Bridget laughed at the obviousness of her statement, then added, "I guess if a person is really ambitious she could put the Infant Daily Records of all the caregivers for a specific day or time on a chart and have a good illustration of care loading for the whole center. Have you ever done that?"

"Yes," Ruth said warmly, "Many times. I do it at random, as a type of spot checking, or I do it specifically to pinpoint problems and make changes. *Task/time plotting,* for a specific caregiver or for all caregivers in a center, shows possible problem times, and so directs us to look closer at specific times and tasks." She looked towards the counter and said, "I think it is time for a cup of cappuccino, don't you?" Bridget had agreed readily.

5.1.2 Actions In A Procedure

As they sipped their cappuccino, Bridget said, "When I first started working in the centers I knew very little about the licensing standards and regulations that governed procedures and I thought I would *never* learn."

"The same with me." Ruth replied.

"You know," Bridget said thoughtfully, "there are many ways you can design a procedure to comply with the licensing requirements, but you don't usually know what actions are best until you try them out."

"True, to a point," Ruth agreed, "you can do a lot of figuring out on paper, but sometimes you cannot use the actions that you think are best."

Bridget looked puzzled and asked, "What do you mean?"

Action Selection Within The Constraints Of Cost, Preference, And Bias

"Well as we have agreed, procedures are made up of actions that caregivers are required to do. Procedures must also take into account the materials and equipment caregivers have to use," Ruth said, and paused to nibble on the carrot cake she liked so much.

"And procedures must also consider the layout of the center in which the caregivers have to work." Bridget said. "For example stepping over infant safety gates can cause accidents." She had noted that rather than unlatching the gates, the staff tended to step over them, sometimes while carrying babies.

"Right," Ruth said. She paused. The remark Bridget made about stepping over the gates did not seem relevant to her and she expected Bridget to expand her statement.

Bridget looked at her inquiringly so she continued, "Procedures must meet or exceed licensing requirements. I also want them to reduce care loading. But cost of equipment and material is also a factor in action selection, as Mikki frequently reminds me. When I redesigned the morning arrival procedures I had to consider the cost of another changing table. Parent preference was also a big factor in the times at which the arrivals and Daily Health Inspections were scheduled, as were caregiver preference for their assigned babies. (see Chapter Four) Then too, I must make allowance for Mikki's biases. I would love to change the reusable cloths, that we use for diapering, for disposable wipes."

"I was planning to suggest that to you. Why don't you make the change? Bridget asked. She was pleased that her other query had come up in their conversation.

"Well the cloths meet the licensing requirements and Mikki has calculated that the cloths are less expensive than the wipes and she wants to get good use out of the small laundry room she had installed. Also, a lot of our parents are concerned about the chemicals in the disposable wipes and diapers, as well as the environmental hazards caused by their disposal. (see Appendix B: DYK 5.1) Although most of the parents use disposable products at home, they seem to think that if we don't use them here, it cuts down on some of the effects."

"Oh! I see you are really outnumbered with Mikki and a lot of the parents favoring the cloths aren't you." Bridget said.

"I do not argue with valid parent preferences. The caregivers would prefer to use wipes and not mess with the cloths. So Mikki, to smooth things over, has designated herself responsible for laundering the cloths. She makes her rounds each day and trots off to the laundry room with her covered pails of soiled cloths and trots back again with the laundered articles. I must say she is doing a good job as a laundry maid." Ruth replied.

Bridget laughed as she said, "Rather her than me. If we just had Mikki to contend with, we could make a good case for using the wipes. But parent preference! That's something else. After all, the children are *their* babies and they do have a valid point about the chemicals."

"Sure. When parents have a strong preference and it does not conflict with the licensing standards, I do not try to make a change. But it highlights my statement that you cannot always use the action or procedure that you think is best. Anyhow, I'm glad we see eye to eye."

Ruth looked at Bridget and said teasingly, "And, I would also like to remind you, that when we select actions in a procedure we also have to consider authority bias, for example, health consultants such as yourself."

Bridget felt her face redden as she thought about a few of her own preferences and biases (apart from removing safety gates that staff tended to step over) that she had persuaded centers to follow. She liked babies to wear loose clothing and favored roomy cotton track suits. She always told the staff and parents of the centers where she worked that track suits are comfortable and can be easily slipped on and off *and* they do not have all that hard metal that some of the designer clothing articles have. She also always checked the babies' socks. She hated tight socks that left red marks on the babies legs or loose socks that fell off leaving babies with cold feet. She spent a lot of time shopping around, looking for the perfect socks.

Her centers flashed before her. She saw the babies dressed in their comfortable, roomy cotton track suits. She suddenly wondered if the babies were deliberately dressed that way on the days she visited the centers. She shuddered as she imagined the staff saying to the parents, "Make sure Carl wears his cotton track suit. You know *who's* coming tomorrow!"

When she confided her thoughts to Ruth, Ruth laughed and said, "Don't worry. Everyone has preferences."

"What are some of yours?" Bridget asked.

Ruth replied readily. "One of my pet peeves is homemade toys and unprofessional materials. You may remember that there are none at the center. I did upset a few people when I first came, by asking the staff to remove a few sloppy charts they had made. I also spoke to Mikki requesting that she type all notices and frame important procedures.

"I think you were right though. It does look better when toys and materials are appropriately arranged and displayed. Then too, good quality toys are more easily sanitized than many homemade ones."

"Yes," Ruth answered, "You would think of that. But no matter how we do things, other people have their own biases and suggest changes accordingly."

Evaluating Actions In Routine Procedures

"A few weeks ago, we had a visitor here from one of the colleges nearby. She told me that she was very surprised about two things that we did, and said if she was the program supervisor she would change them immediately."

"What were they?" Bridget said, wondering whether stepping over the gates was one of the things the visitor noted."

"*One,*" Ruth told her, "was carrying the infants into the food preparation room when we go to get their bottles or food, and *the other* was holding them in one arm while we disinfected the diapering surface of the changing table with the other."

"Oh! Did she have any children of her own?" Bridget asked.

"No." Ruth replied, "Why did you want to know?"

"Parents," Bridget said, "even new ones, soon become very adept at doing all kinds of things with one hand, while holding their babies. They usually see nothing the matter with that kind of action. In fact they think it's clever. But what did you say to her?"

"Well, first of all I thanked her for sharing her concerns with me."

"Of course" said Bridget, taking her opportunity to tease. "You always do the right thing."

"Don't I?" replied Ruth and her voice showed that she was enjoying Bridget's playfulness. "Then, I said that all our procedures were approved by the licensing authority and that we also *evaluated* what we did. So these actions had been discussed and debated, and I showed her the strategy we used. Here, let me show you what we do." Ruth took a pen and some typed sheets of paper from the oversized bag she always carried. There, typed, was an analysis of the actions, *carry baby into the food preparation area to get bottle/food,* and *holding baby in one arm while disinfecting and wiping the diapering surface of the changing table.* (see Table 5.2)

"Wow! What was her reaction to that?" Bridget asked when Ruth had finished.

"She was very impressed and asked for a copy. She has since called

TABLE 5.2: A STRATEGY FOR EVALUATING ACTIONS IN A ROUTINE PROCEDURE

PROCEDURE: FEEDING

ACTION: Carry baby into the food preparation area

Provides for:	
Safety	**Yes**
Sanitation	**Yes**
Supervision	**Yes**
Complies with licensing standard(s)	**Yes**
(Written into the Program)	
Exceeds licensing standard(s)	**No**
Parental Objection	**No**
Caregiver Objection	**No**

ALTERNATIVE ACTION: Leave baby in the activity area

Provides for:
    Safety
    Sanitation
    Supervision
(Dependent upon the availability and cooperation of other caregivers)

CHANGE ACTION	**NO**

RELATED LICENSING STANDARDS

Infants shall be directly supervised at all times.

Each infant shall be assigned to a primary caregiver who shall be responsible for that infant's needs.

Caregivers shall use routine activities to promote language and speech.

Infants shall be taken into the (kitchen) food preparation area only as part of a planned and supervised activity.

TABLE 5.2 (Continued)

PROCEDURE: DIAPERING

ACTION: Hold baby in one arm while disinfecting and wiping over the diapering surface of the changing table

Provides for:

Safety	**Yes**
Aerosol spray not used	
Baby has no contact with disinfectant or surface	
Sanitation	**Yes**
Supervision	**Yes**

Complies with licensing standard(s)	**Yes**
Exceeds licensing standard(s)	**No**
Parental Objection	**No**
Caregiver Objection	**No**

ALTERNATIVE ACTION: Take baby and leave her in the activity area

Provides for:
Safety
Sanitation
Supervision
(Dependent upon the availability and cooperation of other caregivers)

CHANGE ACTION	**No**

RELATED LICENSING STANDARDS

Infants shall be directly supervised at all times.

Each infant shall be assigned to a primary caregiver who shall be responsible for that infant's needs.

Caregivers shall use routine activities to promote language and speech.

The diapering surface shall be disinfected after each use, whether or not a disposable paper covering is used.

me and wants to bring her students out to see the center." Ruth replied.

"I would think so." Bridget said, "The strategy looks great. Getting the infant's bottle or food is just one action in the procedure called feeding, and spraying and wiping the change table are just two actions in the procedure called diapering."

Ruth looked approvingly at Bridget and said, "I think you are just the person to help me with what I am working on now. Would you like to see what I am doing?

5.1.3 Diapering Arrangements And Care Loading

Bridget nodded. She was more than interested in what Ruth had to say, but a little overwhelmed with all the useful information that she was getting so unexpectedly. Ruth carefully pulled from her bag a new yellow folder labeled Diapering. She opened the folder and said, "Care loading during diapering can be increased or decreased depending upon the type of diaper used, and whether it is provided by the center or parent. I am working with four possible diapering arrangements ... you could make other combinations ... which generate tasks related to storage, waste removal, disposal, and cleaning or sanitation." She pointed to the first page on which she had neatly printed an outline of what she had said. (see Table 5.3)

Ruth paused for Bridget to look, then turned to a second page. (see Figure 5.2) "Here is what these arrangements look like in terms of caregiver actions," she said. "Two parts of the diapering procedure involve getting a clean diaper and disposing of the dirty one. The number of actions in these steps depends on the kind of diapers used, and who supplies them. For example, look at the top row. If the parent provides cloth diapers, the caregiver must walk to the infant's cubby hole and find the diaper, and if in the process, clothing spills out, she must replace that. Then she must take the clean diaper to the diapering room changing table. To dispose of the soiled ones, if parents provide cloth diapers, she must place the soiled diaper into a container or plastic bag, seal it, and place the container or bag in that baby's labeled storage space apart from the cubby holes for clean belongings. In contrast, look at the bottom row where a center provides disposable diapers. The diapering procedure requires fewer actions. The caregiver needn't leave the changing table. She just reaches into a box for the clean diapers, and disposes

TABLE 5.3: A PAGE FROM RUTH'S NOTEBOOK DISPLAYING DIAPERING ARRANGEMENTS AND CAREGIVING TASKS

ARRANGEMENT 1:   Disposable   Provided By:
                                                           Center/Parents

ARRANGEMENT 2:   Diaper Service   Provided By:
                                                           Center/Parents
                               (Plastic pants needed)

ARRANGEMENT 3:   Diaper Service   Provided By : Center
                               (Plastic pants needed   Provided By: Parent

ARRANGEMENT 4:   Disposable   Provided By: Center
                               Cloth Diapers   Provided By: Parents
                               (Plastic pants needed)

DIAPERING ARRANGEMENTS GENERATE TASKS:

a. Storage:

    1. Unused diapers

    2. Used diapers

    3. Plastic pants (if needed)

    4. Used diaper receptacles

b. Waste removal and disposal

    1. Removing waste from soiled diapers and plastic pants

    2. Not removing waste from soiled diapers and plastic pants

    3. Waste disposal <u>Where</u>

c. Laundering and sanitation

    1. Diapers and plastic pants (if used)

    2. Used diaper receptacles

of the used ones in one large receptacle near the changing table. (see Figure 3.3) It doesn't seem like much of a difference, but . . . "

Bridget broke in, "No, I can see that it would make a big difference in how much caregiver time would get taken up with diapering. It's too bad that disposable diapers create so much of an environmental hazard. In comparison with cloth diapers they do reduce diapering care loading."

5.1.4 Using Safety Barriers

Ruth peered into her empty coffee cup and said, "Well, it's about time to get back. Do you have anything you'd like to bring up?"

Bridget was happy to be asked. "Well, yes, I do have one thing. I notice that instead of undoing the latches on the little safety gates, the caregivers tend to step over them . . . even when they are carrying infants. I don't know whether or not anyone has tripped yet, but . . .

"So that is what you meant." Ruth interrupted, "Your earlier reference to tripping over safety gates puzzled me. I did not know the caregivers had made a habit of stepping over them. I'm glad you drew it to my attention."

"I know it's a pain to fiddle with latches." Bridget said, "Especially when they are hard to manipulate."

"Now that you mentioned it, I do recall that lately the gates had become difficult to open and close. I am surprised that Mikki did not note this on her Safety Hazard checklist. She is so good about noting such details. Ruth said. She smiled and added, "So we are all not infallible after all!"

"Perhaps Mikki could replace them with half doors which open more easily and are practically impossible to step over." Bridget said with a grin. "I would suggest that she do away with the safety gates into the diapering and feeding area as well as across the nap sleeping room doorway. The crawling area is barrier protected anyway, and the immobile tiny babies in the open activity area are not going to start suddenly crawling or moving across the floor!"

Ruth nodded and said. "I agree. Mikki had the safety gates installed to provide more crawling space apart from the crawling areas, in order to meet a revised regulation, the one that says, 'Infants, each day, shall be given opportunity to crawl and explore in an *open* uncluttered area.' But we do not really need those bothersome gates. The crawling infants use

FIGURE 5.2: A PAGE FROM RUTH'S NOTEBOOK DISPLAYING ACTIONS IN DIFFERENT DIAPERING ARRANGEMENTS

Getting Clean Diaper   Handling of Dirty Diaper

Parent Provided:
Caregiver walks to
individual cubby hole,
selects diaper from
among belongings, and
goes back to changing
table.

Caregiver may or may not
rinse solid waste.
Caregiver places dirty diaper
in plastic bag, seals, and stores
in individual location other than
cubby for clean clothing.

**Diaper
Service**

Center Provided:
Caregiver reaches
below changing table.

Caregiver places dirty diaper into
center receptacle for soiled cloth
diapers.

Parent Provided:
Caregiver walks to
individual cubby hole,
selects diaper from
among belongings, and
goes back to changing
table.

Caregiver may or may not
remove solid waste from diaper.
Caregiver places dirty diaper into
center receptacle for disposable
diapers.

**Disposable
Diapers**

Center Provided:
Caregiver takes diaper
from box in diapering
area.

Caregiver may or may not
remove solid waste from diaper.
Caregiver places dirty diaper into
center receptacle for disposable
diapers.

the open and larger activity area, as a crawling space, only when the immobile babies are asleep or outside. The half doors would be much easier to use. I'll talk to Mikki and tell her about your astute observations. You must think us silly to have had such redundant safety barriers that were not only bothersome but also themselves had become safety hazards."

"Not at all." Bridget replied. "Your concern with care loading prompted me to look at the gates as not only safety factors, but also factors that could increase or decrease care loading."

"I am pleased that you have joined our staff. I know we are going to work well together." Ruth said. And with that, the two of them paid the bill and left.

5.2 ANALYSIS 1:
HOW CENTER FACILITIES AFFECT CARE LOADING

The operator of an infant center when designing or choosing a facility, apart from considering broad fire, health and safety codes, must take into account regulations that specify finer details about how infants are to be housed. An infant center, for example, must be located on the ground floor. Infants and toddlers are usually required to be cared for in areas away from older children. Most state standards specify that crawling infants are to be separated from immobile infants, and from infants who are learning to walk, and that infants are to be separated from toddlers. The program for infants frequently specifies that non walking babies be given opportunities during each day for freedom of movement, such as creeping and crawling in an open, uncluttered, safe, clean area (North Dakota, 1987), or allowed the opportunity to explore the environment outside their cribs (Nebraska, 1987). Age appropriate equipment and furnishings must be provided, and specifications for both indoor and outdoor space must be met.

5.2.1 Meeting Specifications

Space

Licensing standards for the various areas of regulation, as shown in Chapter One, vary, and the required minimum indoor and outdoor space for each infant is no exception to this. Although less space is sometimes specified, the Montana (1988) requirements of seventy-five square feet outside space for each child, and thirty-five square feet indoor space is typical of state space requirements. The manner in which space is calculated varies. Some states exclude certain areas and equipment for example, bathrooms, built in cabinets, furniture, hallways, and stationary furnishings. Others have less specific space regulations. North Dakota (1987) requires centers to have, "sufficient space and appropriate furniture and equipment to provide for support functions necessary to the program, and to provide for the reasonable comfort and convenience of the staff and children." (p. 22)

The use of space and the arrangement of furnishings and equipment are important elements in providing the support functions necessary for the routine care of the babies. They are also important elements that must be considered in any analysis of the care loading of center caregivers.

Layout

Whether or not the layout of a facility increases or decreases care loading depends to a great extent on how accessible the facilities are to the caregivers. Accessibility is considered in most state standards, especially as related to the facilities for diapering and hand washing. But it is not the prime factor in the specifications for the location of one area or room in relation to another. For health and safety reasons licensing standards usually require a diapering area and a laundering area to be separate from a food preparation area, a nap/sleeping area to be separate from an activity area, and an isolation area to be separate from the other areas used for the care of the infants. (see Figure 5.3)

There are various ways a center can be designed. For example, the four units comprising Infant and Toddler Center USA, are self-contained. Such a design incorporates, in each unit, all essential facilities needed to care for a group of children. (see Table 5.4) Essential facilities, in this instance, means food preparation, nap/sleeping, diapering, activity or play areas or rooms and their furnishings and equipment. Another way a center can be designed is by the use of a crossover or sharing plan. This plan does not provide all essential facilities for the exclusive use of a group of children. Instead, some of the essential facilities are shared by more than one group. For example caregivers from other groups may use the same food preparation area or room.

Usually the essential facilities are incorporated in a self contained unit by either separate rooms as in the case of Infant and Toddler Center

TABLE 5.4: SAMPLE STATE DEFINITIONS OF A GROUP
AND GROUP SIZE LIMITS

Group...

A specific number of children and staff assigned to be together throughout the day. This definition would permit more than one group to occupy the same physical space. (Alabama, 1988, p. 10) Group Size Limits: Infant non walkers 6: Toddlers 8

An autonomous unit of children, who together with the staff assigned to them, share a specific room or area and use materials, equipment and furnishings specifically identified for their use. (Maryland, 1989 p. 5) Group Size Limits: Infants 6: Toddlers 9

Two or more children who participate in the same activities at the same time and are assigned to the same staff person for supervision, at the same time. (Massachusetts, 1987, 102 CMR-96) Group Size Limits: Infants 7:Toddlers 9

The children assigned to a specific caregiver or caregivers to meet the staff child ratios set forth in G.S. 110-91 (7) and this Subchapter, using space which is identifiable to each group. (North Carolina, 1988, p. 2) Group Size Limits: 0-2 years 12

Specific number of children assigned to specific staff. (Oregon,1988, p. 3) Group Size Limits: 8

Number of children who interact with each other and with the caregiver to whom they are assigned in a space, which is divided from the space of other groups by a recognizable barrier to define limits and to reduce distraction. (Tennessee, 1987, p. 25 Group Size Limits: Infant 10: Toddler 14

Specific number of children assigned to a specific caregiver. Each child in any group shall have the following things in common with every other child in his/her group: (1) The same primary caregiver responsible for the child's basic needs. (2) The same primary area. (Utah, 1987, p. 8) Group Size Limits or number in a room: Under 2 years 8.

Number of children assigned to a teacher/caregiver or team of staff members who meet together regularly and can be identified with one another as being distinct from the larger population of children in care. (Vermont, 1989, p. (ii) Group Size Limits: Infants 8: Toddlers (older 24 to 35 months) 10.

The children assigned to a staff member or team of staff members, occupying an individual classroom or well defined physical space within a larger room. (NAEYC, 1987, p. X)

FIGURE 5.3: THE LAYOUT OF A CAREGIVING UNIT AT INFANT AND TODDLER CENTER USA

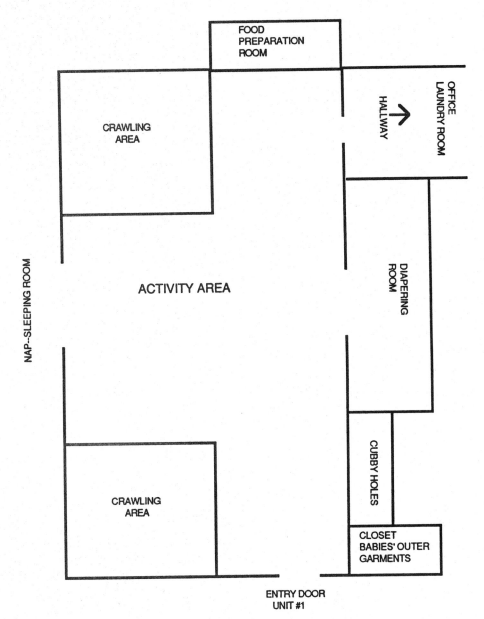

USA, or small areas set aside in a larger open area. Both have their advantages and disadvantages.

Separate rooms provide privacy, lessen disturbance especially at nap/sleeping times, and give staff an opportunity to keep the facilities more orderly. However, as we saw in the narrative, separate rooms can pose a supervision problem for primary caregivers who are assigned a specific number of infants. The degree of the problem is dependent upon the state's definition of supervision. (see Table 5.5) Whenever a caregiver has a caregiving task to perform, in a separate room, either for one or more babies, what is she to do about the supervision of the others? If the infants are required to be under direct visual supervision at all times their caregiver has two options. One, she can ask another caregiver to keep an eye on them, though this leads to increased care loading for that caregiver. Two, she can take them with her. However, this increases care loading for her.

We saw examples in the narrative of caregivers taking a baby with them when they went into the food preparation room, or when they returned to the diapering room to sanitize the diapering table. The staff at Infant and Toddler Center USA felt that these actions provided a workable solution when they had only one baby to supervise. But under some conditions, infants are restricted from certain areas. This leads to questions about non compliance as was illustrated in the narrative by the comments by the visitor from the college. Problems or queries relating to compliance or non compliance were analyzed at Infant and Toddler Center USA by the use of Ruth's Strategy for Evaluating Actions in a Routine Procedure. (see Table 5.2)

Another way to aid visual supervision requires structural modification. Visual observation can be improved by the installation of windows to allow viewing from one room to another. Such modifications were made at Infant and Toddler Center USA and were extended in the nap/sleeping room by the use of mirrors placed on the wall. (see Chapter Two)

However, if the state's definition of supervision requires that a caregiver have her babies not only under visual supervision but also within reach, of course a self contained unit similar to one at Infant and Toddler Center USA clearly would not allow a caregiver to meet the state requirements for supervision.

Small areas set aside in a larger open space may be the answer to the supervision regulations of states that require caregivers to be within reach of their babies at all times. However as we have discussed, infants

TABLE 5.5: SAMPLE STATE DEFINITIONS OF SUPERVISION

Supervision ...

Direct and immediate observation and direction of personnel, a group of children, an activity or function. (Arizona, 1988, p. 2)

The direction and onsite observation of the functions and activities of others in the performance of their duties. (Connecticut, 1988, p. 2)

Watching and directing children's activities within close proximity within the same room inside or within a designated outdoor play area. (Florida, 1986, p. 13)

Occurs when a program staff person is within sight and hearing of a child at all times so that the program staff person can intervene to protect the health and safety of the child. (Minnesota, 1989, p. 4)

The direct observation and guidance of children at all times and requires being physically present with them. (New Mexico, 1987, p. 10)

Visual supervision with the exception of brief periods necessitated by emergencies and day to day child care responsibilities. (North Carolina, 1988, p. 25)

The act of caring for a child or group of children. This includes awareness of and responsibility for the ongoing activity of each child. it requires physical presence, knowledge of program requirements and children's needs, and accountability for their care. (Oregon, 1988, p. 3)

The knowledge of accounting of the activity and whereabouts of each child in care and the proximity of staff to children at all times assuring immediate intervention of staff to safeguard a child from harm and to maintain the program of the facility. (Vermont, 1989, p (iii))

and toddlers are not permitted free access to diapering and food preparation areas. Such areas in an open space must be barrier protected from crawling and walking infants. But barriers and gates, as Bridget pointed out, pose potential safety hazards (if caregivers tend to step over them), and the continual opening and closing of the latches increases the care loading for the caregivers.

Storage

Storage, like other aspects of center care must comply with licensing standards. Centers must provide adequate storage space to store the materials and equipment that make up the center supplies, and to store the belongings of the babies.

When storing center supplies the caregivers must abide by regulations related to safety and sanitation. It makes sense, for example, to store medication and household cleaning products, not only away from food but also out of the reach of children. In Chapter Three we saw how medication is kept in locked storage and also how medication for internal use and medication for external use are stored separately. During the administration of medication, safety procedures, such as opening and closing safety caps and locking and unlocking storage containers or cabinets require additional actions of caregivers. Safety actions must be implemented. So to reduce care loading we need to direct our attention to factors that can be changed.

In the narrative we saw how care loading during diapering can be increased or decreased depending on the type of diaper used, and whether diapers are provided by the center or parents. These two factors, diaper type and provision generate tasks related to storage, waste removal, disposal, cleaning and sanitation. Caregiver actions related to storage for two different diapering arrangements, and two parts of the diapering procedure, getting a clean diaper and handling dirty one, are displayed in Figure 5.2.

In most states, parent provided cloth diapers when soiled, (for each diaper change for each baby) must be placed in an individual labeled container, sealed, and stored away from the babies' other belongings. This not only takes up space (see Figure 5.4) it also increases the number of actions a caregiver is required to do. Visualize a caregiver, after every diaper change, putting a center supplied used cloth diaper in a large receptacle for soiled cloth diapers. Then visualize a caregiver, after every diaper change putting the parent supplied used cloth diaper in a small plastic bag, sealing and labeling it, and placing it in the baby's assigned soiled clothing storage space. Apart from the actions involved in sealing and labeling the plastic bags, the accessibility of the required storage spaces, especially whether or not the caregiver has to run back and forth to them to get or put articles, is a prime factor in decreasing or increasing care loading.

FIGURE 5.4: SOILED DIAPER STORAGE

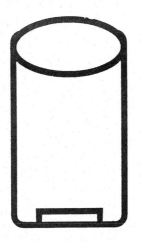

DIAPER SERVICE CENTER PROVIDED: SINGLE STORAGE

Regulation:

Used/soiled diapers shall be stored in a leak proof closed receptacle and emptied daily or as needed.

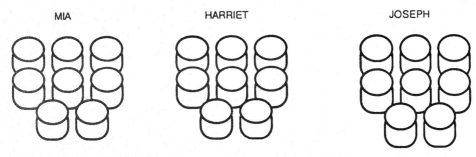

DIAPER SERVICE PARENT PROVIDED: MULTI-STORAGE

Regulation:

Soiled diapers for each baby must be individually sealed, labeled, stored apart from that baby's clean clothing, and sent home with the parent at the end of the day.

5.3 ANALYSIS 2:
HOW PREFERENCES AFFECT CARE LOADING

The various diapering arrangements that are available for use at a center illustrate how the selection of material and equipment affect actions needed in a procedure, and how this in turn affects care loading.

The type of diapering arrangement is sometimes specified by the licensing regulations. Many states, for example, require centers to use disposable diapers, or if cloth diapers are used specify they must be supplied by a commercial service. Other states leave the choice of diapers to the center and or the parents. In Chapter Two, we saw how at Infant and Toddler Center USA, the diapering arrangement for each baby is formally stated and agreed upon by both the center and the parent in the Admission Agreement.

If the decision for the type of diapering arrangement used only considered care loading, disposable diapers would be the obvious choice. But many parents are concerned about the environmental hazards that disposable diapers present. So the decision at Infant and Toddler Center USA, as we discussed in the narrative in this chapter takes into account parent preference. Ruth and Bridget both agreed that if parents' preference do not conflict with licensing standards they should be honored. As Bridget put it, "After all the children are their babies."

Some preferences of parents about the routine care of their infants, may prevent a program supervisor from using actions in a procedure that would reduce care loading. Other preferences are open to suggestions or requests to change. For example, many parents buy clothing for their infants and toddlers and consider style over ease of putting on and taking off an item of clothing. Features of design that facilitate dressing and undressing, such as a roomy cut, few buttons, can be pointed out to parents. Infant and toddler clothing is available in such a variety of styles that it is rather easy to choose clothing that is functional as well as attractive. It is also rather easy to convince parents that dressing their baby in one style instead of another is a big help to a caregiver who has to dress and undress several babies through out the day.

Preferences of center directors, program supervisors, consultants and other authority figures can also increase or decrease care loading. Directors' preferences frequently are influenced by cost and existing center facilities. Mikki, the director of Infant and Toddler Center USA provided washable clothes rather than the disposable wipes the caregivers preferred to use. One they were cheaper, and two, the center had a small laundry where the cloths could be washed. Program supervisors and sometimes designated caregivers are responsible for the way the program material and equipment are arranged. Many prefer arrangements that enhance the appearance of the room or space. Although the center may look attractive, the arrangement may require many additional actions by the caregivers. Health professionals, like Bridget, look at center facilities from the point of view of health, sanitation and safety factors. (See Appendix B: DYK 5.2) Their preferences reflect their medical training and tend to be based on facts rather than whim. It is important to remember, as discussed in Chapter Four, that eliminating necessary health and safety regulations does little to reduce care loading.

Using equipment that has been tested and approved by a recognized consumer protection agency not only safeguards the child but can save a caregiver many unnecessary actions. Fiddling with hard to manouever gate latches, struggling to unfold or fold tight hinges on playpens, fumbling to fasten high chair trays in place, jiggling to remove a child from a swing, searching for pieces of poorly made equipment that has fallen apart, takes time. While a caregiver is spending time wrestling with shoddy equipment she is not tending to her babies. It does not take long for several to be waiting for care. Fortunately parents and caregivers who have had the experiences described above soon learn to prefer sturdy, durable equipment over equipment that may look attractive, but is flimsy and easily broken. This is not to imply that sturdy durable equipment is not attractive. Most regulations, including the U.S. Army's, specify that "indoor and outdoor program equipment and materials be provided in the learning environment that are safe, durable, in working order, and appropriate to age levels, abilities and interests. (U.S. Army 1988, Draft p. 4–18)

5.4: SUMMARY

In this chapter we examined how center facilities and preferences affect care loading, and saw how task/time plotting (the first step in the analysis of care loading) can be used to record what caregivers and their babies do.

Center routine care procedures such as feeding, diapering, putting an infant down for a nap, and recording information, are made of several actions. Looking at procedures as a set of actions makes it easier to measure both care loading and compliance with licensing standards.

Many people are concerned about quality care for children in center care, but have not analyzed in depth the factors that underlie the care loading of caregivers. Regulations that specify what caregivers should do to care for babies are necessary. But specifications need to take into account how requirements generate actions in care giving procedures; whether these actions increase or decrease care loading, and how this impacts quality care.

PART THREE
MAINTAINING AN ENVIRONMENT
FOR BEHAVIORAL CARE

Chapter Six

TEACHING APPROPRIATE BEHAVIORS

ROBERT LEARNS WHY EVERY INTERACTION
IS A LEARNING EXPERIENCE FOR THE CHILD

OBJECTIVES

After you have read this chapter, you should be able to . . .

1. Explain why arranging antecedents and providing consequences are both necessary for teaching appropriate behaviors.
2. Describe how observation and records help a caregiver maintain physical comfort for a baby.
3. Explain why is it important to know what an infant is doing at the moment a caregiver attends to his or her needs.
4. Explain the statement, "You cannot eliminate misbehavior by ignoring it. You must build appropriate behavior to take its place."
5. Describe how given inappropriate behaviors could be unintentionally strengthened by caregiver attention, and explain how to change the timing of that attention to change the child's behavior.
6. Explain the difference between "pushing" an infant or toddler and teaching.
7. Explain why it is important to teach skills *before* they are needed, giving an example like the one about "handing things over" at Infant and Toddler Center USA.
8. Define shaping and reinforcement and give examples.

Both caregivers and parents would like a center environment in which infants and toddlers thrive physically and also learn the behaviors which make babies so adorable and lovable. Yet in many centers, one can find crying or cranky babies, and squabbling or misbehaving toddlers. No one deliberately teaches children to cry or squabble, but caregivers' day to day interactions with children determine how they behave.

Few caregivers are aware of the importance of the details of their interactions with children. But the contingent relationships between children's behavior and staff actions determine the way each child will behave in the future. Even during such seemingly routine operations as diapering, the caregiver's timing of talking, smiling or tickling, relative to the infant's movements, determines whether that baby will wriggle or hold still during future diaperings.

To see how appropriate behaviors are taught to infants and toddlers we will accompany Robert on two visits to Infant and Toddler Center USA.

6.1 NARRATIVE: ROBERT LEARNS WHY EVERY INTERACTION IS A LEARNING EXPERIENCE FOR THE CHILD

Robert drove into the parking lot of Infant and Toddler Center USA and hopped nimbly out of a sleek blue sports car. It was a lovely Monday in October and he was looking forward to his visit with Ruth. He had been more than pleased with the interview visit of the last week, and he and Alison were happy that the center had reserved a place for the baby they were soon to adopt. Robert liked the center's philosophy of teaching appropriate behavior and had decided to learn as much as possible about it before they brought Teddi home. He had called Ruth and told her of his interest, and she had suggested that he come into the center the following Monday. Robert agreed. Being a free lance graphic artist, his schedule was flexible, and he didn't have a rush just then.

6.1.1 Ruth Demonstrates How to Settle In a New Baby

So today was the day for Robert's first lesson. Ruth had told him that a three month old baby girl was being admitted in Unit #2 that day, and that it would be a good learning experience for him to see how she settled in a new baby. She asked Robert to excuse her if she ignored him temporarily while caring for the baby, and reminded him of the center philosophy of teaching appropriate behavior and the corresponding practice of "infant first"

"Rules, rules," Robert had thought, but he was pleased with himself for being so responsible about his new parenthood.

Robert entered the center at 9:00 AM. He paused to watch a busy little group of two infants and their caregiver June. The babies took turns in handing her blocks. June handed them back promptly, and then asked again for the blocks, prompting with her outstretched hand. The babies looked very pleased with themselves and each time the task was completed waited eagerly for their next turn. The caregiver seemed to be having as much fun as the babies.

"Some sort of a game, I guess," Robert mumbled. He was rather surprised how such a simple activity brought the three of them so much pleasure.

He spotted Ruth and she beckoned to him. She was standing by a crib with a bottle and a light receiving blanket in her hand. In the crib, a baby was stirring.

Ruth greeted Robert, and without delay told him that the baby she was watching in the crib was Lori, the new baby. Ruth said, "The teaching of appropriate behavior begins immediately. If we consistently attend to appropriate behaviors those are the behaviors the baby will learn."

"We talked about appropriate behavior, but what exactly do you mean by 'attend to appropriate behavior?'"

"Attend, in this case, means to provide consequences which will reinforce the baby's behavior."

"I've heard about reinforcement."

"Yes. Most people think of reinforcement as something contrived and tangible that you give, but by far the most frequent and important reinforcement is social. Babies respond readily to eye contact, smiles, being talked to, receiving hugs, kisses, or being cuddled. All of these usually strengthen behavior, and of course, are pleasurable not only to the baby but to the caregivers as well."

"Yes. I remember how Alison and I enjoyed the babies all waving to us on our first trip to this center."

Ruth smiled and continued. "The challenging part is to set up the environment so that the baby will behave well in the first place. We call that arranging antecedents. We want to increase the probability that the baby will behave appropriately."

"That sounds complicated," Robert said. "Is it?"

"Not really." Ruth answered, "But it requires preplanning, which in turn requires knowing each baby's physical needs and her own unique behaviors."

"I guess that takes time."

"It takes careful observation. I don't know much about Lori, for example, and she doesn't know much about me. I will learn about her today through carefully observing what she does. Using available information also helps. I can see by her mother's notes on Lori's Infant Daily Record, that she was last fed at 6.00. She drank three ounces of formula, and has been sleeping since she arrived here at 7.00 AM. So I can expect her to be hungry when she wakes up."

"That's why you have her bottle all ready, then." Robert commented.

"Yes," Ruth replied. "But it's more than attending to her hunger. If we give Lori a bottle quickly we accomplish two things. One, we provide good physical care, and two, we prevent her having to cry to get fed, and that's providing good behavioral care."

"I never thought of that." Robert said.

"People always comment on how happy our babies are, and how rarely they cry. We manage that by preventing crying in the first place, and by reinforcing all of the happy behaviors of our babies."

Lori stirred again, opened her eyes, and moved her fist closer to her mouth. Deftly, and in what seemed like one movement, Ruth put the nurser in Lori's mouth and gently picked her up. Robert watched the baby hungrily suck the nipple and swallow the formula. He turned to Ruth and said,

"I don't think I could drink that fast."

Ruth smiled. The two watched in silence as the baby drank. When about half of the formula was finished and Lori's sucking slowed down, Ruth gently called her name a few times. Lori seemed relaxed, and looked calmly back at Ruth.

Ruth addressed the baby. "Come on, darling, it's time to burp." As she waited for the baby to burp, she talked to Robert. "I'll never forget one of the first babies I cared for. He was an adorable four month old who had been at home all the time with his mother. He woke hungry and quickly drank from the bottle I offered him. He snuggled into me and then looked up, expecting to see Mommy. When he saw my face, he spat out the bottle and reacted as though I were Dracula. He fussed and cried for some time. So now with new babies, I try to get them used to me gradually. I mean, how would you like a perfect stranger to grab you and thrust his face right up to yours? I don't get my face too close to the baby's or draw attention to myself by talking too much until they have had a few ounces of milk. Then I just smile quietly, rock them, and hum or talk a little. Over the course of a morning they get used to me."

Robert looked at Ruth. The artist in him noted her fine bone structure and he could not possibly imagine how anyone could think she looked like Dracula.

"Also, Ruth continued, "You may have noticed that I did not change Lori before I fed her."

Robert hadn't noticed anything of the kind, but said nothing.

"Again, I did not want to take the chance of her crying."

At this point the awaited burp arrived in full force. Lori looked surprised. Ruth said to the baby, "That's *burping,* Lori. Now we will go get a clean diaper."

To Robert she added, "This is the first time I have changed Lori, so I must be very careful to reinforce appropriate behavior while it is still occurring. I must attend to every cooperative movement she makes. Reinforcement is mostly a matter of timing."

Ruth placed Lori on the changing table and talked softly to the child. Lori looked uncertainly at Ruth. When Ruth reached for a cloth, the baby began to make a face as if about to cry. Ruth went on with the task of changing her but did not talk to her or look directly at her. The baby's expression relaxed a bit. Immediately Ruth smiled at the child and softly chanted, "Lori, Lori." Lori stared back. Ruth tickled Lori's feet and talked quietly to her as she completed the diapering.

"That looks simple," Robert said, "but I can see that there is more to arranging antecedents and timing of reinforcement than meets the eye."

Ruth replied, "Yes. That's why I always act as the caregiver for new babies. Then little by little, depending upon that baby's behavior, the baby's assigned caregiver takes over."

Ruth continued the feeding, talking now and again to the baby, between explanations to Robert.

"Timing is critical. If I had waited even a second, Lori might have started whining or crying."

She turned to Lori, "We wouldn't want that, would we Darling?" Lori continued drinking, but her eyes flicked up to meet Ruth's. Ruth continued talking to the baby. "You like reinforcement, don't you?" Lori let go of the nipple and gurgled. Ruth cuddled the baby affectionately. "You are settling in very nicely, Lori."

Ruth looked up at Robert. "The baby's behavior is the quality control for behavioral care. Anyone's behavior always reveals their history of reinforcement. For example, whining babies show that someone has been attending to their whining behavior or otherwise reinforced whining. If babies play happily, that shows that playing behaviors have been reinforced."

Lori completed her feeding and Ruth placed her in a baby carrier. She told Robert that Bridget, the consultant nurse, recommended that the babies rest for at least fifteen minutes after each feeding, rather than engaging in activities like dancing that often caused them to spit up.

"Now is a very important time," Ruth said, hunching down by the little girl. "It is the first time Lori is sitting by herself here at the center. I must be sure not to ignore her when she is behaving so well."

"Lori, look." Ruth held up a ring of plastic keys within reach of the baby. Robert noticed that she did not shake the keys or flip them over one by one the way most adults do when trying to interest a baby in a new toy.

"It's fun to play with these toys yourself," Ruth said as if guessing Robert's thoughts. "Particularly the musical ones. But if you show the baby everything a toy can do, you spoil the enjoyment of discovery for the baby. Also, look at the timing. If you entertain the baby *while she is inactive,* you reinforce sitting passively, rather than letting her explore her environment and generate her own reinforcement."

Lori was now reaching for the toy.

She didn't get a good hold and it dropped. Again Ruth held the keys within reach. This time Lori grasped the ring and drew it up to her mouth.

"Now I will leave her for a few minutes," Ruth said, "but I will put her where she has other babies to look at, and I will also catch her eye or smile at her often."

Ruth addressed a caregiver sitting in a little group with three babies, "Edna Mae, Lori is settling in well, so I'm going to let her rest beside you so she can see the other babies." She placed Lori's carrier over in the group of babies by Edna Mae and then stood up.

"I once observed a center where the infants were lined up like soldiers. Each was staring off into space, like a zombie. We always face babies towards each other. You would be amazed at the difference such a simple step makes in the babies' behavior." Ruth said, "Look now at Lori." The little girl was happily moving her arms and legs, and staring intently at the baby in the infant seat opposite her. That baby was also waving his arms and kicking his legs and cooing at Lori.

Ruth leaned over towards Lori and said, "Michael is saying hello to you Lori."

She then turned to Michael and said, "Lori is happy to see you."

Robert said "What you did, facing the babies toward each other, was so easy to do. It seems so logical. I wonder why they didn't do it in the center you mentioned."

Ruth smiled. "You're an artist. You attend to many details that most people wouldn't notice. Learning to be sensitive to each baby's behavior, and reinforcing appropriate behavior is like any profession. You have to know what to do."

It was Robert's turn to smile. "Yes, I suppose that's true." Robert looked thoughtful as he and Ruth walked away from the infants.

They had reached the door. "I need to get back to Lori, now." Ruth said. "Any time you want to discuss more, just call."

Robert said, "I may just do that." and left the center.

As he drove home, Robert visualized himself and Alison picking up a smiling Teddi, playing with her, placing her down while she was still happy, and picking her up again while she was still smiling—to reinforce her appropriate behavior. He could hardly wait for Alison to return from her flight to Chicago to tell her what he had learned.

Six weeks went by. Robert and Alison received their little girl, and followed Ruth's suggestions about reinforcing appropriate behavior, they had a wonderful first few weeks with Teddi. Robert had intended to go back to Infant and Toddler Center USA for another chat with Ruth, but business was hectic, and with Teddi to care for, he never got the chance. Anyway, they hadn't had any problems with Teddi. Everyone said what a beautiful contented baby she was. Then came the awful weekend.

6.1.2 Robert and Alison Visit Friends and Observe a Toddler Who Grabs Noses

Robert and Alison visited some friends who had a thirteen month old toddler called Randolph. Robert now felt confident about the way he interacted with babies, and did not hesitate to pick up Randolph. The baby went to him readily enough, but as soon as he got near Robert's face, he grabbed Robert's nose. Hard. Robert winced and tried to get loose, getting in the process, a scratch which bled.

The father immediately rushed over and caught Randolph's hand as he made another attempt at Robert's nose.

"No, No. Make this a *good* hand," he said, kissing the baby's hand which he had trapped in his own fist. "Don't grab at noses."

He looked pleadingly at his wife, who came to take the child. The parents apologized profusely to Robert. It seemed that the baby continually grabbed his father's nose, and was now starting to grab the noses of anyone who came near him. The father was unable to hold the baby, and even the mother had a difficult time. That fact was underlined throughout the weekend. Both parents were unable to converse without being interrupted by some misbehavior of their child. Teddi, of course, had behaved very well. Their friends had warned them that although the first months were easy, they could expect problems with Teddi when she grew a little older. Robert shuddered. What would he do if Teddi did something gross like grabbing at his nose when he had a client at his home studio?

6.1.3 Robert Visits Unit #3 (Toddlers) and Learns How to Shape Appropriate Behavior to Replace Inappropriate Behavior

The specter of Teddi humiliating him loomed so large that Robert called Ruth and briefly outlined the weekend's trials. Ruth was very reassuring. She told him that no behavior appears in full strength, and it is not hard to get rid of an action if you work on it right away. She suggested Robert pay a brief visit to Unit #3 and observe the young toddler group.

"Now is a good time to visit," Ruth said. "We have a new toddler who hasn't had the advantage of our infant program, so he will probably grab or push or something, and you can see how we handle such behaviors. I'll be free on Tuesday morning at 10:30 if that is convenient."

On Tuesday Robert arrived in the parking lot just as his watch beeped 10:30. Ruth was expecting him and opened the door.

"My, he did give you a scratch," she exclaimed after the hellos.

"What? Oh, that." Robert put his hand up self-consciously.

Ruth showed Robert into Unit #3, one of the toddler units (for babies as soon as they walked independently to twenty-four months of age). The fifteen toddlers were divided into three groups, each supervised by the children's assigned primary caregiver. The caregivers and toddlers said hello, and then turned back to their activities. In one corner a group was busy fingerpainting. Children in a second group were playing in a little play house.

Ruth directed Robert's attention to the third and nearest group. She pointed out a blond child saying, "That's Scott, the toddler I was telling you about." She pulled up two chairs close enough so that she and Robert could observe the group, but far enough away so that they would not disturb the children when they talked. The children were sitting on the floor around a pile of page-sized cards with pictures on them. One of the toddlers was standing by his caregiver Kris. The child was holding up a red colored card. Kris carefully pronounced the word "RED" and the toddlers repeated with various approximations.

Ruth explained that Kris said "red" first because the children were still learning the name of the color. She also drew Robert's attention to the way in which the toddlers were taking turns in holding up the cards.

They continued watching. Kris said, "Peter, pick out the next card."

As soon as Peter picked up a card, however, Scott (the new boy) grabbed it from Peter's hands and stood up. Peter looked puzzled.

"That's OK, Peter. Get another one." Peter moved away from Scott and sorted through the pile. He picked out a picture of a ball. Kris held her arms out to him and he went to her side. "What is this?" she asked and the group, in unison, replied "ball." Scott observed the activity, and then sat down, putting the card on the floor beside him. Kris turned to him and said,

"OK, Scott, now it is *your* turn. Would you like to pick out a card to name?"

Scott, looking around to make sure that all the others were watching, picked out a card showing a bat and strutted to the front.

"Thank you, Scott," Kris said approvingly, as she turned him around so the others could see the card.

The game continued. Ruth and Robert talked quietly as they watched. Ruth said.

"Well, there you saw an instance of grabbing. Notice that Kris did not say anything to Scott. Most people would tell him, 'We don't grab,' or give him a little lecture. But then his *inappropriate* behavior is getting him attention. In fact, many adults strengthen just the behaviors they do *not* want, by criticizing when the child engages in them."

Ruth continued, "Instead of scolding Scott, Kris talked to Peter. But she kept an eye on Scott so she would be ready to catch any appropriate behavior."

"That's all fine," said Robert. "Scott stayed in the group. But what would you do if he walked away with the card or hit another toddler on the head with it?"

"In the first case, leave him be. In the second, we would attend to the child he hit, walking him away from Scott if necessary. But we would be sure to pay attention to anything appropriate Scott does. You cannot eliminate misbehavior by ignoring it. You must build appropriate behavior to take its place."

Robert looked dubious. "So you just let toddlers do whatever they like?"

"In a matter of speaking, yes," Ruth replied, "but when children's appropriate behaviors are reinforced, what they *like* to do changes. It is all a matter of the kinds of consequences children get. For example, our children *like* to name the pictures on the cards. But suppose we kept telling them they weren't pronouncing the words correctly, or told them they picked up the wrong card. If we often showed disappointment in their performance every child would hate naming cards. As it is, they love it, and we have some long words too, such as brontosaurus."

"But isn't that pushing them? I've read that you shouldn't push children."

"Pushing isn't *what* you teach, it's *how you do it.* Pushing is using disapproval or punishment to get a child to do something. It would be pushing to ask a child to do something at which he is likely to fail or to criticize the children for not naming the cards well enough, or making them stay in that activity until they named them better. But the children's behavior shows we are not pushing. Watch them. They love to pronounce the long names." Ruth glanced at the group. "Notice also how often Kris talks, smiles, or nods at Scott just at the moment he is behaving well. She is making sure he is successful so that he will enjoy naming pictures, too. He won't grab much more, because grabbing doesn't pay off."

"You mean all bad behavior pays off?"

Ruth tilted her head and glanced sideways at Robert. "Maybe not every time, but at some point, yes. Babies are sensitive to contingencies and change when contingencies change. What about your friend's nose grabber. What did Randolph get by grabbing at your nose?"

"What do you mean?"

"What happened right after he grabbed?"

"Well . . . The father held the baby's hand and told him not to grab . . . and . . . and, I see it now, he actually kissed the 'bad' hand . . . to make it better, he said. And then the mother came over and took the baby in her arms. You mean the parents have been *reinforcing* their little boy for grabbing?"

"It's a good guess," Ruth said, "but they can find out by changing the contingencies—by turning away when he starts to grab and by. . . . "

"You don't know this kid," Robert interrupted. "He's lightening fast."

"In that case, they may have to begin their efforts by finding a situation in which he is not likely to grab—say when he is watching a dog or something else that holds his attention. If they make sure to pay lots of attention to him and kiss his hands then, when he does *not* grab, even for a few seconds, and if they *never* talk to him when he is grabbing, it won't take long to stop that behavior. It may be a bit hard on their noses for a day or two if the behavior is as strong as you say."

Some toddlers were getting ready to go outside.

"The children are certainly well behaved," Robert remarked. "Alison and I visited centers where it was chaos when the toddlers were putting on their coats and caps. There was lots of squabbling and the caregivers looked harassed. Here the kids look as though they enjoy getting ready."

Ruth smiled. "Yes they do," she agreed, "It's a natural progression from our philosophy of teaching appropriate behavior as soon as a baby enters the center. You remember the first time I changed Lori."

"Oh yes. When you were changing her you caught all of her appropriate behaviors and reinforced them."

"Well that was the first step in teaching a baby to enjoy dressing. We reinforce all the appropriate behaviors. At first the babies learn to relax so it is easy for us to put on their diapers. Little by little we teach them to help with dressing by holding their arms up or out, or putting their foot in their shoe and so on. As their motor skills develop, they take on more of the dressing tasks and get lots of reinforcement for their efforts. The end result is a child who is a cooperative or independent dresser."

"So it's done step by step, or behavior by behavior." Robert said.

"Yes," Ruth laughed, "You can't suddenly get a cooperative and independent child. You build those behaviors by attending all along to little things infants and toddlers do. You've heard the old saying. 'If you attend to the little things, the big things will take care of themselves.'"

The toddlers started leaving the center and their laughter could be heard through the open door. Robert and Ruth headed towards the staff room.

6.1.4 Contingencies: The Importance of Timing

Two caregivers, Amanda and June, were in the staff room. Ruth said, "Robert has just had a look at the toddler group in Unit #3. He was interested in how we teach appropriate behavior to replace inappropriate behavior."

Amanda said, "Well if you had wanted to see inappropriate behavior you should have come when Louise was here."

"Louise?" Robert asked. "Was she a problem baby?"

The caregivers laughed, and June explained, "No, she was a problem caregiver. I'll never forget the day I came into the center and saw that most of the babies were whining and crying."

"I know what you are referring to." Amanda said, "I shall never forget it either. It was an experience that I would hate to repeat."

"I was so surprised." June said. "I had only been working at the center for three days, and had taken the position mainly because whenever I visited the babies were always so happy. Priscilla was away and we had a substitute called Louise. She had been through Mikki's orientation, and had told Mikki she thought the babies were adorable and liked how well we cared for them. So we thought she would do fine, but were we ever shocked!

"It all started early in the morning, when she tried to feed Kayla. She put the nipple in Kayla's mouth and Kayla spat it out. This happened three or four times and all the while she talked in a continuous stream to Kayla. I suggested that she put Kayla down to play for awhile and then offer her the bottle later. She told me that she was old enough to be my mother, had raised three children of her own and did not need *me* to tell her how to care for infants. Remember, I was new at the center and was just learning the way Ruth and Mikki wanted things done. They had told me about how talking to the infants at the center should be contingent upon appropriate behavior. So I was surprised to find out that Louise talked to the babies all the time whether they were behaving appropriately or not."

"I can see it now," Amanda said. "She went on trying to feed Kayla and soon Kayla was crying. Then she started walking up and down, patting Kayla firmly on the back."

"Exactly." June said. "As you can imagine this did not sooth Kayla, but made her cry louder. While Louise was walking around with Kayla, Holly, another of her infants woke up. Holly played nicely in her crib for a while. Louise ignored her. Both June and I had our four babies to care for, and we were also caring for Augustus and Daniel, the other two babies assigned to Louise. So we couldn't help her with Holly. Soon Holly started whimpering. Louise didn't notice that Holly was awake until she started crying. Then she put Kayla, who by now was hungry as well as crying, in the playpen. Then she got Holly out of the crib. She changed her and gave her some of her bottle and then put her in the swing. She went back to Kayla, who was only whimpering now, and took her into the nap/sleeping room to feed her. She said there was too much distraction in the activity area for Kayla and that was why she was crying. She stayed in the nap/sleeping room for *forty minutes,* feeding and then walking up and down holding Kayla until the baby fell asleep. She did this without making *any* provision for her other babies, and we were left to care for them as well as for our own."

"It must have been hectic," said Robert.

"Hectic is not the word for it. It was chaos." June replied, "We raced around red-faced, trying to get one baby fed, changed, put down for a nap, or settled, and then running back for another."

"What I could not believe was her attitude." Amanda said, "When Kayla finally went to sleep, Louise fed and changed Daniel. I don't know what happened, but Daniel started to cry, and she carried *him* around, patting him on the back and saying 'Hush hush'. I suggested she put him in the playpen and change Augustus and put him down for a nap before he got overtired. She said she did not believe in letting babies cry and that she was going to take Daniel into the sleeping area and rock him to sleep. I was flabbergasted that she, who said she did not believe in letting babies cry, was setting up situations which practically guaranteed crying. Maybe she expected us to care for her other babies."

"Where were Mikki and Ruth while all this was going on?" Robert asked.

Amanda said, "Mikki was helping out in Unit #2 where one of the babies had broken out in a rash and had to be isolated until the parents arrived. Ruth was having some emergency dental surgery and was expected back at the center sometime after lunch. When she got back, things were really in a mess. Lorraine's four babies all needed care. Kayla was awake and crying in the playpen, Daniel was awake and crying in his crib, Augustus had thrown up some formula and needed changing, and Louise was carrying Holly who was crying loudly. June and I were trying to get our babies fed and changed and up from and down for naps. The extra tasks the care of Lorraine's babies had heaped on us had interfered with the care of our own babies and we now were too busy to help her."

Ruth laughed. "Really," she said, "I wouldn't have wanted anyone to visit on that day. But I could not have planned a better demonstration of what *not* to do for my other caregivers. Louise really proved my point by showing what happens if you fail to arrange antecedent conditions to prevent crying, and she showed what happens when you wait until babies start to whimper or cry before going to them. But one demonstration was enough. We never asked her back."

Robert spoke to Ruth. "Maybe I should bring Randolph's parents here to learn what to do."

"That's O.K. by me," Ruth answered, "but you will have to be careful. Most parents don't realize their role in teaching inappropriate behaviors and it can come as quite a shock."

"I can imagine." Robert raised his eyebrows. The conversation seemed over, and Robert judged by the light that it was nearly 1:00. He had a client coming at 2:00, so reluctantly, he took his leave.

Ruth accompanied him to the door. Well, I hope that was helpful for you," she said.

"Yes it was." Robert laughed. "If Teddi grabs my nose, I certainly won't kiss her hand."

6.2 ANALYSIS I:
APPROPRIATE BEHAVIORS AND INDIVIDUAL DIFFERENCES

Before we analyze how to teach appropriate behavior, we need to clarify what appropriate behavior is. In Chapter Two we saw that in order to judge whether or not something is appropriate we must consider the situation in which it occurs. Screaming, for example, may be appropriate on the playground, but inappropriate in the classroom. In this analysis we shall discuss appropriate behavior in more detail . . .

In order to decide what behavior is "appropriate" for a particular child, it is necessary to know what is the child's typical pattern of behavior. For one child, saying "wed" to name the color red may be a step forward, for another, a regression to "baby talk." Even behaviors which are generally desirable may not be appropriate for a particular child. For example, children are usually expected to take bumps and pain without crying or complaining. But even that behavior in the extreme is inappropriate. A child who is seriously hurt *should* cry out or complain. You would not want a child to have serious stomach cramps and not let you know, or wear shoes that cause blisters and not complain. Only by observing behavior will a caregiver know that a particular child is too stoical, and that for her, complaining is *appropriate* behavior. Similarly, although sharing is generally desirable, a child may give toys away too much, so that he never has anything himself.

One further point: Many caregivers consider the quiet baby to be a "good" child. For the boisterous child, sitting quietly for a moment or two may be appropriate behavior. But being quiet is often inappropriate behavior. (see Appendix B: DYK 6.1) Children must learn, and to learn they must be active. A baby who sits quietly staring off into space is not manipulating objects, or exercising her eyes, or gaining any reinforcement from her environment. She is at risk, partly because passive babies tend to be ignored more than demanding ones. Caregivers must counteract their own tendencies to leave quiet babies and toddlers alone, and to make sure that they teach such children to interact more actively with their environment.

Many actions can prevent babies from becoming passive. In the narrative, we saw how Ruth gave a toy to the new baby, Lori, without demonstrating how it worked. She explained to Robert that she did not want to spoil the baby's pleasure at discovering what it would do. If the sounds or sights produced by a toy come only when a baby moves it, the baby will learn to explore rather than wait to be entertained. Ruth also placed Lori facing Michael, an active baby. At a very young age, babies find each other interesting. In addition, when one baby moves an arm or leg, or babbles, the other may respond with a noise or movement. Thus the actions of one baby may reinforce the actions of the other. In interacting, both babies improve their vision and coordination. In addition, placing babies facing each other helps them take an active interest in their environment—a prerequisite for all the learning to come.

6.2.1 The Importance of Appropriate Behaviors

In Chapter One, we mentioned that the behavior of the babies in a center is one of the most important quality indicators of center care. The reasons for this are many. A center with happy, active, and cooperative children is a pleasant place for both the children and their caregivers. But more than that, the behavior of children in a center impacts what caregivers can do, and as a result what all of the children will learn.

A center with children who behave inappropriately poses three problems for caregivers. First, babies who are behaving inappropriately are not themselves productively learning. Second, they have a negative effect on other children, who bear the brunt of their crying or bullying, or may imitate their inappropriate behaviors. Third, they preoccupy staff members. In the narrative, the caregivers discussed Louise, the caregiver who attended to babies mainly when they fussed or cried. We saw how the crying of one baby in her care interfered with her giving adequate care to the rest of her babies. Then they too, cried. With a toddler group, a caregiver who ties up her time with a child who grabs or hits or bites, does not have time available for other children.

In contrast, children who have been taught appropriate behaviors enable caregivers to provide better care for all their children. (see Figure 6.1) When children are cooperative, caregivers can provide incidental learning during routine care. A caregiver who is changing a cooperative baby can play and talk with the child. In Chapter Three we saw how Amanda used the changing time to recite little poems to the babies, teaching them the parts of their bodies. Also, when routine care goes smoothly, caregivers create opportunities for "quality time" that is, for relaxed interaction with individual babies. In this chapter we saw how June was teaching two babies to share by playing a game with blocks. Such activities are possible only when other babies are not demanding immediate attention. Similarly, the narrative showed a caregiver teaching a toddler group. Because the children had been taught to participate enthusiastically, caregivers did not have to spend time coaxing children to join the group or to look at the cards or admonishing them not to grab. Instead they could help them master the objectives of the learning activity.

All center personnel and parents would like a center in which children actively explore their environment, interact happily with others, and participate enthusiastically in group activities. Such a goal is not unrealistic. But it requires knowing how to teach appropriate behavior.

6.3 ANALYSIS 2: SHAPING APPROPRIATE BEHAVIOR

In this chapter we have emphasized two points at which environmental events can be arranged; before or after behavior of a child. We call events which precede the behavior of a child antecedent events. Consequences which follow a specific act of a child are called postcedent environmental events.

6.3.1 Arranging Antecedent Events

Before infants or toddlers arrive at a center, facilities are designed to promote health and safety. Centers are safety-proofed by such preventive measures as covering electrical outlets, placing gates or barriers at the tops and bottoms of stairs, and by making sure that toys do not have parts

FIGURE 6.1: THE CYCLES OF BEHAVIOR

AND ENVIRONMENT

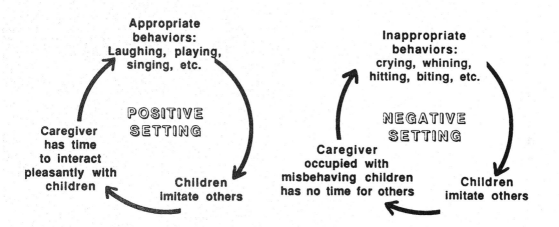

that could cause cuts or choking. (see Appendix B: DYK 6.2) So far as health and safety are concerned, state standards clearly specify procedures which anticipate and prevent problems.

Similar anticipation and preplanning can set up an environment which encourages appropriate *behavior.* Planning includes providing physical comfort, interesting activities, and it also includes teaching behaviors which will be useful later.

Teaching Behaviors Before They Are Needed

No one would wait until a fire is raging to start fire drill training. But the systematic building of helpful behaviors is not as widely practiced. The time to teach toddlers to wait to go outside is *before* they start shoving or squabbling. The time to teach a baby to hand over objects is *before* you need to have something he is holding. We saw in the narrative how June was playing a game involving handing blocks back and forth. Not only did the babies enjoy this activity, but it was teaching them to place objects into an outstretched hand. If, later, one of June's babies grabbed her mother's car keys or someone's glasses, or even a dangerous object, it would be easy to get the objects back without a struggle.

By arranging antecedent events, caregivers set up an environment in which appropriate behaviors are likely to occur. Strengthening those behaviors, so that they become part of a baby's normal activities requires attention to postcedent events.

6.3.2. Postcedent Environmental Events: Shaping Behavior

Important as antecedents are, they are not as important as postcedents, the consequences that follow behavior. The most important kind of consequence is called reinforcement.

Reinforcement

Reinforcement is defined as a procedure which increases the frequency of a behavior it follows. Reinforcement is thus defined by its affects on behavior. A caregiver may praise a child, but if her praise does not strengthen the kinds of acts for which she is praising, praising is *not* reinforcement for that behavior. On the other hand, criticism doesn't seem to be something a person would want, yet it often functions as reinforcement, strengthening exactly those behaviors a caregiver wishes to eliminate.

Although informally people talk about praising or criticizing a child, it is actually the *behavior* which is reinforced. Technically, it is incorrect to say, "The caregiver reinforced Johnny." The correct phrasing would be "The caregiver reinforced sharing." (or whatever the child was doing). By insisting on correct usage, focus is placed on the behavior which is being strengthened. This helps reduce the problem of a teacher who tells a child he has been sharing nicely, but does so *when the child starts to grab*. The caregiver may feel that she is "praising Johnny for sharing", but she is actually reinforcing grabbing. By talking consistently of reinforcing *behavior*, rather than the child, the relationship between caregiver actions and their effect on the child's behavior becomes clearer.

The Strength of a Reinforcer

We defined reinforce*ment* as a procedure which increases the frequency of a behavior it follows. Positive reinforcers are the objects or events which, when presented, strengthen the preceding behavior. The strength of a reinforcer depends on the momentary state of the child. Activities are more reinforcing when we have not had them for awhile. Food, even a food a child likes, will reinforce behavior only if a child is hungry. Getting to play with a particular toy will probably not reinforce behavior in a child who has played with that toy the entire morning. Some activities depend less on the child's state than others. A kind word or smile from a caregiver is usually effective, even when a child has recently received many other kind words or smiles.

Caregivers often over use praise. Not only does too much praise lessen its effectiveness, it may not function as reinforcement at all. For older children particularly, praise may actually weaken behavior. Teachers do not usually go on and on praising their better students. Profuse praise is reserved for poorer students, and may therefore point out to the whole class a student's weakness. Such praise may punish behavior, not strengthen it. Praise can be effective if it is used sparingly and when it is genuine. At other times, simple attention will be enough. A glance, a laugh or smile, or even just watching a baby—a recognition that you noticed—usually will reinforce a baby's behavior.

In this text, we assume that attention is reinforcing. Only in rare instances (such as when a baby does not know you) is attention not reinforcing. If, however, talking or smiling does not seem to have an effect on a child's behavior, you may need to try cuddling, or rocking or some other event. It is incorrect to say, "reinforcement doesn't work." The correct statement is "What I'm doing isn't reinforcement."

Contingencies: The Timing of Caregiver Actions

Contingencies of reinforcement are the relationships between a behavior and its consequences; the timing of caregiver actions *relative to infant behavior.* There is a critical difference between picking up an little boy when he is crying and picking him up when he is holding out his arms. The first will strengthen crying, the second will encourage him to hold out his arms when the wents to get picked up.

Every interaction between caregiver and infant affects behavior. Whatever a baby girl is doing when a caregiver glances at her, or smiles, or talks to her, or gives her a toy, strengthens that kind of behavior. Even within a small time period, behavior varies. In this chapter we saw how, by attending to contingencies, Ruth taught Lori to relax *during the two or three minutes she was changing her.*

What might have happened if Ruth had reinforced Lori at the wrong times? Let's say the baby twisted over to one side a bit, and Ruth said, "Hey, sweetie, hold still." If a caregiver consistently talks when a baby squirms, it will not be long before the baby becomes difficult to change.

In the narrative, the staff told how a caregiver, Louise, shifted contingencies by attending to children primarily when they started to whine or cry. By waiting until a child cried until she went to him or her, she had nearly all her babies crying by the end of one morning.

The inappropriate behaviors seen in toddlers are also inadvertently taught. In most centers, a toddler can usually gain the attention of a caregiver by any of a number of inappropriate behaviors, throwing, grabbing, shoving, hitting, and biting to mention a few. In fact, the "problem" child often gets more attention than his or her victims. Such a child's aggressive behavior is likely to continue: one possible reason for one research finding that boys who have had center care are likely to be more aggressive than their home-raised peers. (see Appendix B: DYK 6.3).

To change inappropriate behavior, caregivers must change the contingencies. Instead of attending to a child when he hits or bites another, you must attend to his appropriate behavior. We saw an example of this in the narrative, where the caregiver, Kris, gave Scott attention, not when he grabbed a card from Peter's hand, but when he sat down and looked up. Kris did not wait until Scott named a card. That would have been too big a step. Instead, she reinforced the first appropriate behavior she observed and that was looking up at the card. Kris could not just wait for Scott to behave perfectly. She had to shape Scott's behavior.

6.3.4 Shaping Behavior

Shaping is the building of new behavior by reinforcing just those responses which are closest to it. In the early stages of building new behavior, frequency of reinforcement is the key. You must continually reinforce the best of what a child does. Those "bests" may not, at first, be very close to the behavior you want. In the narrative, we saw how Ruth worked with Lori while changing her. The baby did not smile or babble. In fact, at first she looked as though she might cry. Ruth had to start by reinforcing a shift in facial expression, because that was the best she had to work with. As Lori's behavior improved, Ruth continued to respond to her most appropriate behavior.

In the diapering example, shaping took place during a few minutes. Other behaviors are shaped over the period of weeks, months, or even years. For example, you cannot teach children to talk, or to share, or to dress themselves in the space of a few moments. Ruth, in the narrative, explained that even teaching babies to relax while being changed, helps teach them to cooperate with dressing. A child who can relax an arm is easier to dress than one who squirms or fights. Similarly, children in Infant and Toddler Center USA started learning to share as young babies. We saw how June played a game with her babies which taught them to place an object in an outstretched hand, and to ask for it back with a similar gesture. Asking nicely for a toy rather than grabbing, helps other children learn to share. A child is more likely to give up an object if approached with an outstretched hand than if approached by a grabbing child. Then, if a nice request works, that is, if the child hands it over following the request, the behavior of asking (rather than grabbing) will be strengthened. Thus by teaching children to hand over an object, you have set the foundations for sharing. (see Table 6.1)

All of the goals promoted for day care such as "sharing", "cooperation", "generosity", "maturity" and "self-esteem" can be analyzed into their component behaviors which can be taught one by one. Unfortunately their opposites can be taught, too. But by arranging antecedent events so that children will be happy and active, and by reinforcing appropriate behaviors when they occur, caregivers can establish a center which meets the goals we all have for our children.

6.4 SUMMARY

What you see children doing in a center is what that center environment is teaching them to do. The environment includes toys and physical equipment, but the most critical part of the center environment consists of what the caregivers do and how they interact with the children. For it is this interaction that determines what the children learn and how they behave. Every time a caregiver addresses a toddler, or nods, or picks up an infant, some behavior of that child is strengthened.

In this chapter we looked at ways to build appropriate behaviors. We saw how Ruth established antecedent conditions to make it likely that the infant Lori would behave appropriately, and then reinforced the appropriate behavior that occurred. We looked at how caregivers can shape such actions as sharing by building them behavior by behavior. We examined contingencies—the timing of caregiver actions relative to each child's behavior—and saw how they determine what a child learns.

An environment which teaches appropriate behaviors benefits the

TABLE 6.1: TEACHING SHARING, BEHAVIOR BY BEHAVIOR

Sharing is best taught, not at the moment a child grabs something and clutches it to his chest, but behavior by behavior from birth on. The initial activities below are developmentally appropriate as soon as the baby begins grasping and releasing objects. They are also developmentally appropriate for an older child who has not yet learned to share.

<u>Behavior</u>: **Handing things to a caregiver.**
<u>Comment</u>: This involves two parts; (1) Learning the motor skill of releasing an object, and (2) Learning to hand over something when asked for it.In the narrative we saw how very young babies can learn to place objects into an outstretched hand -- IF they are taught to do so in a game-like situation.

<u>Behavior:</u> **Asking for something from a caregiver.**
<u>Comment:</u> While this does not seem like a component of sharing, it actually helps in teaching that skill. It is more likely that a child will share a toy when asked for it, than if another child tries to grab it. Thus by teaching a child how to ask, you help others learn to share. In the narrative, part of the handing game taught babies to hold out their hands to receive an object. This is one way of asking for an object.

Behavior: Handing a toy to another baby when asked by a caregiver.
Comment: It is easier to use prompts to teach a child to share than to try to get him or her to share freely in an unstructured situation.   At first, set up a situation to increase the likelihood that the baby will give an object away by 1) using a neutral object, rather than a baby's favorite blanket or toy and 2) picking a time when the baby is about to drop an object rather than when he first starts playing with it.   Use gestural and spoken prompts. For example, guide a baby's hand while saying, "Give the toy to Kayla."Lastly, don't forget that behavior is maintained by its consequences.   A smile, an approving glance, an offer of another toy, a cuddle, or a few words will usually reinforce sharing behavior.

child, the caregivers, and ultimately society itself. The baby benefits when she learns to interact in positive ways with others. Staff members benefit when babies play happily and get along well with each other and with staff members. Society benefits when children entering early childhood already approach the world full of the curiosity, spontaneity, and a positive self-concept which comes from successful experiences in life.

Chapter Seven

THE ABC'S OF INFANT DEVELOPMENT

GEORGE, A BEHAVIOROLOGIST, GIVES
AN INSERVICE ON HOW BEHAVIOR DEVELOPS

OBJECTIVES

After you have read this chapter you should be able to . . .

1. Explain why physical behaviors, such as crawling, can develop without help from parents or other caregivers.
2. Describe social behaviors such as sharing or holding out one's hands to be picked up, and explain the role of a parent or caregiver in their development.
3. Analyze a given behavioral episode in terms of the three term contingency.
4. Define verbal behavior and identify examples of the mand and tact.
5. Give an example of how a child could mand or tact before he or she could talk.
6. Diagram a discrimination using the three term contingency analysis.
7. Describe how to teach tacting, for example, naming colors, without using any punishment.
8. Explain why interaction between baby and caregiver is so important for the development of verbal behavior.

Babies develop in many different ways. Their physical development depends upon such factors as proper nutrition, appropriate exercise, fresh and unpolluted air, and regular and adequate sleep. For children to develop physically to their full potential, they must encounter an environment which provides all of these factors.

But physical care is not all a baby needs. From the very first moment of birth a baby begins to develop socially. No one knows to what extent babies are born "friendly" or "unfriendly", "gregarious" or "shy", but we do know that a baby's day to day experience profoundly impacts his or her outlook on life. The baby's social world consists of hundreds of little glances, touches, laughs, and expressions from peers and from those who care for them. The cumulative effect of and timing of these interactions determine the kinds of social behaviors that children learn. In this chapter we look at the mechanisms through which behavior develops.

7.1 GEORGE, A BEHAVIOROLOGIST, GIVES AN INSERVICE ON HOW BEHAVIOR DEVELOPS

Saturday, inservice day. All of the staff of the four units were required to attend, and were paid for doing so. Mikki liked to say that paid inservice was one of the benefits of working at Infant and Toddler Center USA. The full time staff of *Unit 1*, Amanda, Eve, and Priscilla, and the part time staff of *Unit 1*, Joyce, Marilyn, and Beverly arrived early. They knew that Ruth had arranged for coffee and fruit as well as the danish pastries the staff liked so well. While they breakfasted on the refreshments, the staff all talked animatedly about the finer points of care.

The presenter this day was a professor that Ruth knew, from a nearby university. Mikki went to the front of the room and motioned to Ruth. The caregivers dispersed and made their way towards the chairs.

7.1.1 Selection by Consequences

When all were seated Mikki asked Ruth to introduce the speaker. She turned towards a tall well built man with thick black hair and a charming smile.

"This is Dr. George Lorca," Ruth said, "My advisor from my Masters program."

"Thank you," George said. "I'd like to run this session informally, so if you have any questions, feel free to raise your hand at any time. I thought we'd begin with an overview of how behavior develops and then get to particulars. O.K.?'

The staff nodded agreement.

George leaned against the table at the front of the room and began.

"As you know, the human infant is born with very few behaviors. All of us inherited a few specific reflexes (like the sucking reflex) and we inherited physical characteristics such as perhaps overall energy level or height. But we inherited first and foremost a capacity to learn. From the moment of birth, behavior begins to develop through the infant's interactions with his world."

"The process by which behavior develops is similar to natural selection in the evolution of species. Both require variation. In natural selection, animals differ in their physical and behavioral traits. Animals whose traits enable them to mate and pass on their genes, increase the numbers in future generations that resemble them both in physical characteristics and in behavior. Gradually, over the course of many generations, the characteristics of the species shift in the direction of the surviving individuals, and we say the species evolves."

"In the development of *behavior*, variation occurs in the individual acts of a single living being. We all engage in a variety of behaviors. No one can repeat everything she has ever done. Some of our acts survive to be repeated, some do not, causing a shift in the pattern of how we generally behave. Behaviors are selected by their consequences. Selective strengthening operates all the time in all of our lives. It's happening right now as I talk. When you smile or nod, that strengthens my making a particular point, or phrasing something a particular way."

The staff smiled. George laughed. "Behavior develops through the child's moment to moment interaction with its environment. For example, take learning to reach. I'm sure you have seen young babies trying to reach. Their arms move all over the place. Some of the motions bring the baby's arm closer to objects, and are strengthened. Gradually the ineffective actions (which move the arm farther away from an object) die out, and those that bring the arm closer to objects occur more frequently. The consequence of the hand approaching an object (and eventually touching the object) selects movements for an effective reach.

The Development of Physical Skills

The consequences for effective reaching occur without help from caregivers. Babies learn many behaviors through direct contact with their physical world. No one has to teach a child how to reach or to walk or to pick up things. They will learn on their own through natural consequences. *Touching* is the natural consequence for successful reaching. *Moving forward* increases the movements involved in crawling, scooting, or walking. Babies get constant feedback from kicking, putting things in their mouths, catching their toes, and so on. They learn to bring their hands together from the physical contact. They learn to focus their eyes correctly by producing a clearer picture. They learn the movements involved in speech through the sounds those movements produce." George paused and then asked, "Can you think of other skills that a baby learns through consequences from the physical world—which don't need consequences provided by people?"

The staff was silent.

George prompted, "Think of physical skills."

Eve spoke. "How about throwing a ball?"

"Good." George smiled. "You may say "good throw", but the path of the ball itself provides the most effective feedback for proper aiming and releasing. Gradually the more effective combinations of aim and release survive and the less effective ones die out. A child could learn to throw without being taught."

George paused, then continued. "Youngsters are constantly moving, and every movement provides feedback to the baby. But while the physical environment provides consequences for development of most *physical* skills, people must provide the consequences for much of what a child needs to learn, including all social behavior.

Social Development

Social behaviors develop through selection also, but the consequences for social behaviors are provided, not by the physical environment, but by other people. You could not learn to talk, or to share, or to wave "Bye-bye" if you grew up apart from other people. You must learn those behaviors through interacting with others." George paused, consulted his notes, and continued.

"Behaviors are dependent, or contingent, upon events in the environment. These events occur before and after our behavior, and provide the framework in which behavioral and environmental interactions or relations are analyzed."

7.1.2 The Three Term Contingency Analysis

"To analyze behavior we identify the antecedents events that come before the behavior, and the postcedents events or consequences which come immediately after the behavior." George turned on the overhead projector and placed a transparency with the headings on it. He pointed to *Behavior,* and said, "We identify the behavior of interest first." He then looked towards the group and said, "We usually refer to the three terms Antecedents, Behavior, and Consequences, as the ABC's of behavior. (see Figure 7.1).

FIGURE 7.1: DIAGRAM OF THE THREE TERM CONTINGENCY ANALYSIS

<u>Antecedents</u>	<u>Behavior</u>	<u>Consequences</u>
Events occurring **immediately** before the behavior occurs, so that the behavior interrupts those events, or particular objects or people that are present at the time the behavior occurred	The behavior you are interested in explaining	Events happening **just after** the behavior

An Example:

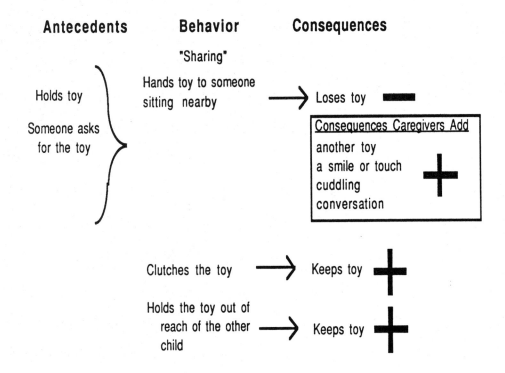

Antecedents

Holds toy

Someone asks for the toy

Behavior

"Sharing"

Hands toy to someone sitting nearby

Clutches the toy

Holds the toy out of reach of the other child

Consequences

Loses toy

<u>Consequences Caregivers Add</u>
another toy
a smile or touch
cuddling
conversation

Keeps toy

Keeps toy

7.1.3 Why Social Consequences are Important for Teaching Sharing

"Let's look at, say, sharing. Ruth tells me that you teach your children to share very early." What specific behavior might be an example of sharing?"

"A baby could hand a toy to someone sitting near her."

"Good. The antecedents of sharing would be what?"

Since George was facing her, Eve continued. "Hmm. Whatever was happening before."

"Yes," George said and added. "Or any relevant aspect of the situation in which the sharing is to occur. For example, a child can't give a toy if she's not holding one."

"Or if no one else is nearby," Eve continued, "so I suppose some antecedents would be holding a toy and someone asking or reaching for it for it."

George wrote them down. Now what is the opposite of sharing?"

"Clutching the toy, or holding it so the other baby can't reach it."

George wrote "clutches the toy" and "holds the toy out of reach of the other baby."

"Most people look for causes in something that happens BEFORE the baby acts. How, for example, do most people explain a child's clutching a stuffed bear?"

Several caregivers answered at once.

"They say she's afraid that someone will take it away."

"They say she's selfish."

"They say she's too young to share."

Ruth added, "An infant is too egocentric to share. That's the explanation that drives me crazy."

"Good," George replied, and then looked towards Ruth. "I'm glad you mentioned stages. Saying a baby is afraid that someone will take the bear away, or saying he is selfish or egocentric doesn't explain anything. It just is another way of saying he clutches objects. You still need to explain why one baby hands a toy over and another clutches it. In fact, the reason for both behaviors lies in the consequences—in the history of behaviors that have been strengthened in the past. Let's look at the natural consequences for sharing. What are they?"

"There really aren't any." Eve looked at Ruth for support, and went on. "Actually the baby loses the toy if she gives it away. I guess Ruth has told you that when we teach babies to hand us things, at first we give them right back." George nodded.

Edna Mae joined the discussion and said, "So at first the babies only lose them for a second or so. We gradually increase the time we hold the toy and eventually do not always give it back."

George had written "loses toy" under "consequences." Now he spoke. "You are quite right about losing the toy. That's why sharing does not develop naturally, the way walking does. A child cannot learn to share through natural consequences. He must receive a positive consequence provided by parents or caregivers. What do you do here when you see someone sharing?"

Several caregivers spoke. George wrote down their suggestions: to give the child another toy, to talk to him, to smile, to touch or cuddle him. Then he leaned back and surveyed the chalkboard.

"If no one provides positive consequences for sharing, that behavior will not develop in the youngster. You cannot not teach sharing by continually telling a youngster to share. In fact, if you urge a baby to share at those times when he is holding tight onto something to prevent its being taken away, you are providing attention for the exact opposite of sharing. You are strengthening clutching, not giving up, the object. If a baby gets to keep things only by clutching them tightly when someone else wants them, the baby will learn behavior we call selfish. That's why it is so important to look at the contingencies, as you do here in this center."

"Though you can overdo the sharing," Ruth said. "We taught one baby, Russell, to hand over objects too well and he started to hand all of his toys to any caregiver who came near him. We had to teach him when it was appropriate to give us what he was holding."

The staff nodded, laughing at the memory. George took up his pen again and continued.

"Teaching when it is appropriate to share brings me to discrimination — how the antecedent stimuli gain control over behavior."

7.1.4 Discrimination

"Much development involves learning discriminations. If a child shakes a rattle, but runs a toy car along the floor, we say the child discriminates between the two toys. He behaves differently with them. Discrimination is defined as responding differently to different situations, objects, or people. Let's look at your example. Here we have the antecedents of 'holding a toy'. What else must we add for the appropriate situation?

What would be the antecedents when you wanted him to hand over and object?"

Several of the staff raised their hands. George called on Edna Mae.

"Asking for it by holding out your hand."

George turned to the board. "So we will add 'hand held out' to the antecedents for the response." George wrote it down. "How about when it was not appropriate for the baby to give you the toy?"

Several staff members spoke:

"When we were busy with another child."

"When we were just walking by."

"When we had our back turned to Russell," they said.

George wrote their statements down. (see Figure 7.2)

"And what consequences did you provide for each case?"

"We stopped saying 'Thank you, Russell', when he handed us a toy unless we had asked for it. Really, you'd be surprised how quickly he learned."

"Yes." George added the consequences. "If you are consistent, discrimination occurs very rapidly. All it requires is reinforcing behavior in the appropriate antecedent situations and not reinforcing it otherwise. In this case," George pointed to the diagram. "When you held out your hand, you reinforced Russell's behavior of handing you an object, but when you did not ask for it, that behavior got no consequence from you and thus stopped occurring." He drew a big X through the behavior for the first situation. (see Figure 7.2) Note that you do not need to punish the inappropriate responding, that is, when the child responds incorrectly. I know you don't use punishment at your center," George hastened to add, "but I always emphasize that it is not needed for discrimination."

June had her hand raised, and George nodded for her to speak. "But how do you stop something like mouthing everything. I have a new baby who sticks everything into her mouth. I mean everything. I don't think that's healthy. I mean, its not only the germs, but . . . " June paused, and Amanda came to her rescue.

"When the baby has a toy in her mouth, she's not manipulating the object, and she's not even looking at it. She's missing out on experiences she will need to develop good eye-hand coordination. But it's O.K. to suck a pacifier if the parents have left her one. That's discrimination isn't it, sucking a pacifier, but not toys?"

FIGURE 7.2: DIAGRAM ANALYZING DISCRIMINATION

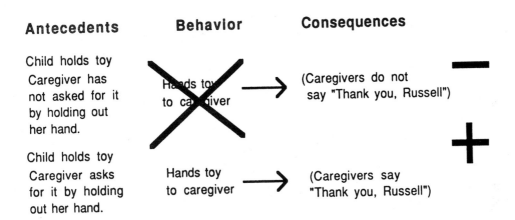

Teaching a Child to Discriminate Between What Goes In the Mouth and What Doesn't

"Yes." George replied. "That's a good example. The child should suck a pacifier, but play with toys." George grabbed a clean transparency and wrote the headings A, B, and C. "What antecedents can you arrange so that the child will not be likely to suck a toy? No answer. . . . Well, What is reinforcing sucking?"

"Oh, we don't give her attention for it, if that is what you mean."

"That's good. But something must be maintaining the behavior. What does the baby experience when she puts a toy in her mouth?"

June spoke slowly. "You mean she likes the feel of it?"

"Exactly. The feel of an object in the mouth is a strong reinforcer for most babies. After all, feeling something in the mouth is paired with food from the very beginning of its life. It is also a consequence that occurs automatically, like getting a sweet taste when you eat candy. But to reduce the probability that sucking a specific toy won't occur, you can try giving her that toy after she is fed, not when she is hungry."

"That's what Ruth said, and we have done that."

"Then you must work on teaching the baby to play with toys. Curiously enough, some babies have to be taught how to explore a toy. What would you consider appropriate exploring behavior for a baby under a year old?"

The staff were all used to this kind of question from Ruth, and they all spoke up. George summarized their contributions.

"If you work on building these two behaviors the way you would work on waving bye-bye or finding the parts of your face, you will find that the baby will be less inclined to suck on toys. In fact, the best way to get rid of inappropriate behavior is to work on shaping the appropriate behavior that should occur instead, as I'm sure Ruth has told you."

George continued. "You could start by picking toys she rarely sucks. Does she suck some more than others?"

"Not really." June said, but then changed her mind. "Well maybe so. I notice that she sucks cloth toys more than plastic ones. So I should start by giving her plastic toys, shouldn't I?"

"Yes. That would be a good idea. Then when she doesn't put those toys to her mouth, try a few toys which are more like those she usually sucks. If you select the toys carefully, you should be able to solve the problem in a week or so."

June had turned to Amanda and was saying, "Let's try the toy train. I don't think she'd try to suck that."

George asked about other discriminations the staff wanted to teach. They mentioned how they taught the babies to discriminate between "good" books and cloth books. They told him how they worked on teaching the babies not to touch the pages roughly in the "good" books, nor to try to turn the pages. With the cloth books, however, the babies could do whatever they liked. George had each staff member make an ABC diagram of the book problem, and went around making sure that everyone understood the method of analysis. Then he said, "It looks to me as though you all understand the general framework of discrimination. Now let's turn to color discrimination."

Teaching Color Discrimination

George noticed Eve perk up, and suggested she explain her procedures to the rest.

Eve went up to the front and spoke readily. "First, you must start with at least two different colors, say red and green. Otherwise the child memorizes that the answer to 'What color is this?' is always 'red' just like the answer to 'What is your name?' is always 'Sheri'. Ruth suggests gathering several red toys or blocks and several of another color."

Eve stopped and looked at George. He was nodding, and started to talk. "You know, Montessori had a good sequence for teaching. First she would point to a red object, and say 'This is red. Say "red."'". The child would repeat 'red'. Next, she would play a kind of game, mixing up red objects with those of another color, say green. Then she would ask, 'Find me something *red*,' and approve or just take the object when the child picked the right one. When the child could do that easily, she would point to a color and ask the child 'What color is this?' Then she would add more colors. Montessori's children learned very subtle color discriminations. She could show a four year old a spool of thread in one room, and without seeing it again, the child could walk into another room and pick out the exact same color in a whole rack of colored threads. I couldn't do that!"

George turned the session back over to Eve, and she continued.

"We do it very much like Montessori. First we ask the toddler to 'find the red one'. Then 'the green one'. We mix the things up until the child can pick out green and red without any difficulty. Sometimes we ask if they can find other things in the room that are red or green, too. They love to run around finding a red shirt or a green tree. Then we ask them to name the colors. At first, we help them. You know. We say 'Reh...' and then they say 'red'. Actually, we don't have any trouble teaching the colors, though some children learn them faster than others."

George thanked Eve and said that she'd covered the topic nicely, and that he had nothing to add. He suggested a break before turning to a topic Ruth had asked him to discuss, namely verbal behavior.

7.1.5 The Development of Verbal Behavior

When everyone had reconvened, George began.

"Since babies can do very little for themselves, they must get what they want or need through the actions of others. We looked at the three term contingency. Well, verbal behavior involves *four* terms (E. Vargas, 1989). Instead of obtaining a consequence directly, consequences of verbal behavior are mediated by another person. (see Table 7.1) For example, instead of climbing up to get a cookie, a toddler may say 'cookie' or point to the cookie, and receive the cookie through the action of another person." George placed a transparency on the projector and adjusted it.

A diagram of verbal behavior contains a pair of behaviors in the middle. Unlike motor behaviors that operate directly on the environment in physical ways, verbal behavior is social and, like the other social behaviors we discussed, achieves its affect throught the actions of others. "We tend to think of verbal behavior as vocal, but much verbal behavior

TABLE 7.1: THE ABBC ANALYSIS OF VERBAL BEHAVIOR

Antecedents	Behavior Toddler	Behavior Caregiver	Consequences
cookie out of reach	says "cookie"	hands toddler a cookie	Gets cookie

does not involve speech. For example, a baby may push away what he does not want, or bang when no one has noticed him for awhile. B F. Skinner (see DYK 7.1) has classified different kinds of verbal behavior by the way in which the actions function. We will look at two of the most basic categories, mands and tacts.

The Mand

"B. F. Skinner coined the term mand to describe verbal behavior which brings a particular consequence. If raising arms up to a caregiver usually results in getting picked up, we say that raising of the arms is a mand for being picked up. If squirming is maintained by the consequence of being put down, the squirm is a mand for getting down."

"Since, at birth, babies have few ways of getting attention as effective as a cry, a baby's first mands are usually cries. Look, for a moment at the infant's situation. Imagine being in a plane crash and waking up in a Chinese hospital unable to move. The sheet is rumpled and lumped under you which is painful. You cannot move the lump yourself, but must get rid of it *through the action of others.* Imagine that although you cannot move, you can make a kind of groan. Your Chinese nurse talks rapidly to you in Chinese, but you do not understand. He brings you water. You groan, and he brings the glass to your lips. You groan and he takes it away. Your nurse raises the head of your bed, but that increases your pain and you groan again. The nurse lowers it immediately. He brings you a bedpan, he opens the window shades, clearly doing his best to meet your needs, but failing completely. Imagine your frustration."

George let the caregivers visualize the situation. "The infant that can only cry no matter what he wants is similarly ineffective at controlling his environment. He cannot yet communicate *what* it is he wants."

"Now suppose that you just happen to shut your eyes tightly. Immediately the nurse comes over and adjusts your position, smoothing out the lump in the process. If shutting your eyes tight consistently results in someone rearranging your bed, you will soon learn to shut your eyes when you are uncomfortable. Perhaps, when you raise your eyebrows, someone raises the blinds. When you open your mouth, someone brings you food. Soon you will be able to ask for many different things, though you cannot say one word. The more different things you can do to produce different results, the more effective you will be at communicating."

"Similarly, the more different mands a baby learns, the more control he has over his environment. A baby that cries for everything is less effective than one who raises his arms to get picked up, jounces when he wants to dance, and goes to his jacket to go outside. Can you think of other mands?"

"How about babies turning their heads away when they don't want food." Victoria demonstrated.

"Yes. Turning is a very effective way of saying "no." Of course, parents and caregivers also teach manding directly, particularly after the child starts to imitate sounds. Parents may, for example, start to ask questions and respond only when the baby utters something close to the correct word. For example, they may ask 'Do you want *milk?*' Upon saying "Mih" the baby gets milk right away (and probably a delighted smile of approval), but when saying nothing, or "Mama," or something else, no milk follows (or at least, it is not given to the baby as readily). Soon, when wanting milk, the baby says, "Mik."

Again, note that the consequences for verbal behavior are provided by people. Unlike reaching for a bottle, there is no mechanical effect from saying "milk". The consequences are *mediated* by the action of another person. That is why children learn to walk without help, but cannot learn to talk unless someone provides the required contingencies."

"The way I have described it," George said, "the changes sound like they occur in steps, but the process is really one continuous flow. Gradually, adults expect more and more of the baby, always responding particularly enthusiastically to his or her best. Really, most people do a beautiful job of shaping up verbal behavior."

"Though some parents encourage baby talk." Ruth said.

George agreed. "Yes. Or even worse, the respond to their child's grunt or whine. In fact, many of the problem behaviors seen in children are *mands*. They disappear when the child learns to mand in other ways. (see Table 7.2)."

TABLE 7.2:   THE MAND – DIFFERENT WAYS IN WHICH
BABIES "ASK"

The mand is verbal behavior which typically brings a characteristic consequence. If, every time a baby squirms, he is put down, soon the baby will squirm when he is uncomfortable being held.   Similary, an infant who gets fed when she nuzzles her mother's chest, learns to nuzzle when hungry.   When these babies behave because of the consequencs which follow their behavior, we say they are manding. Some ways in which babies often mand follow. This list includes only gestural mands:

Behavior	Characteristic Consequence
squirm	gets put down
nuzzles	gets fed
bounces up and down	gets danced with
clutches mother and whines	gets to stay in mother's arms
shakes barrier to food preparation area	gets fed
holds out hand	gets object someone else has
points	gets object pointed to
shakes foot	gets out of swing
pulls hair	gets put down for nap
hold hands up	gets picked up
waves	gets to go on a walk
kisses caregivers bye-bye	gets chatty mother to leave
brings jacket	gets to go out

Of course, crying and other inappropriate behaviors bring all of the consequences listed above as well as others.   On the positive side, vocal behavior begins to replace many of the gestural mands as soon as the baby begins to talk.   New "cute" words are particularly effective at producing consequences.

The Tact

George looked at his watch and then at his notes. "We have talked about one kind of verbal behavior, the mand, in which a particular form of behavior typically produces a particular result. A second kind of verbal behavior is the tact. A tact is defined as verbal behavior whose form is determined by a particular object or event or property of an object or event. A toddler who says 'red' when seeing a red block is tacting. His behavior is determined by a property (namely color) of an object. A baby that says 'milk' when he sees milk is tacting. What he says depends upon the antecedent stimulus. Note that, unlike the mand, tacting does not result in getting what was named. Speaking loosely, a child mands when he wants or needs something, but people tact to report on features of their environment. What are some tacts you teach at Infant and Toddler Center USA?

Ruth volunteered, "Parts of the face."

The others added, "The names of animals. Kinds of dinosaurs. Butterflies—the different kinds."

George looked up at the caregivers. "The distinction between manding and tacting may seem academic, but it is important to realize that asking for something and naming it are really two *different* behaviors. You may teach a baby to say 'milk' when you show him milk (a tact), but that does not mean that he can ask for milk when he is thirsty or hungry (a mand). Few elementary teachers would make the mistake of assuming that just because a student can read a word that he can spell it too. But teachers of infants and toddlers make just as unreasonable assumptions. A baby can experience much frustration when he is expected to have learned something he has not been taught.

George looked at the intent expression on the caregivers' faces. "I realize," he said, "that you may not have looked at verbal behavior in this way before. But I invite you to watch your babies this next week, and notice their mands and tacts. Note what your babies do to get you to provide particular consequences—what mands they have learned. I think you will be surprised at how many ways they ask for things. (see Table 7.2) Note also what tacts you are teaching. Do you have any questions?"

Several of the caregivers could still think of things to ask, but it was getting on towards noon, and time to stop. Ruth thanked George for his presentation, and everyone left, chatting mostly about verbal behavior.

7.2 ANALYSIS 1: THE DEVELOPMENT OF BEHAVIOR

It was not until the middle of this century that scientists began to look at the role of interaction in the development of behavior. Before that, children were thought to unfold much as a flower does, and schools for the young were called Kindergartens (child gardens). With the initiation of behavioral science, however, it became increasingly clear that while physical movements might unfold without much adult contribution, social and verbal behavior would not. Without interacting with others, a child will not learn to share or to talk.

The behaviorological principles through which social and verbal behavior develop were first researched by B. F. Skinner in 1938. (See Appendix B: DYK 7.1). Like Mendel and Darwin before him, Skinner spent years studying his science in species much simpler than man. The *particulars* of applying the principles of behavior are, of course, different, and more complex with members of the human species than with the rats and pigeons of Skinner's labs. But human behavior can be explained by basic behaviorological laws, just as physical movement can be explained by the laws of physiology and of physics.

The basics of behaviorology are deceptively simple. The unit of analysis is behavior-environment relations; the interaction between behavior and environment. Behavior shifts through a selection process in which, in a given situation, certain kinds of responses are reinforced, but others are not. The analysis thus considers three terms: the antecedents (or setting in which a person acts), the behavior itself, and its consequences.

Originally, behavior analysts concentrated on the consequences end of the three term contingency, but the field has matured, and recent analyses have focused on antecedents as well as consequences. (see Appendix B: DYK 7.2) Researchers and applied workers have also become more sensitive to the kinds of reinforcement employed. In particular, behaviorologists are sensitive to the source of reinforcers, that is, whether they are produced by the behavior itself, or added by others.

7.2.1 The Role of Natural Consequences and Consequences Arranged by Caregivers

Reinforcement is often divided into two categories, natural and added. Natural reinforcement is reinforcement produced by the behavior it strengthens. Thus the sound of a rattle is the natural, intrinsic, consequence of shaking the rattle. Marks on a page are the natural consequence of drawing. Getting closer to something is the natural consequence of crawling. Added consequences, also called extrinsic, artificial, or contrived, are not an inevitable result of the behavior, but supplement those natural consequences. A touch, a smile, a hug, a word of approval, these are not automatically produced by a child's behavior, but are provided by others. A parent may smile at a child when she shakes a rattle, or praise a drawing or pretend to race the crawling toddler. These consequences are added to the natural consequences produced by the behavior itself.

Sometimes it is difficult to tell whether a consequence is natural or not. If a baby does something funny, and people laugh, the consequence is in one sense added, but it is also a natural result of being funny.

Since natural reinforcement is produced by the person behaving, it is a consequence which does not require the presence or attention of a caregiver or parent. No one has to be around for a baby to hear the sound of a rattle he shakes. A baby can enjoy the marks she produces without the attention of a caregiver (as anyone who has discovered a child's early artwork all over a wall will verify). No one has to praise a baby for crawling towards an attractive object. She will produce her own reinforcement by getting closer with each movement.

The Development of Natural Reinforcers

In the last chapter we mentioned that the reinforcing effect of all objects or events depends on whether the child has had them recently. Milk is a reinforcer for babies at birth, yet even then it will not reinforce a child who has just finished nursing. Still, being held or cuddled, motion such as rocking, and non-frightening stimulation (seeing moving objects, hearing pleasant sounds) can be counted upon as reinforcers for most babies. However, many things which do not at first reinforce children become reinforcers. In other words, many natural reinforcers are created by a child's history of reinforcement.

It seems illogical for a natural reinforcer to be created. But think of cigarettes or alcohol. Few smokers or drinkers enjoy their first cigarette or drink. It is only after being paired with other consequences, such as peer approval, or bodily effects, or parental horror, that the taste of the cigarette or drink *itself* becomes reinforcing. Similarly, it is only after being paired with other reinforcers, that the consequences of eating with a spoon, or using a potty, or fitting pieces into a puzzle become reinforcing.

After it becomes reinforcing to have dry pants, or clean hands, or a completed picture, caregivers no long need to add reinforcers for those behaviors.

Caregiver actions such as hugs, smiles, attention, talking, picking up, and bringing toys, thus both strengthen behavior *and* create reinforcers. A caregiver who rushes to an infant's side when he strikes another child not only strengthens his tendency to hit, but also strengthens the power of the cry or protest of a victim as a natural reinforcer for the child. If such a pattern is repeated, a child learns to enjoy harming others: A bully has been created. In contrast, generosity can be taught. Making another child happy is no more naturally reinforcing than making another child cry. But by consistently reinforcing children for kind or generous actions, a caregiver turns the smile or quiet pleasure shown by the befriended child into an effective reinforcer. (see Figure 7.3) Saying, "Look, now Stephen has something to play with too." or "Stephen really likes the ball you gave him," helps the child focus on the positive social effects of her action. The resulting behavior—actions which a child engages in to produce smiles and pleasure in others—we call "kind" or "generous." Because caregiver actions both strengthen behavior and transform consequences into reinforcers, the timing of their actions has a double impact on behavior.

Using Too Strong an Added Reinforcer

When appropriate behavior is maintained by natural reinforcers, additional powerful consequences may destroy the effect of the natural reinforcers. Let's say that you mow a neighbor's lawn because he is too old to do it himself. You have never asked for payment. His appreciation is enough. One day, after two years, he starts paying you very well. You may be hurt or insulted, but let's assume that you could really use the money, and that he insists you take it. Over a period of weeks, you come to count on the pay. Then one day he does not pay. You might tell yourself that you shouldn't require pay, but you would feel the loss. You might even resent not getting paid, and not go to cut the lawn anymore, or go only reluctantly. The natural consequences that maintained your behavior for two years no longer suffice. The added reinforcement has taken over.

Added reinforcement can similarly take over control of babies' behavior. A child who *already* loves doing puzzles may stop enjoying the activity if given too much attention and praise for her work. Instead of watching

FIGURE 7.3: THE TWO EFFECTS OF ADDED
REINFORCEMENT

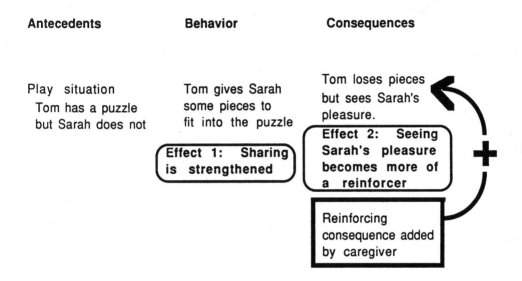

Antecedents

Play situation
Tom has a puzzle
but Sarah does not

Behavior

Tom gives Sarah
some pieces to
fit into the puzzle

Effect 1: Sharing
is strengthened

Consequences

Tom loses pieces
but sees Sarah's
pleasure.

Effect 2: Seeing
Sarah's pleasure
becomes more of
a reinforcer

Reinforcing
consequence added
by caregiver

the pattern she is creating, she may start looking around for approval after fitting in a piece. Or take a baby who shares for the pleasure of seeing another baby have a toy. Now assume that one day a caregiver gives the baby her favorite snack as reinforcement for sharing. Soon, instead of sharing for the natural consequences of making a peer happy, she will start to share in order to get a snack.

How, then, does a caregiver know when to add reinforcement? Certainly, if a behavior does not exist, added reinforcers must be used to shape it. No one starts to share, or to wave bye-bye, or to name colors without added consequences. However, for most children, as we mentioned before, simple attention, a few words, a smile, a pat, or even just a look, usually suffices. Now we can see why simple consequences achieve a center's goals better than edibles or overdone praise. There is one exception to this principle. Severely retarded or handicapped children may not respond to simple attention. For them, more powerful reinforcers may initially be needed.

When a behavior already is established, added reinforcement may not be needed, but a few words or smiles of approval now and then will insure that the behavior continues, and will not weaken the natural reinforcers. Caregivers need not worry about overdoing simple consequences. So long as they are contingent on appropriate behavior, a laugh, a few words, or a smile cannot go wrong.

In the narrative we looked at how social behaviors develop. We analysed sharing in some detail. We saw how one natural consequence of sharing is losing an object, and how, therefore, the behavior will not develop without added social consequences. In this analysis, we have shown how caregiver approval for sharing also begins to turn other natural consequences into reinforcers. Part of development, then involves not only the building of behavior, but the shift from added to natural consequences.

The shift from added consequences to natural ones is particular conspicuous in verbal behavior, and we will look at it now.

7.2.2 Verbal Behavior

A baby is born with vocal cords which soon develop so that they are capable of producing every sound in every language in the world. Babies all over the world babble at first with sounds characteristic of English, Chinese, French, and all other languages. But by around six months, certain sounds and combinations of sounds begin to be selected and others drop out. (Reese and Lipsit, 1970) Sounds which resemble those produced by others in a baby's environment are more likely to get a favorable response than other sounds, and are thus strengthened.

Verbal behavior emerges gradually. At first, parents or caregivers pay attention to single syllables that sound kind of like words. "Ma," or "Da," for example. But pretty soon the baby is "Ma" and "Da-ing" all over the place, and the parents do not pay as much attention to those syllables as they did. But "Ma*ma*" or "Da*da*," that's an accomplishment! Gradually the sounds the baby makes shift. He or she says more "Mama's" and "Dada's" and fewer "Ma's" and "Da's".

Note that babies make many sounds. New behavior emerges when some are more effective than others, and tend to be repeated more and more. The baby learns to talk best when his vocal cords and mouth muscles become strong enough to produce a variety of sounds, when the baby makes *many* sounds, and when others in that baby's environment selectively attend to only some of the babbling. If any one of these is missing the baby will not learn to talk. Interestingly, a baby does not need to hear in order to make sounds. Deaf babies babble. Unlike

hearing babies, however, they cannot get the auditory (natural) consequence of hearing their own noises. By about six months of age they stop
vocalizing unless a caregiver consistently provides consequences for
making sounds. If they are worked with early on, they will continue to
babble and they can eventually learn to talk.

The first word-like sounds babies make are just sounds. The baby does
not know when to say what sound. The sounds have no meaning for the
child. But soon the infant learns which sounds are appropriate for which
circumstances.

One of the first kinds of verbal behavior to develop in the infant is the
mand. The development of mands involves sharpening the relationship
between actions or vocalizations and the consequences they bring. George
mentioned how a baby who cries or whines for everything she wants is
less effective at fulfilling her needs than a child whose actions corre-
spond to different consequences. The more mands a child learns, the
more she can communicate what it is she wants.

The tact, in contrast to the mand, involves sharpening the relationship
between antecedents and behavior. A child tacts when he responds to an
object or event in his environment or to some feature of an object or
event. A child who says "ball" to a red ball is responding to an object. A
child who says "red" or "round" to the ball is responding to a feature
(color or shape) of the ball.

In tacting, a child is also discriminating, because he is responding
differently to different objects or features. Discrimination is easiest when
there are conspicuous differences between two or more objects. It is
easier for a toddler to learn the difference between a dinosaur and a
whale than the difference between two dinosaurs. Similarly, babies usually stop calling women "Dada" well before they stop calling other males
"Dada," a source of teasing for many new parents.

When teaching more academic discriminations, such as naming colors
or shapes, contrast between stimuli is also important. You would not start
to teach colors with red and red-orange, nor shapes using a square and
nearly square rectangle. Similarly, in teaching toddlers to tell apart the
sounds of different instruments, a caregiver will have more success by
starting with two that sound very different (such as drums versus flute),
than with instruments which are more similar in sound (such as clarinet
versus oboe) (see Chapter Nine). In teaching tacting, a caregiver helps
children become aware of their surroundings. By teaching babies to

enjoy identifying things, caregivers are also helping them to develop curiosity.

George in the narrative, mentioned that discrimination training does NOT require punishment, not even the mild punishment of "No, that's not green, that's red." A caregiver need only prompt with the correct response when a child hesitates, or blurts out an incorrect response. It is very important NOT to punish youngsters. Each time you tell children that they are wrong, you chip away at their self-confidence and enthusiasm for learning (see Chapter Eight). In contrast, by showing pleasure at your babies' performance, you build not only their skills, but their self-esteem as well.

Self-esteem comes from being effective within one's world. A baby develops self-esteem partly by becoming effective physically and socially. By teaching social and verbal behaviors, therefore, you are also building self-esteem.

7.3 ANALYSIS 2:
LEARNING AND STAGE–RELATED BEHAVIORS

The development of behavior involves interaction, and the nature of that interaction determines how behavior develops. Although there are, no doubt, genetic differences in temperament, no child is born destined to be generous or selfish. Children learn the behaviors that earn them such labels.

Stages of development also involve contingencies. People tend to treat infants differently from toddlers, and toddlers different from older children. Adult reaction to a toddler climbing onto a dining room table is much different than their reaction to a six year old doing the same thing. The patterns of behavior that are typical of the two year old reflect similar contingencies provided by parents and caregivers as much as any physiological development of the child. Because behavior patterns are produced by contingencies, they can be changed by changing contingencies.

7.3.1 Why Stages, Such as "The Terrible Twos" Are Not Inevitable

When parents or caregivers attribute a child's behavior to "a stage he's going through," they imply that the behavior is inevitable. Usually such a statement is made about inappropriate behavior. One does not usually say "Oh yes, she plays independently, but that is just a stage she is going through." Rather one hears, "She refuses to do anything I ask of her, but that's just a stage she's going through." The names of the stages reflect their negative image; The terrible twos, the stage of separation anxiety, the egocentric and the clinging stage, and so on.

In this chapter George discussed how behaviors develop. If toddlers seem selfish, that is, they clutch objects and do not give them to other children or adults, that does not show a "stage" in their development, but rather a history of losing things by handing them over. In this chapter and the last, we saw how very young children can be taught not only to hand things over, but also to do so in order to please others. If parents and caregivers routinely taught such behavior, there would be no such thing as "an egocentric stage" and the corresponding inference that young children are naturally too selfish to share. (Elder, 1988)

The same analysis can be made of other "typical" behaviors, for example "separation anxiety." The fact that many two year olds cry when separated from their mothers shows that they have learned that cries often bring mothers back. Look at a typical scenario. Say a baby has always been with his mother outside of the home. One day he is taken with his mother out to lunch. He sits on his mother's lap while an infant seat is brought. His mother feels warm and soft. Then his mother starts to place him in the seat. He protests and clutches his mother. "Oh, he loves his Mommy," the mother says, and takes him back. If one were to design instruction to teach a child to protest when separated from his mother, one could not pick a better first step.

It is not difficult to prevent "separation anxiety," but it requires teaching "parting" like any other skill, behavior by behavior. Here is one way. At first, the mother conspicuously leaves just for a few moments when her child is involved in something interesting. Perhaps the mother could wave "Bye-Bye" to make it clear she was leaving. By gradually lengthening the periods of separation, a child learns that his mother will return and he gets used to playing without having his or her mother around.

A similar analysis can be made of other behaviors commonly found in two year olds. The point here, however, is not to explain "stages," but to show that the behaviors associated with them are learned like any other behaviors. By providing different contingencies you produce other behaviors.

7.3.2 The False Dicotomy Between Development and Learning

In the narrative George discussed how behavior develops through the moment to moment interaction between child and environment. Although the fields of Development and Behaviorology bear different names, they are simply different ways of looking at the same change and growth over time. Development focuses on the characteristics which are typical of most children at each age, where Behaviorology explains how behavioral changes occur. When one talks of the development of individual behavior, however, the two fields merge. Even physical development depends upon factors in the environment. Social development, as we have seen in this chapter, cannot occur at all without interaction with other people. Development requires learning, and learning results in development.

7.4 SUMMARY:

Members of the human species are born quite helpless. Newborns exhibit a few behaviors, such as sucking, soon after birth. Sucking seems to be an inherited response to objects placed in the mouth and it is shared by infants in all cultures. But only a few of the behaviors that a child will need in life are inborn. Most of what a baby will need to survive and succeed, the baby must learn through his or her interactions with the physical environment and with other human beings. In this chapter we have looked at how behavior develops in the infant and toddler through the interactions a baby has with her physical and social world. We have analyzed the interaction between infant and environment by looking at the antecedents of behavior, the behavior itself and its consequences. By teaching appropriate behaviors, caregivers insure that children develop in ways that will help them along in their world.

Chapter Eight

DISCIPLINE

RUTH, THE PROGRAM SUPERVISOR, AND KRIS, A CAREGIVER, EXPLAIN TO A PARENT WHY INFANT CENTER USA NEVER USES PUNISHMENT

OBJECTIVES

After you have read this chapter you should be able to . . .

1. Explain the difference between punishment and discipline.
2. Describe how a biting incident would be handled without using punishment.
3. List some of the harmful effects of punishment.
4. Define corporal punishment and explain why it should be prohibited.
5. Identify examples of redirection and timeout.
6. Explain why timeout is really a punishment procedure.
7. Describe alternatives to punishment when handling: (1) an inappropriate behavior which occurs for the first time (2) an inappropriate behavior which occurs often.
8. Identify methods of discipline which are, and are not, permitted by your state licensing standards.
9. Explain how positive methods of discipline teach self-control, self-direction, self-esteem and cooperation.

Discipline. The very word conjures up visions of stern schoolmasters, paddles in hand, and cowering and fearful students. The Random House College Dictionary lists several definitions for discipline. (Revised Edition, 1982) The first three are as follows:

"**1. Training to act in accordance with rules; drill: military discipline.**
2. Instruction and exercise designed to train to proper conduct or action.
3. Punishment inflicted by way of correction and training." (p. 378)

Most people think of discipline as punishment used to eliminate undesirable behavior. Because discipline and punishment are not synonymous, the use of the term discipline is unfortunate. In fact the best discipline techniques do not employ punishment at all. Instead they use positive methods, which "encourage self-control, self-direction, self-esteem

177

and cooperation." (Vermont, 1989) Although most licensing standards require caregivers to use positive methods few define the term discipline. (see Table 8.1) Further they do not tell caregivers what to do in order to produce the desirable behaviors the regulations specify.

In this chapter we will: (1) look at what licensing standards have to say about discipline; (2) discuss why punishment is a poor discipline technique; (3) describe how alternatives to punishment teach the behaviors referred to as "self-discipline" and "self-control."

TABLE 8.1 SOME STATE DEFINITIONS OF DISCIPLINE

Only a few states define discipline. Some definitions are listed below:

The ongoing process of helping children to develop inner controls so they can manage their own behaviors in socially approved ways.
(Illinois, 1985; Kansas, 1985)

Training that corrects inappropriate behavior, teaches an orderly way of life and protects and maintains the integrity of the individual.
(Indiana, 1985 p. 2)

The ongoing process of helping children develop self control and to assume responsibility for their own actions.
(Oregon, 1988 p. 2)

An educational process by which staff assist children to develop self-control and self direction necessary to assume responsibilies, make daily living decisions, and learn to live in conformity to accepted levels of social behavior.
(Wyoming, 1985 p.1)

8.1 NARRATIVE: RUTH, THE PROGRAM SUPERVISOR, AND KRIS, A CAREGIVER, EXPLAIN TO A PARENT WHY INFANT CENTER USA NEVER USES PUNISHMENT

Kris was happy. Today only four of her toddlers had come, and she was enjoying a relaxed afternoon. Now, at 2:30, two of her children were with another group for outside play, and the remaining two were playing quietly. Ursula was over in the book corner, looking at books, and Leigh was seated at a small table beside Kris putting a puzzle together. Kris glanced at the clipboards above the cubby holes and thought, "Record keeping will be easy today."

8.1.1 Handling Biting Without Using Punishment

Suddenly the situation changed. It happened so quickly that Kris was taken completely by surprise. Ursula, the little girl who had been in the book corner, got up, walked over to Leigh, bent down, bit her hand, and nonchallantly strolled away. Leigh let out a squeal of protest. Without thinking, Kris exclaimed, "Ursula," and then stopped herself. Leigh meanwhile had turned to Kris holding out her hand.

Kris was shocked. Teeth marks were clearly visible. But she was relieved to see that the skin was not broken.

"Here, baby," she said to Leigh, "Let's go tend your hand."

She took the toddler's other hand and led her towards the cabinet where the first aid supplies were kept. She unlocked the door and took out an antiseptic wipe. Leigh looked at the supplies and said, "boo-boo" and pointed towards the adhesive tape.

"You want some tape on your hand?" Kris asked.

Leigh looked serious and nodded.

"O.K," Kris replied and proceeded to disinfect and tape the bite.

Meanwhile, Ursula had followed them and stood by watching. She moved towards Kris's arm, but Kris was not about to let another biting incident happen. She moved her arm out of the way and picked Leigh up out of reach. Ursula swung her arms around as though she was dancing.

"Ursula," Kris asked, "Do you want to dance?"

Ursula repeated, "Dance," and clapped her hands.

"Come on, then," Kris said. She put Leigh down, and took both children, one in each hand, to lead them over to the music corner. She glanced at Ursula who looked as though butter wouldn't melt in her mouth. "Whew," Kris thought. "It's amazing how quickly you can shift behavior. It's just like Ruth says."

As the music filled the room, the other toddlers came in from outside. Their caregiver, Carol, noticed that Kris was not dancing and said, "Anything up?"

"Um Hum." She shot a glance toward Ursula who was skipping around happily. "Can you look after these two for a minute? I need to make a phone call." As she went by she whispered to Carol, "Ursula, out of the blue, bit Leigh. Keep an eye on them for me."

"Sure. Take your time." Carol said.

Kris went to the phone and looked at Ruth's posted schedule. She was in Unit #1. Kris dialed, and when Ruth answered she asked her to come to Unit #3. While she waited Liz, the caregiver who relieved Kris at 2:45 arrived. Kris briefed her about the biting and said that she would put all the details in the Infant Daily Records of both children, and fill in an Injury Report for Mikki to file in the center records. "So much for easy record-keeping," she mumbled.

Ruth arrived and was quietly told what had happened. She did not want to draw attention to the bite, but she did need to check the extent of the injury. Passing among the children she said a few words to each. When she reached Leigh, she commented on her taped hand, and quickly peeked. She was relieved to see that the mark was hardly visible. Kris caught Ruth's eye and by mutual agreement they met outside.

"No damage done," Ruth said, "No need to contact the parents at work. But give me some more details about what happened."

Kris told her, stressing the unexpectedness of the incident. "Ursula has never done anything like that before."

"Well," Ruth commented "It sounds as though you handled the incident well."

Kris said, "I wonder how the parents will react to this. Leigh's mother notices any tiny scratch or mark."

"It might be a good idea for you to be here when I talk with them." Ruth suggested. "If you're free, I'm sure Mikki will pay you for your time." Kris nodded, and Ruth added, "You could take a break and come back in a couple of hours."

"That sounds good." Kris said. "I think I'll go down the street and check out the sales."

"Fine. I'll see you later." Ruth said as she walked away.

8.1.2 Ruth and Kris Talk With the Parents of the Two Children Involved in the Biting Incident

Leigh's mother, Natalie, arrived first, and Leigh ran to meet her pointing proudly to her taped hand. Ruth joined in the greeting, informed Natalie about the bite, then said, "Leigh's hand is taped, not because it was needed, but because Leigh wanted it." After Natalie checked beneath the tape and saw no mark, she took the whole incident lightly, and as she walked out the door said, "I hear biting is common in most centers, but this is the first time I've heard of biting here." (see Appendix B: DYK 8.1).

Kris looked relieved, and said "That was easy."

A few minutes later Ruth who was looking out the window said, "Well here comes Ursula's mother Peggy, I wonder if this will be easy! Let's meet her outside and take her to the office."

"Good idea." Kris replied.

They met her before she entered the Unit, and told her about the biting. Ruth mentioned that Kris had been on duty when the biting occurred, and suggested the three of them talk in the office.

When they were settled, Ruth asked Kris to describe the incident for Peggy. As she listened Peggy nodded knowingly.

"It doesn't surprise me," she told them. "Ursula spent the weekend with her father. He informed me that she bit a neighbor's child. Can you believe he told the neighbor's child to bite Ursula back?"

Ruth shook her head, and asked, "What would you do?"

"I don't know." Peggy replied. "She never bites me. I suppose I'd tell her biting is not nice. What do you recommend?"

Ruth answered. "We follow the center's philosophy of teaching appropriate behavior rather than using punishment. In fact, what Kris did is what we recommend. Kris attended to Leigh. She did not want to reinforce the biting behavior so she ignored it. At the same time, she kept an eye on Ursula so she could reinforce her appropriate behavior."

Kris said, "It didn't take long."

Ruth continued "Now that we know that Ursula has bitten, we'll be especially careful to make sure that Ursula is productively occupied. It's always easier to prevent biting than to handle it afterwards. But, since her biting wasn't reinforced, I wouldn't expect Ursula to bite again in the center."

Peggy sighed. "I don't know. She'll be visiting her father again."

"But she will learn that biting doesn't work here with us." Kris reassured her.

Peggy looked doubtful. "Well what should I do if she bites me or someone else? I know a parent who sits her child in a chair facing the wall whenever he misbehaves. She calls it "timeout" What do you think of that?"

Peggy had addressed Kris, so after glancing at Ruth, Kris answered. "Timeout is still punishment. If you reinforce appropriate behavior, with infants and toddlers, you don't need to use punishment. Besides, facing a child towards the wall is prohibited by our state licensing standards."

"Oh?" Peggy sounded surprised.

Ruth explained. "You can sit a child apart from the group, but the child must not face the wall. But we don't use timeout for two reasons. First, to get the child to the chair, you must pay attention to him or her. In fact, some caregivers, not in *this* center of course, but in others, stay with children during timeout explaining why their behavior was not appropriate. You run a danger with that procedure. You might be reinforcing the behavior rather than punishing it. Second, if timeout is really punishing the behavior, you get all of the damaging by products that punishment generates."

"By products?" Peggy asked.

"Yes. Punishment begets punishment. You know how you feel at the end of a really bad day? You are much more likely to snap at others or to refuse to cooperate or to lose your temper. It's no different with children. When they are punished, they are less likely to cooperate and more likely to engage in withdrawal or in antisocial behaviors than on days when everything goes well." (see Appendix 2: DYK 8.2)

Peggy looked at Ruth. "But I thought that a certain amount of discipline was good for children, that it built character."

Ruth spoke slowly. "Discipline and punishment are not the same thing. It is good to have standards, and to expect children to live up to them. But the way you show your expectation makes a big difference. At the most basic level, you can reinforce appropriate behavior or ignore behavior that does not meet your standards. It is more complex than that, but by using positive methods you produce self-discipline, whereby the child *wants* to behave well. With primarily negative methods, you risk producing resentment, sneaky behavior, and unhappy children."

Peggy looked alarmed.

"Don't worry." Kris said quickly. "Ursula will learn to take punishment from her father just as she has learned to take bumps and spills from the physical environment. You are very supportive of her. She's not going to become sneaky or resentful."

"No," added Ruth. "Anyway, no one grows up without any punishment. But in general, the less the better. I like to use an analogy with germs."

Kris smiled. She had heard this analogy before.

Ruth explained. "No one recommends deliberately exposing children to filth and sickness in order to build resistance to disease, though it would probably do just that in the ones that survived. Rather, we keep youngsters away from harmful germs as much as possible, so that when they do meet harmful germs, their bodies are strong enough to fight them off. On the other hand, a *completely* sterile environment would not build up any resistance at all. So it is with punishment. Generally, by eliminating punishment as much as possible, we help a child develop the strong adaptive behaviors that come from reinforcement. Of course, in order to learn to take bumps or criticism, children must occasional experience them. But they will get plenty of punishment without our adding any. Deliberately adding more punishment makes as much sense as deliberately adding more germs."

"Then you wouldn't recommend any punishment by parents either?" Peggy asked.

"No. We don't recommend punishment at all." Ruth said. "But parents rarely know other ways to keep their children from doing dangerous things, or even just things that annoy them. We try to help parents learn how to reinforce appropriate behaviors so they can at least reduce the amount of punishment they use, as you know." Ruth smiled.

Peggy nodded. "Yes. I don't know how other parents feel about it, but I really appreciate the time you take explaining things." She looked at her watch. "I do have to go, now, and I am sure you have lots to do. If Ursula bites me I will try to ignore her behavior. But my friends will expect me to punish her if she bites their children."

"If you ignore Ursula and make a big fuss over the child who was bitten, the other parent will appreciate the concern you are paying to her child. It may not be as hard as you think." Ruth said.

"I'll give it a try. But I hope Ursula doesn't bite again." Peggy said as she stood up.

"We do too." Kris and Ruth said in unison. The meeting ended.

Several weeks went by and, as Ruth had predicted, Ursula had not bitten again in the center. One afternoon, just before a holiday, all of the babies but Joseph had left early, and he was sleeping. The caregivers resting in the activity area began talking about an inservice on discipline planned for the holiday.

Eve said, "Boy I wish we had had these inservices when Lorraine first came."

"Lorraine," repeated Marilyn, "wasn't she the 'screaming baby'?"

8.1.3 The Screaming Baby

Eve, Lorraine's caregiver, burst into a broad smile. "Oh yes, Lorraine was the screaming baby. She came into the center screaming, left the center screaming, and screamed on and off throughout the day. Funny though, when she wasn't screaming, she would flirt and laugh and charm everyone, just like she does now."

"With her big green eyes and thick black hair, even as a screamer, she was very appealing." Amanda remarked.

"The screaming would have driven me crazy," said Marilyn.

Beverly jumped into the conversation. "It was very upsetting for us. But believe it or not, the other babies got used to her after a couple of days. Whenever she started her screaming they would look at her, or at each other, as if to say, "That's just Lorraine." All the parents knew about her and their interest in her really surprised us. Mikki used to say that the other parents were sympathetic about her screaming because they were so thankful she wasn't theirs!"

They all laughed and Marilyn asked, "What were her parents like?"

Beverly thought for a few seconds and then replied. "They seemed rather helpless. They always looked exhausted when they brought Lorraine into the center in the morning. They were both teachers and worked at the same school. She was their first baby and it was obvious that they adored her. But they acted embarrassed that she was, as they said, "so willful and hot tempered.""

"Did she have some type of painful physical problem?" June asked.

"No," answered Beverly. "Her parents assured us that she had been checked and rechecked and there were no abnormalities noted in her medical reports."

"How did you all cope with her?" Priscilla wanted to know.

"We really did not know what to do with her." Beverly told her. "She was a big strain on us. You know how upsetting it is to listen to a baby cry, so you can imagine what it was like to listen to a baby scream nearly all day long. She would stiffen her arms and legs and just howl. It was very difficult to change her or place her in a high chair or swing. Really, it was exhausting. We also found that she was taking so much of our time we were getting behind in the care of the other babies."

"Why didn't Mikki ask her parents to find another source of care for her, or advise them to seek professional help?" June asked. "I read in one of my journals that there are many programs for troubled babies." (see Appendix B: DYK 8.3)

"Well, we wanted to give the baby time to settle down. Actually, we thought that maybe her parents had spoiled her, and we believed that we would be able to help her get out of her moods. But after eight days, Mikki was just at the point of asking her parents to consider placing the baby elsewhere, when Ruth came to the center for an interview."

Amanda nodded and said, "Ruth sure came at the right time. We had talked and talked about Lorraine. We couldn't find a pattern to her screaming, or calm her down once she started."

"I will never forget the day Ruth came for an interview." Beverly said. "Mikki was just about to open *Unit 2*, and could no longer act as both director and program supervisor. So she had advertised for the new position and Ruth applied. Lorraine had been at the center only eight days, but it seemed forever to us. We were starting to admit that we were unable to cope with her. Remember, this was before we had any behavioral training. When Ruth walked in, I was dancing with Anthony, and Lorraine was sitting in the playpen screaming." Beverly looked over at Ruth. "Remember, Ruth?"

Ruth nodded, and Beverly continued.

"Mikki told Ruth that she had tried everything to pacify Lorraine. She had picked her up, offered her toys and food, changed her diaper, put her on the floor, and placed her in the swing. Mikki had even tried to sing and dance with her. Nothing had worked. In fact, she seemed to scream louder. We had all agreed that the best thing to do was to leave her in the playpen for awhile."

"Wow, what an introduction to the center," Marilyn said. "But how did Ruth react to all the noise?"

"She made no comments." Beverly answered and looked over again at Ruth. "She just listened as Mikki told her about the center and the duties of the program supervisor. She answered Mikki's questions and asked Mikki for details about the center. Right from the first they got on well together. I guess they had been talking about thirty minutes when Mikki said, 'I think Lorraine likes you Ruth, see how she is smiling at you.' Ruth asked for permission to pick her up and we all watched as she danced with Lorraine. Lorraine laughed and clapped her hands. In between the dancing, Ruth sat her on the floor for a few seconds and played peek-a-boo or patty-cake with her, and then picked her up and continued dancing. She seemed to enjoy everything that Ruth did. I'm afraid that we were not very polite. We just stared."

Ruth said she believed Lorraine needed a diaper change, and Mikki suggested that since Lorraine was being so nice for her, that perhaps Ruth could change her. The rest of us watched, in awe, as Lorraine let Ruth change her without crying or trying to roll over or grab hold of Ruth, things she always did while we changed her. We were *very* impressed."

"Mikki told Ruth we could not believe that Lorraine had not screamed, even once, and complimented her on her way with babies," Beverly continued. "Ruth then explained that she had worked on Lorraine from the moment she arrived in the center. She explained about contingencies to Mikki, but not in those words. She said that while she and Mikki had been talking, she had not looked at Lorraine when Lorraine was screaming, but had looked over when the baby stopped, even if it was just to draw in a breath for the next scream. She mentioned how quickly even young babies learn. . . . "

I suppose Mikki hired her on the spot." Marilyn interrupted. "I would have."

"Pretty much. Mikki didn't even interview anyone else."

Marilyn excused herself, to check on her baby Joseph. She had been glancing frequently at the mirror that gave her a view of the nap/sleeping room. She saw that he was stirring.

"Wait," she asked. "I'll be right back."

"Here," volunteered Ruth. "I'll take care of Joseph. I know the end of the story."

The rest laughed, and Eve continued.

"When Ruth was hired, to help me learn what to do, she volunteered to help with the care of Lorraine. She offered to work out a *Plan of Care* for her. The first thing she wanted to see was all the records we had on Lorraine. She noted that Lorraine's food intake was a little low for her height and weight. She said that Lorraine was long and lean and tall for her age and was probably using a lot of energy when she screamed and thrashed about as strenuously as she did. She suggested that we talk to her parents about increasing the frequency of her feeding, both at home and at the center. Then she explained about preplanning to prevent crying situations." (see Chapter Six)

"I'll never forget when Lorraine's parents came to pick her up after Ruth's first day. Mikki introduced Ruth as the new program supervisor and told them that Ruth was going to work with Lorraine. They were relieved to see their baby laughing and babbling, and commented that it was nice to see her 'in a good mood.' ".

Ruth finished diapering Joseph and returned to the group. The baby held his arms out to Marilyn. He was still a little sleepy from his nap, and cuddled up to her as she held him on her lap.

Ruth Talks About a Baby's Physical State

Ruth explained, "Before I knew about teaching appropriate behavior, I had an experience with one of my own babies. It taught me alot."

"Really, which one?" Amanda asked.

"My daughter Annabel." Ruth replied. "You know she's a preteen now, but when she was eight months old, and had been sleeping through the night for four months, she started waking up again. She would cry, and I would run downstairs and get her a bottle. She would drink a little and then start to fuss. I would pick her up, change her, offer her the bottle again, and again she would drink a little and then fuss or cry. After this had gone on for three or four nights, Annabel started screaming. I became worried, and took her to the doctor. The doctor couldn't not find anything the matter with her. That night when Annabel woke up and started screaming, I took her downstairs with me while I prepared the bottle. I was living in the Panama Canal Zone, and there was large stalk of bananas hanging in the kitchen. As I walked by them, Annabel grabbed one and started gnawing on it as though she was starving. I took the cue, and prepared some solid food for her. To my surprise, she ate everything and went contentedly back to her crib and was soon asleep. I was shocked that my baby had been so hungry. I felt like a fool when I called the doctor and told her what had happened. The doctor said that it was possible that since Annabel had started walking . . . she walked at eight months . . . she was using more energy and needed an extra serving of food before she was put to bed. I followed the doctor's advice and Annabel went back to soundly sleeping through the night."

"What did you say you learned from that?" Beverley asked.

"I haven't said yet." Ruth told her. "I didn't want to spoil the story. But what I learned was to check out the physical state of the baby. That was why, apart from shaping Lorraine's appropriate behavior, I suggested to her parents that they try increasing her food intake . . . with consultation with their baby's physician . . . of course."

"It was a good suggestion." Amanda said, "She certainly was using a lot of energy with her screaming and thrashing about. But she soon thrived on Ruth's Plan of Care that addressed both her behavioral and physical care."

"Anyway," Eve commented, "you know how adorable Lorraine is now. Really it's hard to imagine her screaming."

Marilyn shook her head. "I wonder," she said, "what I would have done with such a child before I came here. The licensing standards contain no directions for behavioral care."

"True," Eve agreed. "I took a child development course once. I learned a lot about how an infant develops physical skills, but I didn't learn much about discipline. Luckily we get training in behavioral care here."

The arrival of the last parent broke up the discussion and the caregivers gathered up their things and left.

8.2 ANALYSIS 1: DISCIPLINE AND LICENSING STANDARDS

Most standards, both civilian and military have a section related to "Discipline". But some include the topic under other titles such as "Behavior Guidance" (Minnesota, 1989), or "Management of Behavior" (Virginia, 1988). Though the sections vary in length and specificity, they all include one or more of the following:

(1) A general statement about the intent of discipline.
(2) A requirement that discipline policies be in writing.
(3) A statement about rules, for example, that they must be clear and appropriate for the age level of the child, or that limits must be clear cut.
(4) A list of recommended or permitted methods of discipline
(5) A list of methods which are not permitted.

The lists of prohibited methods reads like a list of child abuse methods. (see Table 8.2, and 8.2.1). The list is all the more horrifying when you consider that specific prohibitions often find their way into regulations because of actual instances of use.

Throughout this book, we have continually highlighted the teaching of appropriate behavior. If caregivers teach infants and toddlers appropriate behaviors they should have little need for traditional "discipline." Nevertheless, inappropriate behaviors occur, sometime, and how to handle them needs to be addressed

Many of the suggestions allowed or proposed by one or more state licensing standards cannot be recommended as being in the best interests

TABLE 8.2: SAMPLE STANDARDS LISTING METHODS OF DISCIPLINE PROHIBITED IN CHILD CARE CENTERS

Most licensing standards list methods of discipline which <u>cannot</u> be used. Specific actions <u>disallowed</u> vary from state to state, but include the following:

1.   "medications or mechanical restraints and devices shall not be used to discipline children" (Arizona, 1988, p.21)

2.   "deprivation of 'food or toilet use'" (Delacare, 1988, p. 38)

3.   "loud, profane, threatening, frightening or abusive language" (Kentucky, 1988 p. 13)

4.   "rough handling, shoving, hair pulling, ear pulling, shaking, slapping, kicking, biting, pinching, hitting, and spanking." (Minnesota, 1989, p.18)

5.   "threaten a child with the loss of love of any person ... threaten a child with punishment by a diety." (Nevada, 1989, p. 21)

6.   "being placed in a "locked room, closet, or box" (North Carolina, 1988, p.62)

7.   "binding to restrain movement of mouth or limb" (U.S. Army, Draft 1988, p. 4-8)

8.   "Children may not be punished for lapses in toilet training." (U.S. Marine Corp, 1983, p.11)

8.   "forcing a child to assume an uncomfortable position (e.g. standing on one foot, keeping arms raised above or horizontal to the body." (Virginia, 1988, p. 29)

9.   "Mechanical restraints may not be used. These include but are not limited to: Hanfcuffs, belt restraints, and locked time-out rooms.Physical restraints which could be injurious are not to be used. These include but are not limited to: A large adult sitting on or straddling a small child, sleeper holds, arm twisting, hair holds, and throwing children and youths against walls, furniture, or other large immobile objects (Washington, 1987, 9. 7)

of the child. In this Analysis we will look at the following three: Corporal Punishment, Redirection, and Timeout. In Analysis 2, we will discuss how to teach "Self-Discipline or "Self-Control."

8.2.1 Corporal Punishment

Corporal punishment is the infliction of pain upon the body of a child as a penalty for a disapproved action. More specifically it is defined in the Arizona (1988) standards as:

"Shaking, spanking, punching, hitting, hitting with instruments, pinching, biting, pushing, slapping, twisting, jerking, kicking, pulling hair, strangling a child or other acts which causes bodily pain and may result in bruises, welts, abrasions, contiusions, lacerations, burns, fractures, wounds, cuts, punctures, subdural hemorrhage or hematomas, internal injuries, sprains, dislocations, or other forms of physical damage." (p. 1)

It is an outmoded, harmful method of punishment. In child care centers for infants and toddlers it is also a barbaric and unnecessary method of control. The United States and South Africa are the only two industrialized countries that still permit corporal punishment of children in schools and child care centers. (see Table 8.3) In the United States, criminals in prison can not be subjected to methods of punishment which in some states are legal with children.

There are good reasons for abolishing corporal punishment. First of all, any person who spanks or otherwise hurts another individual is modeling undesirable behavior. Children imitate adults. What, then, do children learn from receiving a spanking or seeing others spanked? They learn to hit or strike people when they do not like what they are doing. Needless to say, that is not a lesson caregivers wish to give. Secondly, it is much more difficult to control the severity of a blow than to outlaw hitting altogether. Even people who approve of mild spankings (and the authors are not among those) balk when the spankings get severe. But how can you control those who hit to make sure that they hit just hard enough, but not too hard? Remember that people tend to punish when they are angry or frustrated, or when they have been unable to stop a situation by other means. Under such circumstances, it is no wonder that spankings turn into beatings and beatings turn into hospital cases. But even if spankings were administered "objectively" and with controlled strength, causing pain is in conflict with all of the goals of child development.

TABLE 8.3: SAMPLE STANDARDS THAT SPECIFY THE USE OF CORPORAL PUNISHMENT IN CHILD CARE CENTERS

1. "no form of corporal punishment may be used on newborns, infants, and children with special needs; only with prior parental permission may controlled hand spankings with the open hand be used, when appropriate, with:

    (A) no more than one slap on the clothed buttocks of a toddler; and

    (B) no more than three slaps on the clothed buttocks of a pre-schooler or older child.

    (C) no other form of corporal punishment may be used."
    (Alaska, 1988, p.25)

2. "if the policy of a facility includes physical punishment for children age three (3) and over, it shall be administered only with the prior written consent of the parent or guardian with the following guidelines being met:

    a. Punishment shall be directed by the director or person acting as director.

    b. An adult witness shall be present

    c. Any spanking shall be administered below the waist and preferably with an open hand on the buttocks. Physical punishment shall not be administered to children under the age of three." (Arkansas, 1986, p. 11)

3. "if the center's written discipline policy permits spanking, the center shall receive signed permission from the parent or guardian of the child in order to administer spankings, and shall on the same day of administering a spanking notify the child's parent or guardian in writing that a spanking has been administered." (Ohio, 1985, page2 of 2)

Corporal punishment, in any case, is not needed. It is specifically prohibited in all but twelve states, and there are groups working to abolish it altogether. (see Appendix B: DYK 8.4) Then, when you understand that most inappropriate behavior is shaped and maintained by consequences provided by caregivers, and thus can be changed by changing the timing of reinforcement, you see that there is no reason ever to deliberately inflict physical pain upon a child.

While most state's licensing standards specify what caregivers may *not* do to discipline a child, less than half have regulations that tell caregivers what to do. Of the sanctioned methods, we can endorse only a few. Two that cannot be recommended with infants and toddlers are redirection and timeout.

8.2.2 Redirection: The Right Action at the Wrong Time

Redirection is a technique of discipline in which a staff member tries to distract a child who is behaving inappropriately. Perhaps when a baby girl is fussing the caregiver shows her something more interesting than the toys in front of her. Or when a toddler grabs a toy from another child or starts a fight, the caregiver tries to distract him by suggesting one of his favorite activities. Drawing a child's attention in order to get him or her involved in appropriate behavior would be a good idea except that redirection sets up the wrong contingencies. In redirection, the toy or attractive activity is offered while the child is behaving inappropriately. Usually caregiver attention, a new toy, or an offered activity is reinforcing. Presenting them at the moment the child is behaving inappropriately strengthens the very kinds of behavior the caregiver wants to stop. Of course, if the caregiver succeeds in distracting the child, it seems as though the "redirection" worked. It does interrupt inappropriate behavior, but it creates more problems for the future.

Offering new toys and changing activities is part of a caregiver's job. But caregivers need to attend to a child *before* the baby gets into trouble or becomes bored with what he or she is doing. By changing activities or offering toys while a child is behaving *appropriately,* caregivers strengthen positive behaviors (see Analysis 2), so that "discipline" is rarely, if ever, needed.

8.2.3 The Trouble With Timeout

"Timeout" refers to procedures in which a child is removed from a group. Usually the child is asked to sit where he or she can watch the other children. In most uses of timeout, the child may rejoin the group after a specified time period or as soon as he or she is behaving appropriately again.

Timeout came from the laboratory. In a typical experimental setting, a pigeon worked in a box, receiving food for pecking a key. Timeout consisted of some conspicuous change in the environment (usually a light going off) during which time the food hopper was turned off, so the pigeon could not get grain for pecking. When the light came back on, the pigeon again had the opportunity to earn grain. The distinguishing features of true timeout are therefore (1) a clear stimulus or sign that (2) reinforcement is no longer available for working. In the laboratory setting, the animal was never removed from the apparatus.

Since timeout did not require harming an animal in any way, it seemed to be a punishment method that might be appropriate with children. But changes were made in the application. There was no way to disconnect the reinforcement dispenser in a group of active children. So instead of a pause in activities, the child was removed from the group.

Timeout Compared With Redirection

Timeout proved to be punishment for children just as it had for animals. One study in a center for one-year and two-year-old babies compared timeout with *redirection*. The timeout procedure involved having children who disrupted group activities go to the periphery and sit and watch for a brief period. When caregivers used timeout, disruptive behavior fell to less than half the levels that occurred during the "redirection" phases. (Porterfield, et. al, 1976) In addition, six raters listened to tapes of the play periods, and all six judged the center more pleasant during the times when disruptions were handled by timeout rather than redirection.

Why, when timeout is effective, is it not recommended as a treatment for inappropriate behavior? There are two parts to the answer. First, timeout may not involve physical harm to a child, but it is still punishment, with all the damaging by products. Second, judging from current regulations in licensing standards, inhumane procedures can occur under the name of timeout.

Timeout is Punishment

Punishment is applied to reduce or eliminate behavior. We have seen that a caregiver may *intend* to reduce a behavior, for example, by "redirection, but actually strengthen it. In that case, the procedure redirection, is reinforcement, not punishment. Timeout, however, usually reduces the behavior it follows and therefore is a punishment technique. Unlike ignoring a behavior, (which also weakens it), timeout requires doing something to the child. Usually caregivers physically remove the child to a timeout chair or playpen, or area of a room set aside for the purpose. While such an action is usually less harmful than inflicting pain, it still involves physical contact with the child (making it possible to lift the child roughly), and like any punishment technique, can cause counterattack, resentment and insecurity.

Timeout and Regulations

Timeout seems to have become a popular punishment method. It is mentioned by name in many licensing standards. So are restrictions on its use. Even before the word had become popular, separation from a group had been used as punishment. In fact, severe punishments, such as solitary confinement in prisons, or confinement in a closet, differ from traditional timeout only in the extent of separation and time left alone. If a child is to be removed from a group, where do you put him or her? Suppose the child does not stay in a timeout chair, or at the edge of a group from which he or she was removed. In the study described above, a playpen was used for such circumstances. The playpen was also used for quiet play, so that it would not be associated just with punishment, but it still posed physical barriers between the child and others.

Most licensing standards which mention timeout require that a child be within sight of an adult at all times during the separation period. Some regulations specifically mention places that cannot be used. For example, the U.S. Army (1988) regulations state that "Highchairs will not be used for discipline purposes." (p. 4–8) California (1989) prohibits confinement to cribs, high chairs, playpens, or other similar furniture or equipment as a form of discipline or punishment. (Issue 399)

Regulations also place limits on the amount of time a child can stay in timeout. Arizona (1988) specifies "When a child is isolated from other children for unacceptable behavior, the isolation period shall not be longer than three minutes after the child begins to gain control or composure, but under no circumstances longer than ten minutes without personnel/child interaction using methods described in this section." (p. 20) The U.S. Army (1988, Draft) specifies that the "use of time out methods, e.g., chair, will not exceed one minute per year of age. (p. 4–8)

Unlike redirection, timeout procedures do work to decrease the frequency of inappropriate behaviors. But because the procedure is a punishment procedure, and shares the disadvantages of punishment, we cannot recommend it as a discipline method.

The methods of discipline we recommend were illustrated in the narrative with the biting incident and with the screaming baby. They are included in many licensing regulations as recommended methods, and are involved in the almost universal goal of helping children to develop "self-control" or "self-discipline".

ANALYSIS 2: SELF–DISCIPLINE

When we say that a child shows good self-control or that he or she has the ability to be self-disciplined, we mean that a child behaves appropriately in a situation where other children might not. No one considers it self-control when an infant operates a moving toy, appropriate though that might be. But when a hungry infant sits quietly while food is being brought and does not struggle, whine, or cry, that's likely to be called self-control. When a toddler asks for a toy instead of grabbing it away from a smaller child, or goes around him instead of pushing him out of the way, we say he is showing self-discipline. He is behaving better than most children would in such a situation.

Self-control and self-discipline are the effect of a child's shaping history. In the preceding chapters of this book, we have discussed at length how to build appropriate behaviors. By teaching appropriate behaviors, you are automatically teaching a kind of self-control, since sharing, taking turns, cooperating, and so on, require a child to give up something he or she wanted. Still, we have not dwelt on what to do when you encounter inappropriate behavior. The procedures differ somewhat depending upon whether the behavior appears for the first time, or whether or not it is a persistent, frequent problem.

8.3.1 The First Time an Inappropriate Behavior Occurs

When a child bites, or shoves, or hits another child for the first time, you are not dealing with a well established behavior. If the behavior does not bring attention, and if more appropriate behaviors do bring attention, the inappropriate behavior may very well not occur again. The key, however, is to make sure that the child is soon reinforced for more appropriate behavior. In the narrative, Kris occupied herself with dressing Leigh's hand, and ignored the biter's, Ursula's behavior, until the little girl swung her arms around. That was not outstanding behavior, but it was appropriate enough, and Ursula was clearly not getting ready to deliver another bite. Kris immediately spoke to the child, thus reinforcing her body movements and then took her over to dance. The narrative described a first instance of biting. Ignoring it, while reinforcing other behavior, could thus suffice.

For more persistent biting, however, ignoring the behavior and waiting for something better to reinforce may not prevent the behavior from reoccurring. For one thing, although *you* may ignore the biting, the child who is bitten probably will not. A cry of pain or surprise may serve as reinforcement, as may a toy or equipment relinquished by the victim.

Still, punishment is not necessary. But rather than just handling the situation on the spot, a persistent problem requires a more comprehensive program of treatment.

8.3.2 Designing a Program
to Handle Persistent Inappropriate Behavior

The example of Lorraine, the screaming baby, illustrated a persistent inappropriate behavior. Clearly, simply ignoring the behavior would not make it go away. More had to be done. First, Ruth used the technique of reinforcing incompatible behavior—something the child could not do at the same time as scream. Initially, Ruth looked over at the child when she drew in a breath for a scream because that was the closest to appropriate behavior the baby exhibited. By consistently attending to Lorraine's least vigorous cries, she managed to get the baby to stop crying within about twenty minutes.

But Ruth did not stop when she had handled the immediate problem.

Instead she drew up a Plan of Care for Lorraine. She looked at Lorraine's records to find any information which could help prevent Lorraine's crying. In this episode, increasing the frequency of feeding helped. In other cases, other notations might provide ideas of programs to try. For example, a child who has a record of biting usually bites more at some times of the day than others. (See Appendix B: DYK 8.1) Records will show not only when the child is likely to bite, but the activities during which the problem occurs most. A different planned activity at the "danger" times can help caregivers build alternative social behaviors. Or perhaps, at a peak time, children can be temporarily positioned in the room so that fewer are located near the biter and his caregiver, enabling the caregiver to make sure that appropriate behaviors receive attention. Records can reveal many approaches to reducing the likelihood of inappropriate behavior, so that alternative behaviors can be strengthened. Persistent problems require more than reacting to each occurrence. They require a long term strategy for change.

8.4 SUMMARY

When a person talks of "disciplining a child," most people imagine punishment being metered out. Indeed, punishment has been used for inappropriate behavior since the beginning of mankind. But punishment has damaging side effects. For onlookers, a caregiver who punishes is, whether she likes it or not, modeling methods of social interaction. Most caregivers would not want to teach children to use corporal punishment or time-out or withdrawal of privileges with each other. Yet even young children tend to imitate, and they pick up the methods of control used by adults. For the punished child, the effects are even worse. Punishment produces many undesirable behaviors, ranging from aggressive acts to withdrawal and fear.

But discipline does not require punishment. Discipline refers, ultimately, to adhering to standards of behavior, that is, to behaving appropriately. All of the techniques discussed in previous chapters thus contribute to discipline in that they help children learn to behave appropriately. In fact, by teaching appropriate behavior, a caregiver creates the kind of self discipline recommended in state licensing standards.

Still, caregivers will undoubtedly encounter some inappropriate behaviors. In this chapter we looked at how to handle such problems without using punishment. By shunning punishment in favor of preplanning to avoid problems and careful attention to contingencies of reinforcement, caregivers can change the kinds of things children do, so that they learn to interact more effectively with others.

Chapter Nine

DESIGNING A PROGRAM
FOR PLAY AND BEYOND

NAOMI, PATRICK'S GRANDMOTHER, VOLUNTEERS
AND LEARNS ABOUT THE CENTER'S PROGRAM
FOR BEHAVIORAL CARE

OBJECTIVES

After you have read this chapter you should be able to . . .

1. List requirements for volunteers at a licensed center.
2. Describe the components of a program for infants and toddlers.
3. Explain the purpose of a Unit Board.
4. List criteria for the selection of toys and material for infants and toddlers.
5. Select routine activities to teach verbal behavior.
6. Describe why the positioning of toys for infants is important.
8. Draw up a schedule of play activities for infants or toddlers
9. Describe how you would interest infants and toddlers in books.
10. Explain several ways a center can teach infants and toddlers about music.
11. State the long term effects of quality child care for the participants and the nation.

In Chapter Two we described how Ruth, the program supervisor of Infant and Toddler Center USA, told the "new" parents, Robert and Alison about the center's philosophy of teaching appropriate behavior. The reader may recall that Robert and Alison were both surprised and a little taken back. When they had talked together about placing their soon to be adopted baby, Teddi, in a licensed child care center, like many parents, they were concerned about her being well cared for in the sense of being, fed, changed, played with, talked to, loved and so. They had not thought at all about a center staff teaching her to behave. Although they found it an intriguing idea, they also found it a frightening one.

Caregivers teach the infants and toddlers in their care how to behave each time they interact or fail to interact with them. Behaviors such as clinging and refusing to let go, crying to get things, throwing toys, and spitting out food are often unintentionally taught by well meaning staff. Many caregivers do not know how babies learn to behave and are not trained in even the basics of behavioral care. So perhaps Robert's and Alison's reaction was reasonable and well founded.

But as we have shown infants and toddlers can "rather easily" be taught to behave appropriately, and correspondingly caregivers can "rather easily" be taught the components of behavioral care. Teaching appropriate behavior is the basic tenet of behavioral care, and the contingencies of reinforcement are the means through which behavior is taught and learned. By using the positive methods for behavioral care described in previous chapters, caregivers can teach their babies all the appropriate behaviors that make infants and toddlers so adorable and loving. Thus the time spent in the center for the children and their caregivers, can not only be a pleasurable experience for them both, but can give our youngest citizens a good start in life.

In the Narrative that follows we will see how Ruth, the program supervisor of Infant and Toddler Center USA, tells a "new" volunteer, Naomi, about the center's program and activities through which caregivers teach, and infants and toddlers learn appropriate behavior.

9.1 NARRATIVE: NAOMI, PATRICK'S GRANDMOTHER, VOLUNTEERS AND LEARNS ABOUT THE CENTER'S PROGRAM FOR BEHAVIORAL CARE

Naomi was familiar with the content of written programs for infants and toddlers. (see Table 9.1) Although she had preferred family type care to center based care, she had decided to cooperate with her daughter, Claire, and help her find a suitable center for the baby she had been expecting. Before Patrick, Claire's baby, was born, Naomi had called every local facility, and requested they forward to her their pamphlet for prospective parents and a copy of the current program. She and Claire had spent many hours studying the information, and Naomi believed she had learned a lot about the language used in center literature. Her friends were somewhat surprised about her new vocabulary. She enjoyed impressing them by speaking about quality care indicators, child/staff ratios, and developmentally appropriate activities and practices for infants and toddlers.

TABLE 9.1: SAMPLE PROGRAM STANDARDS
(OREGON,1988)

The Program means all activities and care provided for the children during their hours of attendance.

(1)   The center shall provide a written program of activities for each group of children according to their ages, interests, and abilities.

(2)   The program schedule shall be planned to provide:

(a)   Positive learning experiences appropriate to the individual developmental needs of children in care;

(b)   Regularity of such routines as eating, napping, and toileting with flexibility to respond to the needs of individual children;

(c)   A balance of active and quiet activities;

(d)   Individual and group activities;

(e)   Daily indoor or outdoor activities in which children use both large and small muscles;

(f)   Periods of outdoor play each day when weather permits; and

(g)   Opportunities for a free choice of activities.

(3)   The program as implemented, shall reflect the written program plan.

Each infant and toddler shall be:

(a)   Allowed to form and follow his or her own pattern of sleeping and waking periods;

(b)   Given opportunities during each day to move freely by creeping and crawling in a safe, clean, open, warm, and uncluttered area.

On the days when Naomi picked up Patrick at the center, or made other visits there, she had learned about caregiving routines. She had observed the caregivers caring for the infants in various situations, at different times throughout the day, and felt she had a good idea about the organization of the center.

Although she had been reluctant to admit it, Patrick had thrived at Infant and Toddler Center USA. Everyone said how adorable he was, and how talkative he was for his age. At first she was startled when she heard her self saying, "All the babies at *Patrick's* center are like that."

Claire was surprised and pleased with Naomi's positive statements. But when Naomi told her that she had spoken to Mikki about working as a volunteer at the center, Claire knew that she still had a lot to learn about her mother.

9.1.1 Orientation to Caregiving

Despite the fact that she was familiar with the center, and knew the staff and the babies in Unit 1#, Naomi was nervous about her first volunteer session. Ruth had told her that she did not need Mikki's usual preliminary orientation, which was designed to give basic information. She had been in and out the center for over a year, and had attended several center Advisory Board meetings with Claire, so she already knew the center's policies. But she had been required to go to Mikki's office and read and sign for the state's booklet on Child Abuse and Neglect. Thinking about the possibility of something happening to one of the babies while she was assisting in their care had made her worry about the responsibility she was taking on. She had discussed her fears with Ruth who had told her that her fears were legitimate and that many people were concerned about infant and toddler safety. (see Appendix B: DYK 9.1) Ruth assured her that as a volunteer at the center she would *not* be counted in the staff/infant ratio and would be working at all times under her direction and supervision.

"Also," Ruth had said, "there are many other things you can do to help, apart from directly assisting with the care of the babies."

When Naomi walked into Unit #1, the staff complimented her on her suitable attire. Naomi always looked immaculately dressed and elegant. But she usually wore clothes that were unsuitable for caring for infants and toddlers, such as fashionably cut wool suits, silk shirts, and linen dresses. Since Ruth had suggested she wear something washable, she had gone shopping. Today she was wearing a sample of her purchases; an A-line jean skirt, a soft cotton sweat shirt with pink and blue rabbits across the front, and low heeled white leather loafers.

Ruth greeted her. "I have been thinking about your program orientation and have designed something new. I have been meaning to make up one of these for some time, now." She pointed to a four feet by four feet white board covered with writing mounted on the wall near the diapering room. (see Table 9.2)

"This is what I call a Unit Board. There is one in each unit. It lists the caregivers and their infants and contains pertinent information about each baby." Ruth said.

Naomi could see that Ruth had used colored felt pens to highlight information. The dates of birth (DOB) were written in blue, the times of arrival and departure in green, allergies in red, type of diaper in purple, brand of formula in orange, and the rest of the information about feeding was written in black.

Ruth explained further. "The caregivers do not use the Unit Board. They already know most of what is on here. I made it for visitors, substitutes, or volunteers like yourself. As it gives an overall view of each baby, it saves pulling out records to learn about each baby's routine care. I hope you will find it helpful."

Naomi studied the Unit Board.

"Yes, I believe it will," she said. "I can see already which formula each baby takes. Having it all here will save me asking questions about who gets what."

9.1.2 Sanitizing and Arranging Toys and Materials

Ruth pulled on her rubber gloves and suggested that Naomi help her sanitize the toys.

"We are not permitted to do major cleaning jobs . . . except spills and such . . . when the infants are present. But we do sanitize the toys. Janet, our consultant nurse, recommends that we sanitize each toy that a child has mouthed before another child picks it up. Many states are beginning to require sanitizing any toy mouthed by one baby before another plays with it."

Ruth pointed to a yellow pail on top of the toy shelf. "The caregivers place the mouthed plastic toys in that pail, and the first person with free time sanitizes them. We also sanitize the little plastic baskets after each use. They are the ones we put the toys in for the infants for individual play. Come on, let's take them to the sink and I'll show you what we do." Ruth took down the pail and picked up a stack of small colored plastic baskets.

Naomi looked at the toys which half filled the bucket, and said, "Some days when everyone is busy, the soiled toys must mount up. It's just as well you have plenty of toys."

"We are required to have at least three age appropriate toys for each infant under two, but we have many more. There are so many great toys

TABLE 9.2: PART OF A UNIT BOARD INFANT AND TODDLER CENTER USA UNIT #1

CAREGIVERS: Amanda: 7:0 AM - 2:45 PM: Marilyn: 2:45 PM - 6:30 PM

INFANTS:	PATRICK DOB	TINA DOB
ARRIVAL:	7:10 AM	7:45 AM
DIAPERS:	center	center
	cloth d. service	cloth d. service
PLASTICS:	parent	parent
FORMULA:	Similac +	Infamil
BREAKFAST:	center	home
	cereals all fruits	
LUNCH:	center	center
	all vegs chicken beef	all vegs fruits
ALLERGIES	NO	NO
PACIFIER:	No	No
DEPARTURE:	5:45 PM (Mother)	6:0 PM (Father)

INFANTS:	MARK DOB	RUSSELL DOB
ARRIVAL:	8:0 AM	8:15 AM
DIAPERS:	center	center
	cloth d. service	disposable
PLASTICS:	parent	
FORMULA:	Infamil +	Infamil +
BREAKFAST:	center	home
	cereal bananas apricots	
LUNCH:	center	center
	peas beans s. potatoes	all fruits + vegs
ALLERGIES	NO	NO
PACIFIER:	Yes: Type: Nuke	NO
DEPARTURE:	6:15 PM (Mother)	6:30 PM (Father)

on the market. If you shop around you can get them at a good price. For people in our line of work, it is hard to resist buying them. The parents too, give us toys." Ruth led Naomi towards the sink. Ruth took a clean bucket and started mixing the disinfecting solution. "Each day we make a fresh solution of a half cup of bleach to a gallon of water." (California, 1987) Ruth placed the toys into the bleach solution. "We leave the toys soaking for a minute or two before rinsing them well in warm water."

"Do you want me to bring in the large plastic baskets?" Naomi asked. "I know you keep all the same type of toys together."

"Good idea, we'll sanitize them too." Ruth replied, "You're right, we keep the grasping toys like rattles in the yellow basket, the nesting toys like the graduated bowls in the blue basket, the stacking toys like the blocks in the white basket and so on. I guess you have also noticed that the baskets are labeled so you don't have to remember what goes where."

"Yes. That will be a big help." Naomi said. Then she walked towards the toy shelves to collect the baskets.

"On your way back," Ruth called out, "bring the plastic place mats. They are under the shelf. The babies used them this morning and we may as well sanitize them too."

Naomi returned with the large baskets and mats. "I love the simple lines and bold colors of these mats." Naomi said as she handed Ruth the stack of plastic place mats. "The babies enjoy looking at them so much."

Ruth smiled. "I like some of the Disney characters, but I think I prefer the dinosaurs. Brontosaurus was Patrick's favorite. Before he could even sit up he would lay on the floor and study the Brontosaurus. Do you remember?"

"I do indeed." Naomi replied. "In fact, I bought him one of those dinosaur towels . . . the Brontosaurus of course. It started a fad with the grandmas in my set. They all thought it was a novel idea to use a clearly illustrated towel as a wall hanging for their newest grandchild."

"They're washable," Ruth said, "and like the illustrated pot holders the babies like to look at, they can be easily sanitized in the washing machine."

"Do you launder the cuddly toys?" Naomi asked.

"Yes, every toy we have here is washable and easily sanitized. I would not allow anything else. I also *hate*," Ruth said with emphasis, "home made toys. I discourage the caregivers from making them by requiring to see plans, samples, and a rationale for their use, before I give my approval." (see Table 9.3)

"Good." Naomi said. "I've seen a lot of shoddy home made toys. You cannot be too careful about the toys and materials that infants use. If I were responsible for the toys in a center, I would insist that they be safety tested and designed especially for infants and toddlers. (see Appendix B: DYK 9.2)

The soaking time for the toys was up, and Ruth gave Naomi a pair of rubber gloves and asked her to rinse the toys in warm water and place them in a drying rack at the side of the sink. Then as Naomi worked, Ruth explained to her the center's approach to teaching verbal behavior.

9.1.3 Using Routine Activities for Teaching Verbal Behavior

"An important part of our program," Ruth began, "involves verbal behavior. We want the babies to learn to understand what we say and to begin to talk themselves. We often talk to the babies about what is happening around them, so that they will learn words related to their everyday care."

"Yes, I know." Naomi replied, "It has worked very well with Patrick. He can name so many things. He even holds out his hands and says 'wash' when he is finished eating."

"Yes, he does very well. I love the way he calls me Wooof." Ruth said.

"Wooof," Naomi replied, "It sounds almost like a dog's bark, but I guess it's close enough."

"It is better than some names I have been called." Ruth saw Naomi make a funny face, and quickly added, "No, I don't mean those kinds of names. In one center a baby called me "Nanana." She loved bananas and every time I fed them to her I said the word, 'banana' and talked about bananas. The baby learned to say "nanana" as soon as she saw a banana or smelled banana baby food. One day I went out of town. When I walked into the center the next morning, the baby started clapping her hands and singing out "Nanana." I turned to the staff and jokingly said, "Didn't you feed her yesterday?" They all laughed and said, "That is not what she means. She thinks that Nanana is your *name too.*" Yesterday, when we were getting ready to go outside for a walk, she saw your scarf hanging over one of the strollers and started chanting "Nanana," and looking around for you."

Ruth laughed and looked at Naomi. "Right there I realized that although I had taught all the babies everyone else's name, they had not used *my* name enough for the babies to learn it. So now we all use each other's names often."

TABLE 9.3 A SAMPLE MEMO TO STAFF ON TOYS AND MATERIALS

MEMO TO STAFF: REQUIREMENTS FOR TOYS AND MATERIALS

From the Program Supervisor

There are a lot of toys and materials on the market. Many are suitable for infants and toddlers. Most are attractive and reasonably priced. Staff suggestions and rationale for the purchase or making of toys and materials should be written and given to the program supervisor.

1. Toys should be:

    a. Safety tested   c. Easy to clean and sanitize

    b. Non toxic   d. Designed to meet an objective(s)

2. <u>Staff made</u> toys and materials must:

    a. Meet professional standards in safety, construction, and all patterns and printing must look professional.

    b. Fit within the center's purchase and cost policy (This was included in your staff orientation packet and can also be obtained from the director).

    c. Be made to a written Toy and Material Plan approved by the program supervisor. A Toy and Material Plan should include:

        (a) Objectives and positioning (if applicable)

        (b) A written description detailing: material, measurements, colors, safety features, and ease of sanitation

        (c) A sample or Illustration: picture or drawing: scaled down layout: print ... type, size, spacing

Remember: The program supervisor is professionally accountable for the toys and materials used at Infant and Toddler Center USA . No toys or materials are to be used without her prior approval.

The toy and basket sanitizing was finished, so Ruth and Naomi walked into the activity area of Unit #1. Ruth introduced Naomi to Daniel. He was just learning to stand and was using the barrier around the crawling area to pull himself up and down. When Ruth entered he caught her eye and smiled. Ruth returned the smile and said.

"Daniel, this is Naomi." She repeated the name, "Na-o-mi," and clapped out the three syllables as she did.

She then turned to Naomi and joked, "We wouldn't want him to call you "Nanana"

Naomi smiled and wondered what the babies would do with her name.

Talking To Babies

Ruth explained, "If we say too much, too quickly, at one time to the babies we make it harder for them to distinguish one word from the other. It would be like us listening to rapid Russian. So we talk to the babies often, but in simple sentences, and we repeat the key words that we want them to learn. Here is a memo that covers our approach." (see Table 9.4)

Ruth pointed to the memo. "Here, under 'What to do', we give examples of how to help infants learn to name objects in their environment. Look at number two. What might you say to an infant when you are putting on his boots?"

"Well," I could say, "Patrick, let's put on your boots. Here are your *boots.*"

"Good," Ruth said. "You've got the idea. Let's see. We've covered sanitizing toys, and talking to the babies. Next, we should discuss play."

9.1.4 Play

Ruth led Naomi over to the file cabinet and pulled out a copy of the state's licensing standards. She flipped the pages quickly and found the section she wanted to show Naomi. "See," she said "our licensing standards specify that infants shall not remain in their cribs when awake, except for a short period of play that does not exceed fifteen minutes."

"That's no problem at *this* center," Naomi replied, "I don't think I have ever seen a baby left in a crib to play."

"No, here cribs are for sleeping. We do let our very young babies look at crib mobiles for short periods and occasionally place a gym in a crib

TABLE 9.4: A SAMPLE MEMO TO STAFF TEACHING VERBAL BEHAVIOR

MEMO TO STAFF: TEACHING VERBAL BEHAVIOR

From the **Program Supervisor**

From a very early age, infants are capable of responding to the spoken word. To help infants learn to identify people and objects in their environment, the following suggestions are offered:

What To Do:

1. Speak in simple, but complete sentences, repeating important words, and pointing to or touching the corresponding object : "See your fingers." (Showing the baby his fingers, repeat "fingers".)

2. Describe or talk about events in the infant or toddler's environment: "Tina and Patrick have their bottles." "Amanda washed Mark's hands." "That's generous, you shared your toy."

3. Ask the babies questions which give them an opportunity to show what they have learned, giving help if needed. "Gregory, what is this?" Holding a ball (pause) "This is a ball." (for a toddler) "Where's your coat? Is it in the closet?"

4. Explain what you are going to do before doing it. "Russell I will dance with you, after I talk to Woodrow." "Kayla, I am going to get your yellow cap, then we will go outside." "I am mixing the cereal for Brett's breakfast. "

5. Encourage babbling and talking by answering or responding with smiles, cuddles, speech, or by repeating what the baby said.

6. Pick certain words that you are going to work on at particular times, rather than working on everything all the time.

for a baby to use. But we want the babies to engage in lots of different activities and we like to move them from one to the other before they tire of a position or a toy. Also the babies enjoy watching each other play and, of course, we want to supervise what they do. So it benefits the babies and helps the staff to have awake babies here in the activity room rather than in the nap/sleeping room. Oh! while I think of it, you might like to have a copy of this memo I made for staff on the positioning of toys." Ruth took the memo out of the file cabinet and gave it to Naomi. (see Table 9.5)

Positioning of Toys

"You can see," she continued, "that we follow infant development research and place toys in positions that let the babies focus on them easily. Mobiles look nice hanging high over the center of the crib, but the infants aren't likely to see them there, and they wouldn't be able to focus on them if they did. So we put the mobiles on the side the infant usually faces and close enough so they can see them clearly."

Naomi pointed to the heading *Toys for the Hand Watcher,* and said, "I think I can tell a hand watcher. When Claire was little, I was holding her in the kitchen one day, when she flung out her hand. Suddenly she turned her head and stared at her hand as though it were something extraordinary. Then she moved her hand, examining it like some kind of scientist looking at a prized specimen. I hadn't noticed her watching her hand before. It was a dramatic change." Naomi sighed. "I wish I had known then all of the things I'm learning now."

Small and Large Muscle Development

Ruth smiled sympathetically. "Me too. I didn't know much about development when my teenagers were little." Her tone became more businesslike. "Some activities help small muscle development and others strengthen large muscles. Both are necessary so we do make sure to do a variety of activities. We play movement games even with the tiny infants. You've probably seen us do it. The babies enjoy it and love us to move their limbs in, then out, and up and down."

"Yes, it's fun to do." Naomi replied. "I took Patrick to a gym program at a community college. It was organized for babies and grandparents."

"Those intergenerational programs are becoming popular." Ruth said. "I have visited a few."

"You can learn a lot from what other people do." Naomi commented.

Ruth agreed, then added, "It is important to have unstructured exercises too. That's why we have the crawl area with open space for crawling. Then, of course, we have the outside play area that the toddlers like so much."

TABLE 9.5: A SAMPLE MEMO TO STAFF ON POSITIONING OF TOYS

MEMO TO STAFF: POSITIONING OF TOYS

From the Program Supervisor

Remember: Babies change very quickly during the first year of life. A toy that is suitable to a three month old baby may not be suitable for one who is six months old.

Toys for the Looker: Looking behaviors, especially looking at other people's faces and her own hands, are the first signs that a baby is attending to things in her world. Although babies are traditionally bought rattles as their first toy, a mobile is a more appropriate choice.

Using A Mobile {For the baby between three and nine weeks}

1. Babies this age rarely look directly over head. About four out of five babies look to the right most of the time, so a mobile is best positioned to the baby's far right. At times babies will shift their head position and turn to their far left. If a baby tends to favor the left side place the mobile to the left. A mobile on both sides is a good idea.

2. Babies this age do not focus well on objects that are closer to them than eight or nine inches, or farther away than about sixteen or eighteen inches. So a mobile is best positioned between ten to thirteen inches away from the baby's eyes.

3. Babies this age like to look at faces, especially the eyes and nose, and they respond to bold colors and areas of high contrast. The design of the mobile should reflect this preference.

Using a Mirror: A mirror is another suitable crib toy. Choose a good quality, unbreakable mirror that is at least six inches in diameter. It is best positioned just out of the baby's reach ... seven to eight inches away from his or her face, and placed on the side the baby favors.

Toys for the Hand Watcher: A baby who becomes a hand watcher shows that he or she is now visually ready to look at small nearby objects. From this point on, the baby will not only look, but will also touch. The beginning touches often consist of striking or batting objects with a fist.

Using batting toys: Although fisted hands restrict hand activity, objects within striking distance should be provided. Make sure that crib toys such as stuffed

TABLE 9.5 (Continued)

animals, rattles and beads, pot holders, are <u>not</u> attached to a crib, playpen, or stroller with string, elastic, or ribbon that may entangle a baby.

Toys for the Reacher: Touching leads to reaching. The baby continues batting and banging with a fist, and progresses to bringing both hands towards the object, clasping them together or fumbling to grasp it.

Using reaching toys: Small, attractive, safe objects, within reach of the baby can be suspended across the crib. Objects suspended by strings swing freely when hit. So it is better to use a semi rigid mounting that permits the object to yield when struck and return to its place when untouched. A toy that produces a noise when struck is recommended. Make sure that crib gyms are installed securely so they can not be pulled down into the crib. Make sure all toys are removed from cribs and playpens when babies are nap/sleeping.

Note: Visually directed reaching can be identified by offering the baby a small object ... for safety's sake larger than one and a half inches ... on the favored side and about five inches from the face. If the baby brings her hand directly to the object and either begins to open or close it just before contact and grasp, she has acquired the skill.

(Information taken from an article in American Baby, 1986, by Dr. Burton L. White, the Director of the Center for Parent Education and the author of the First Three Years of Life.)

Outside Activities

"Everyone enjoys going outside," Ruth continued, "even if it is only for five or ten minutes. When the weather is nice, we stay out longer or go out both in the morning and in the afternoon."

"I know the babies love to go for walks. I've noticed that even the little ones show excitement when they see the strollers or their jackets and caps." Naomi said.

"Yes," Ruth replied, "and the toddlers enjoy playing on the outside climbers and slides. Of course, we must watch them carefully. We do not want any accidents. If you would like to help later, we can always use another hand strolling the infants or helping the toddlers on the outside equipment."

"Maybe later," Naomi said. "I think I'd be more comfortable reading to the babies."

"Great," Ruth replied, "the babies love to be held while we read to them. Another lap is more than welcome."

9.1.5 Book Sharing and Reading With Infants and Toddlers

"Do you know what my first impression of the center was? Naomi asked Ruth.

"A bee hive," Ruth guessed.

"No," Naomi laughed and said, "It was the babies looking at books. The first time I came here with Claire, two of them were lying on the floor and each was looking at one of those big soft cotton books. Another was in a playpen looking at the accordion type that open up into a long strip. I had never seen babies look at books for such a long time. I thought they were all professors' babies."

"No, not at all. We teach the babies to take an interest in books. Right from the beginning we hold the babies and read to them even for just a few minutes. When they start to look at the pictures we talk to them about what they're seeing." Ruth pointed to a small set of shelves above the big bean bag in the corner. "Here, we keep the books that *we* read with the babies. The other books that the babies handle by themselves are over there in the toy shelves."

Naomi said, "When Claire was a baby I could not have held her, and read a *good* book to her the way you all do here. She was more interested in pulling and tearing the pages than at looking at the pictures or listening to the words."

"You know, when my own children were little, I had the same experience. But now I know that you can teach an interest by setting up the antecedent conditions beforehand and responding to babies when they show an interest by pointing or babbling. Before long books *become* interesting to them."

"What kind of antecedent conditions?" Naomi asked.

"Well, for one thing, we choose a time when a baby has been active and is ready to sit for awhile. Then we pick a book we know the particular baby would like. Even young babies show preferences for some pictures over others."

"I see what you mean." Naomi replied. "Patrick became interested in and learned to like music here."

9.1.6 Learning About Music

"We always start the morning with music, as you know." Ruth explained. Naomi nodded. "Surprisingly," Ruth said jokingly, "we call it morning arrival music."

Morning Arrival Music:

Ruth continued further, "We wanted some songs that had a nice rhythm for moving and dancing. We also wanted songs that the babies could learn to recognize. So I picked out two tunes that had different themes and rhythms. I'm sure you know them. One is the Winnie the Pooh song, and the other is an oldie called the Sidewalks of New York. We play these tunes continually from 7:00 AM to 9:00 AM."

"Oh yes, I know them." said Naomi. "All the parents know them *now*. I remember wondering why you played the same thing over and over. In fact, I asked Amanda whether the staff didn't get sick of it."

"What did she say?" Ruth asked.

Naomi replied, "She said that at first they liked the tunes and thought the lyrics were funny. About the time the staff began to tire of them, they started to hear encouraging stories from the parents. Several parents told the caregivers about how, when they pulled into the parking lot, their babies started moving backwards and forwards in their car seats as soon as they heard the music. One mother left her baby with her sister over a long weekend. The sister wasn't used to babies, and the baby cried nearly all the time. On Monday, she had trouble getting him ready, and he cried over breakfast and all the way to the center. When she reached the parking lot the baby heard the sound of the music, and stopped crying. Then, to the sister's relief and amazement, he started a sing-song babbling and began clapping his hands. He came into the center red-eyed from the crying, but smiling and swaying in time to the rhythm."

They both laughed. Then Naomi asked, "You remember how excited Claire was when Patrick showed he could tell Winnie the Pooh from other tunes, don't you?"

"You mean what happened at the mall?" Ruth asked.

"Yes," Naomi said, "there was music playing and Patrick ignored it. But all of a sudden Patrick began jouncing up and down, and Claire became aware that Winnie the Pooh was playing. She was thrilled that Patrick had recognized the piece, and even more pleased when she realized that he was clapping in time to the beat. He was only nine months old, you know."

Naomi continued, "Amanda said that the parents all wanted to get a copy of the song and asked for the words. Before long, even the parents played the tape as they drove to work. It started a Winnie the Pooh craze. Many parents brought books, and Winnie the Pooh stuffed animals and wall hangings. Now the Winnie the Pooh song seems to be the theme song here.

"That's true," Ruth said. "I suggested a contest to choose new morning arrival songs but the staff and parents protested and all said, 'No! We like the ones we have!' Anyway, the children hear other music the rest of the day."

Background Music and Dancing Throughout the Day

"I've noticed that you play a variety of types of music." Naomi said.

"Yes, we all have different tastes in music." Ruth replied, "When the arrivals are over, the staff choose the music they like. We bring in our own tapes. Priscilla likes country, Eve favors a honky tonk piano, Amanda is a jazz addict, and Mikki prefers classical. I know I surprised everyone when I brought in my rock and roll tapes."

"I guess they expected you to bring in some more Disney tunes." Naomi teased. Then she said, "I like softly playing background music and the babies seem to like it too."

"We turn it up a bit louder when opportunities come to dance with the babies," Ruth said. "We all love to dance with them and do so almost as soon as they are inside the door. When we dance they can feel us move in rhythm with the music. Pretty soon, when you hold them, you feel their little bodies starting to move in time to the beat too."

"Yes, that's another thing I never thought about doing with Claire when she was a tiny baby." Naomi told Ruth. "But when I saw everyone here dancing with the little ones, I started to dance at home with Patrick. I enjoy it as much as my grandson does. You know, in the beginning, I wasn't in favor of center care for Patrick. Now, I believe differently. You all have opened my eyes to a lot of ways to play with and enjoy babies."

Ruth smiled and said. "We appreciate the well chosen toys you so generously donated. In fact, it sounds as though the babies are using the bells and shakers right now. Would you like to have a closer look at the individual musical activities we do with them?"

Naomi agreed and they both walked towards the sound of the shakers and bells.

Using Hand Instruments such as Bells and Shakers

"The babies seemed to learn to use the hand instruments easily." Naomi said.

"Yes. It was almost a natural progression for the babies." Ruth explained. "They were used to moving to music. Susie even moved her head in time to the beat. Of course, they do not always keep the beat as you will see. When we teach them rhythm we use music that matches the natural rhythm of a child's hand movements. That way they can be more successful in shaking the bells in time to the music."

"They are having great fun learning." Naomi said, looking at the children. "See how that little boy is concentrating."

"That's Benjamin. Yes, he really tries to keep in time. Some of the others just like to make lots of noise. But even they speed up or slow down according to the tempo."

"The instruments that you gave us helped. Because they were especially designed for infants, with soft plastic rings and firmly embedded bells, the children can handle them easily. Then too, the fact that they were designed for safety means that we can allow the babies to use the instruments in their own ways. Most people don't think about it, but drum sticks or handles of many instruments can poke an eye or go down a throat. And parts of other instruments might come loose and get swallowed. But a baby can shake, bang, and move a specially designed instrument up or down as he wishes."

"It pays to use properly designed toys." Naomi agreed.

Ruth continued. "Sometimes we have the babies play together. Amanda calls it giving a concert."

"A concert?" Naomi asked. "You mean they play for somebody?"

"Not usually, but if you want they might play for us now." Ruth spoke to Amanda. Can we have a concert?"

Amanda nodded and asked, "Who wants to do a *concert.*" Two babies bounced up and down. The other two turned to look at the "audience".

Amanda explained, "They love to perform."

Then she smiled at the babies and said, "O.K. Let's get ready." The babies looked at Amanda. They had done this many times, and waited for her to say, "1, 2, 3, Start." All four babies started shaking or banging their instruments. Amanda waved her hands like a conductor for a few moments, and then said "1,2,3 Stop." The sounds of the instruments slowly came to a halt. The babies looked at the audience and started clapping. The caregivers smiled and joined in the applause. While Mikki bent down to talk to the group of little performers, Ruth turned to Naomi and said, "Amanda is really so pleased that the babies are not only enjoying playing the instruments, but are also learning to follow directions so well."

Amanda laughed, "They are eager to start, but they are reluctant to stop."

Naomi squatted beside Mikki and said to the babies, "Well that's the shortest, but nicest concert I have attended. Thank you all."

"Well if you enjoyed that, you'll love the toddlers." Amanda told her. "They have learned to stop as well as start, and they even do solos where they take turns playing."

Musical Instruments and the Sounds They Make

Amanda continued the music activity. She held out her hand to collect the instruments and the babies all handed them over. On the table next to the tape player lay a trumpet and Amanda picked it up. Noticing Ruth's inquisitive look she said, "It's mine. I play jazz trumpet, and I thought I'd let the babies hear what it sounds like."

Ruth said, "Just don't scare them."

Amanda made a face at her, pretending to be insulted. "Actually, I play rather well." She turned to the babies. "This is a trumpet." She put the instrument to her lips and played a soft low note, then ran up a scale.

"Maybe this is the right time for me to leave," Naomi teased.

"Maybe." Amanda replied as she held out the bell of the trumpet for the babies to feel. "But you're not getting out of it so easily. Claire told me you play the violin."

"Did she? Do you know she plays the harmonica?" Naomi asked.

"Good." Amanda quickly said. "I'll put you both on my list."

"What list." Ruth asked?

Amanda stood up and replaced the trumpet on the table, "The list of performers and instruments," she replied. "We're planning to bring in musical instruments so the babies hear how they sound."

Ruth said, "By the way, do you know I have a snare drum and some bongo's at home. I haven't played them in years, but I could dust them off."

Amanda picked up Emily, one of the musicians, and as she walked towards the crawling area she said. "Can I take that to mean I have another instrument to add to my list?"

"Sure, why not." Ruth said. She was more than happy with the initiative the staff showed in expanding and organizing the musical activities to include this component.

9.1.7 Contingent Reinforcement

Ruth looked at the clock it was getting near lunch and time for Naomi to leave. Without saying anything to each other, they both started towards the staff room where Naomi had left her coat and pocketbook. Each was pleased with the morning's orientation and when Naomi had collected her things Ruth walked her to her car. As they crossed the parking lot Ruth said, "Naomi you know the center has a philosophy of teaching appropriate behavior to the infants and toddlers. Do you know what we mean by teaching?"

"I think I do," Naomi replied. "I have heard you all say often enough that you reinforce appropriate behavior, and those are the behaviors the babies learn. It is the reinforcement that increases the probability that the appropriate behavior will occur again."

"I couldn't have said it better myself." Ruth said. She paused before she continued. "The timing of the reinforcement is critical."

"I know." Naomi told her. "It is contingent on the baby's behavior, and it must be given while the appropriate behavior is still occurring. I learned how to teach appropriate behavior by observing what you all do here." Naomi laughed before she said. "Then I tried it out on Patrick. It worked! That's what made me decide to ask Mikki about becoming a center volunteer."

"Well I'm glad that you did." Ruth replied. On that note they parted both looking forward to the next session.

9.2: ANALYSIS 1: THE CARE OF INFANTS AND TODDLERS IN CHILD CARE CENTERS

Throughout this book we looked at the care of infants and toddlers in a center based environment specified by state standards under which a licensed center must operate. We examined the standards from the point of view of the routine care procedures they generate, and saw how the selection of actions that make up procedures, can increase or decrease care loading. We illustrated how task/time plotting can be used to gather information about what caregivers and their babies do, when they do it and how long it takes. We showed how information gathered by such directed observation can be used to preplan routine care. We also showed how the information can be used to change the sequence of actions in a procedure, and streamline tasks to reduce routine care loading, thus enabling caregivers to have more time for the behavioral care of their babies. (see Analysis 2, for a final discussion of behavioral care)

We will use Analysis 1 of this chapter, to examine some broader concepts that underlie licensing standards, and will discuss (1) how these concepts were activated, and (2) how they impact the care of infants and toddlers in child care centers.

9.2.1 Current Socio-economic Variables that Affect Many of Our Youngest Citizens

Whether or not infants and toddlers should be cared for in child care facilities was once a hotly debated issue. As late as the beginning of the eighties, most people frowned at the thought of a working mother leaving her young baby in a child care center. In fact many states prohibited center care for children younger than the established state definition of a preschooler. For the poor and those from ethnic backgrounds, child care was an extended family arrangement. For the wealthy it was an in-home luxury only the privileged few could afford (Woolsey, 1977). But today as we enter the nineties available, affordable and reliable nonparental child care is a necessity that the majority of families need. Many parents, both male and female must work to support or help support their children. Young teen-age mothers depend on child care to enable them to complete their education and or enter the workforce. While for others child care is the means that lets them follow a chosen career or live a lifestyle that a single income could not provide. In the United States, within the past two decades, many socio-economic changes have occurred. (see Appendix B: DYK 1.1) These changes have altered not only *who provides* for our nation's children, but *who takes care* of them. Although a large proportion of children of working parents are still cared for by family members, the number of licensed centers and family type child care facilities has steadily grown.

National Concern for Our Children and the Future of Our Country

Despite the shocking socio-economic conditions in which many of our youngest citizens live we have some reasons to be optimistic for the future. Children's advocacy groups not only have a long history of being concerned about the plight of the nation's children, but have an outstanding history of doing something about it. (see Appendix B: DYK 9.3) Recently their efforts have been strengthened by a large group of corporate and academic leaders known as the Committee for Economic Development. This committee published a landmark report called *Children in Need* (Committee for Economic Development, 1987). This was the first report by a major business organization to address the need for a national campaign to provide support for disadvantaged children in order to break the cycle of welfare dependency. (Butler, 1987)

A main point of the report stressed that the health and social development of poor infants and toddlers are crucial factors in their readiness for formal schooling. In line with this point two recommendations were made. One applied to disadvantaged mothers and called for prenatal care, parent training and further education. The other applied to disadvantaged infants and children up to the age of five years; and called for improved infant care, easier access to child care services, as well as quality pre-school programs for all disadvantaged three and four year olds.

Future Employability and Early Intervention Services: In April 1985, a group of Minneapolis business and community leaders made similar recommendations to those of the Committee for Economic Development. (Minneapolis Community Business Employment Alliance (McBA) 1985). This group had formed a task force to study the problems related to the city's unemployed population. They concluded that the employment training for the unemployed or potentially unemployed, that traditionally began when they were in their teens or older, began too late. Instead they advocated prevention of future unemployability by early intervention rather than later training and stated:

> A sense of responsibility and an interest in learning, for example, begin to develop in the first three years of life. Thus employability becomes a continuum of step-by-step emotional, psychological and intellectual learning that begins at birth. (p. 17)

Accordingly they recommended that high quality child development services be made available to young children, (from birth to five years) who come from low income families.

Good News About the Long Term Effects of Early Childhood Programs

Several studies that investigated the effects of early educational intervention for disadvantaged preschoolers, have shown that quality child care can help children overcome the disadvantages of being born into poverty. (Consortium for Longitudinal Studies, 1979; Weikart, 1981, 1984; Maeroff, 1985); Scholastic benefits for children who attend preschool, compared to those who do not are better grades and fewer absences in elementary school; less need of special education services; and a greater likelihood of completing high school and continuing with further education. (Endelman, 1989) What is even more encouraging is that the benefits to the children and thus eventually the nation exceed the cost. One estimate is that $1 invested in preschool education returns $6 in taxpayer savings. The savings result from lower education and public welfare costs, reduced crime rates and higher worker productivity.

However, as stated in Appendix B: DYK 6.3, the results of studies on the effects of center care on infants and toddlers have varied. Some show the superiority of home care, others show the superiority of center care. But as we pointed out, one reason no clear cut results have emerged is that researchers have not looked at the *contingencies* in effect in the centers investigated. This will be discussed further in Analysis 2.

9.2.2: The Influence of
the National Association for Education of Young Children

The question of whether or not infants and toddlers should be cared for in child care facilities is no longer relevant. The relevant question *now* is *how* they should be cared for. Accordingly, the debate on one hand, has moved to issues related to quality care, and on the other hand to issues related to adequate compensation for caregivers and affordable child care for parents. (Willier, 1988) Although the monetary issues have not yet been resolved, a reasonable consensus about the components of quality care has emerged. (Kagan, 1989)

During this century views on how young children should be cared for in child care facilities have radically changed. In many states, less than a decade ago, child care meant only protective care. But today, as explained in the introduction to the Alabama (1988) standards:

"As our knowledge and understanding of young children has increased, the focus of child care has shifted towards programs which provide growth and learning for children in their physical, emotional, social and intellectual development." (p. 5)

Programs, such as those referred to in the Alabama standards, that take into account the total development of the child are called developmental. Although becoming rare, care that provides only for the protection of children is called custodial. (U.S. Navy, 1983).

Developmental Programming

The swing from custodial care to developmental programming was initiated by the child oriented organization known as the National Association for the Education of Young Children (NAEYC). (see DYK 1.4) NAEYC (1987) sponsors the definition of a high quality early childhood program as:

"One that meets the needs of and promotes the physical, social, emotional, and cognitive development of the children and adults—parents, staff, and administrators—who are involved in the program." (p. 7)

The prominent role played by NAEYC in changing the focus from custodial to developmental care can be seen in the content of state licensing standards. Most have incorporated in their standards NAEYC's definition of a high quality early childhood program. Increasingly state standards refer to the social and emotional development of the child, mention developmental programming, and use the NAEYC coined term developmental appropriateness (which is considered a critical indicator of quality care, see Table 1.3) when specifying activities, materials, and caregiver expectation of children's behavior. (see Table 9.6)

Following the concept of developmental programming, there is an increasing tendency to include in the program both the routine care procedures and the developmental activities a center provides. (Oregon, 1988) This transition was facilitated by NAEYC's foresight in initiating program accreditation on a national level.

Criteria for High Quality Early Childhood Programs

Bredekamp (1987) says "one of the most ambitious initiatives that the Association has ever undertaken was launching the National Academy of Early Childhood Programs in 1985." (p. ix)

TABLE 9. 6: SAMPLE PROGRAM STANDARDS RELATED
TO DEVELOPMENTAL APPROPRIATENESS

Kentucky,1988 : The day care center shall provide planned program activities geared to the individual needs and developmental levels of the children served. (p.12)

Arizona, 1988: Teacher-caregivers shall provide infants with a variety of age appropriate toys, sights, sounds and textures suitable to their level of development. (p.11)

West Virginia, 1988:   The program conducted in a day care facility shall provide experiences and equipment appropriate to the age and stage of development of the individual child. (p. 24)

U.S. Navy, 1983: Each program shall provide developmentally appropriate activities for each age group which promote the intellectual, social, emotional and physical development of the children. (p.14)

Virginia, 1988: The daily program for children shall provide experiences which promote growth, well-being, and the age-appropriate development of gross and fine motor skills, language skills, cognitive skills, social and emotional skills, positive self-concept, curiosity, interest , and exploration. (p.33)

U.S. Marine Corp, 1983: Developmental care should be offered in a prepared environment to children receiving full-day or part-day care. (p.2.)

New Mexico, 1987: Each facility must offer children activities and experiences which are developmentally appropriate and which promote positive growth and well being in the areas of social,emotional, physical, and intellectual development. (p.48)

The Academy categorized early childhood programs into ten components. (see Appendix B: DYK 1.5) The standards by which these components are judged are referred to as criteria, and "represent the current consensus of the early childhood profession regarding the definition of a high quality program for young children." (p. ix).

Caldwell, 1984, says the criteria not only had to specify standards to judge the program components, but had to allow for the philosophical diversity that exists among early childhood professionals. The aim she explained was to:

"Formulate criteria which are general enough to cover different types of settings, yet specific enough to be objectively observable: which are precise enough to convey the true meaning of each component, yet comprehensive enough to allow for individual variations. We have not attempted to impose a narrow stereotype of quality in early childhood programs. Rather, we have identified specific aspects of program realities which respect the diversity of educational philosophies without compromising what we know to be the developmental needs of young children." (Foreward) (see Table 9.7)

To formulate criteria to not only judge program components but to allow for philosophical diversity is a difficult task. In Chapter One when we talked about specifying an environment for behavioral health we referred to the program components and said,

"While in most respects, the National Academy of Early Childhood Programs presents valuable components, it has not been precise enough in specifying the kinds of interactions needed for the behavioral care of infants and toddlers. Possibly for this reason behavioral health is adressed in some state standards in only the most general terms." (p. 20)

To illustrate our point we stated that caregivers are usually told to "promote the child's positive self-image" or to "foster a sense of independence" as though everyone would know how to accomplish these goals. We also asked the reader to imagine a caregiver with four babies who wishes to work on building "positive self-esteem," and asked, "What exactly is she to do.?" (see Appendix B: DYK 9.4)

We speculated that the lack of precision in specifing the kinds of interactions needed was due to two factors: (1) The principles governing how behavior evolves have not yet become widely known. (2) It takes time for information from research to be applied and thus an information lag exists. To these two factors we can now add a third and that is: (3) Allowance for philosophical diversity.

TABLE 9.7: SAMPLE CRITERIA FOR HIGH QUALITY EARLY CHILDHOOD PROGRAMS NAEYC (1987)

A-5: Staff encourage developmentally appropriate independence in children. Staff foster independence in routine activities such as picking up toys, wiping spills, personal grooming (toileting, hand washing), obtaining and caring for materials and other self help skills. (p. 9)

A-9: Staff foster cooperation and other prosocial behaviors among children. (p. 10)

B-1: The curriculum is planned to reflect the program's philosophy and goals for children. (p. 11)

B-5: Developmentally appropriate materials and equipment which project heterogeneous racial, sexual, and age attributes are selected and used. (p. 12)

B-6: Staff members continually provide learning opportunities for infants and toddlers, most often in response to cues emanating from the child. Infants and toddlers are permitted to move about freely, exploring the environment and initiating play activities. (p.13)

B-11: Routine tasks are incorporated into the program as a means of futhering children's learning, self-help, and social skills. Routines such as diapering, toileting, eating and dressing, and sleeping are handled in a relaxed, reassuring and individualized manner based on developmental needs. Staff plan with parents to make toileting, feeding, and the development of other independent skills a positive experience for children. Provision is made for children who are early risers and for children who do not nap. (p.14)

Caldwell 1984, in the quote cited above pointed out that no attempt was made to impose a narrow sterotype of quality care, rather specific program realities were identified which respected philospophical diversity without compromising what was known about the developmental needs of young children.

For those concerned with quality care for infants and toddlers allowance for philosophical diversity is an interesting issue that raises some critical questions, for example, "Is allowance for philosophical diversity a quality indicator or an indicator of quality problems."

Throughout this book, while allowing for the *developmental* needs of young children, we have emphasized and described the components of *behavioral* care. Teaching appropriate behavior, is the basic tenet of behavioral care and the contingencies of reinforcement are the means through which behavior is taught and learned. The contingencies of reinforcement (the ABC's of Behavior) are to behavioral care, what developmental appropriateness is to developmental care. As the timing of reinforcement is a critical factor in teaching appropriate behavior, the word "precise" becomes an important element. As behaviorologists we believe that the components and criteria related to the behavior or interactions between the caregivers and the children for whom they care must be precisely specified.

As we mentioned in Chapter Seven, although the fields of development and behaviorology have different names, they are simply different ways of looking at the same change and growth over time. While development focuses on the characteristics which are typical of most children at each age, behaviorology explains how behavioral changes occur. However, in the area of the development of individual behavior, the two fields merge. The physical development of an individual depends upon factors in the environment, and an individual's social development cannot occur without interaction with other people. Thus development requires learning, and learning results in development.

In the coming decade of the nineties and beyond, the two fields of development and behaviorology, will have the opportunity to work closer together. This opportunity has been made possible through another innovative step by the National Association of the Education of Young Children, namely professional preparation for caregivers.

Professional Preparation For Caregivers

Child care is an example of an industry where professionalism is just starting to emerge. (Woolsey, 1977) The National Association for the Education of Young Children together with the federal government, made the first move to lift the nonparental care of children out of the category of a cottage industry by establishing a national system for credentialing those who care for young children. Now with the increasing tendency of parents to place their young children with family type providers or in child care centers NAEYC once more is a forerunner. To meet the demands of the future a Child Development Associate Credential Professional Preparation program specifically designed for currently employed child care workers, or individuals who have no experience or wish to become trained in child care work is geared for implementation. (see Appendix B: DYK 9.4)

The curriculum for this new national training program was designed by staff and consultants from the Council for Early Childhood Professional Recognition. The instructor's manual lists topics to be covered, but how and when they will be covered is left up to the instructor. The instructors must come from state recognized post secondary institutions, such as vocational-technical schools, junior, community and four year colleges. The selection of institutions to carry out the CDA Professional Preparation Program will be based on a letter of intent sent to the Council by the institution. This letter of intent is actually a proposal which must include specifications of the program objectives, content, time framework and staff qualifications. Once more, the National Association for Early Childhood Education has made allowance for philosophical diversity. It is possible that behavioral care will be incorporated with developmental care. It is also possible that behavioral care will be recognized, in the history of child care during the twentith century, as the second major shift in the care of our youngest citizens.

9.3 ANALYSIS 2: BEHAVIORAL CARE

The opening statement in Chapter One referred to how the quality of care the children, who comprise our next generation, receive sets a foundation for both their physical and behavioral health. As we mentioned there has been much debate about what comprises quality care and we defined it as, "care that ensures the physical health and development of the child, and which provides experiences and interactions for behavioral health." The experiences and interactions that provide for behavioral health we have referred to as behavioral care. If caregivers are to provide behavioral care they need to be trained to use the behavioral methods described in this book, and they also need the time to apply them. We have described how routine care loading can be reduced through the design and streamlining of procedures and how parents can be asked to help. Both parent participation and reduced routine care loading give caregivers the time they need to provide for the behavioral care of their babies.

9.3.1: The Basic Tenet of Behavioral Care: Teaching Appropriate Behavior

What babies do in a center is what that center environment is teaching them to do. The behavior of the children in a center is not only a quality indicator, it is also the quality control for the basic tenet of behavioral care, namely the teaching of appropriate behavior. A child's behavior is evidence whether or not a caregiver is teaching the child to behave appropriately.

We have stressed that every interaction, or lack of interaction between a caregiver and a baby affects the way that baby will behave in the future. Thus we agree in essence with the statement made in the report by the Minneapolis Community Business Employment Alliance (1985), that "employability becomes a continuum of step-by-step emotional, psychological and intellectual learning that begins at birth." But, as we hope our readers now recognize, we would phrase it a little differently. "Employability," we would prefer to say, "becomes a continuum of behavior-by-behavior that can be specified and learned from birth." We also agree with our nation's economic and academic leaders, as well as the members of the many children's advocacy groups, that early intervention programs should be made available to the majority of our youngest citizens.

But we do disagree with child care professionals who oppose structured learning experiences for infants and toddlers. As we stated in Chapter Six all of the goals promoted for quality child care programs such as co-operation, sharing, independence, curiosity, self-esteem, can be analyzed into their component behaviors and taught behavior by behavior. Not only can these behaviors be taught, but they can be taught through the use of positive reinforcement that makes learning a pleasurable experience, and the use of any punitive measures, even the frequently recommended timeout, unnecessary. We recognize that many child care professionals who oppose structured learning experiences for young children do so because they do not want children subjected to "pushing" and this is a valid concern. Others believe that focusing on skills is detrimental to motivation. (Elkind, 1988)

"Pushing," is related to the consequences that follow a behavior, rather than the components of the task itself. As we have emphasized throughout this book the behaviors that are shaped and reinforced are the behaviors the children learn. If a caregiver reinforces playing a baby is more likely to play; if a caregiver reinforces whining (by attending to it) a baby is more likely to whine.

Without "pushing," that is by not using punitive methods, and by using the positive methods recommended in this book it is possible to have, happy, curious, confident, co-operative, and competent young children. Children whose behaviors are positively reinforced learn to like what they do, and are more likely to repeat those behaviors. For example young children whose book looking and book handling behaviors are reinforced want to look at and like to handle books. We tend to say that young children who look at and handle books are interested in books or motivated to read. Interest and motivation are produced by the positive reinforcement that follows behavior and are not necessarily directly related to unstructured experiences. Since reinforcement can be designed and changed, an interest such as an interest in books, or an interest in playing with toys can be produced as a behavioral product of a individual's reinforcement history.

Not that we recommend it for young children, but it is possible for children, or adults for that matter, to enjoy doing tasks that are recognized as difficult. Stewart (1977) gave children the option of reading text that was considered difficult for them, and reading text that was considered easy for them. When given positive reinforcement, both social and tangible (green labels that said "good work this is difficult reading"; and extra points that could be spent later in activities such as typing, art, cooking) for selecting the difficult text the children did so. Further they read the difficult material without showing the "symptoms of reading difficulty," such as crying, stuttering, refusing to read, that children under the usual punitive methods used in the school system exhibit. This study showed that the children's behavior was dependent upon the consequences that followed the reading of the text, not the level of difficulty of the reading material. It demonstrated once again that reinforcement contingencies influence the acquisition and maintenance of behavior.

The Scientific Foundations For Behavioral Care

This last statement brings us to the validity of the research basis that underlies the teaching of appropriate behavior and the contingencies of reinforcement through which behavior is taught and learned. The scientific foundations of teaching appropriate behavior which give it the status of an applied behavioral science came originally from work done in the laboratory. (see Appendix B: DYK 7.2) By the 1960's, researchers had begun to apply the basic principles of behaviorology to human behavior. It became increasingly clear that contingencies of reinforcement determined many complex properties of behavior as well as more simple ones. Behavioral methods, both in research and applied settings, have repeatedly demonstrated their effectiveness.

9.4: SUMMARY

The need for behavioral training and for information about licensing standards became apparent to the senior author of this book when she worked for ten months as a program supervisor in an infant center. Since then, the authors have visited many centers. They have consistently noted a need for training in behavioral principles and in the licensing standards that regulate the environment in which caregivers work. This book was written to provide that information. It not only describes behavioral care, but shows precisely how to provide it while designing and selecting procedures which meet or exceed licensing standards. Caregivers will now have available the information they need to arrange the best possible interactions for the infants and toddlers under their care.

REFERENCES

All references to state, territory and military standards can be found in Appendix A.

Axelerod, S., Apsche, J. 1983. The Effects of Punishment on Human Behavior. New Jersey: Academic Press

BankAmerica Foundation. 1987. California Child Care Initiative Program Summary. San Francisco (5 page leaflet)

Belsky, J. 1986. Infant Daycare: A Cause for Concern? Zero to Three, 6 (5), p. 1–7.

Bond, James, T., Lovejoy, Meg, 1988. Mothers in the Workplace Working Paper. The Role of Managers/Supervisors in Easing Work-Family Strain. New York: National Council of Jewish Women.

Bredekamp, S. (Ed.). 1987. Accreditation Criteria & Procedures of the National Academy of Early Childhood Programs. Washington DC: National Association for the Education of Young Children.

Butler. 1987. Zero to Three.

Caldwell, B. 1984. Accreditation Criteria & Procedures of the National Academy of Early Childhood Programs. Washington DC: National Association for the Education of Young Children.

California Task Force to Promote Self-Esteem, and Personal and Social Responsibilit. (no date). Goals and Objectives. Information Paper.

Cherlin Andrew. J. (Ed.). 1988. Changing American Families and Public Policy. Washington DC: The Urban Institute Press

Child Care Action Campaign Information Brochure. (no date) New York

Child Care Action Campaign. (no date). Examples of Employer Involvement in Child Care Assistance. (5 page leaflet)

Child Care Employee Project. (CCEP) (no date). Information Brochure: Berkley

Children's Defense Fund. 1988. What Every American Should Be Asking Political Leaders in 1988. Washington DC: Children's Defense Fund

CDA National Credentialing Program (1989). The Child Development Associate Credential. Washington DC: CDA National Credentialing Program

CDA National Credentialing Program. (no date) Improving Child Care Through the Child Development Associate (CDA) Program. Washington DC: National Association for the Education of Young Children

CDA Professional Preparation Program. 1989 April. Competence, vol 3, No. 3. p. 1–4.

Child Welfare League of America. 1983. Standards for Day Care Service. New York: Child Welfare League of America, Inc.

Child Welfare League of America. 1988. The Children's Presidential Campaign '88 Issue Briefs. New York: Child Welfare League of America, Inc.

231

Children's Defense Fund. (no date). Alliance for Better Child Care: Washington, DC: Children's Defense Fund.

Children's Defense Fund. (no date). Information Brochure. Washington, DC:

Children's Defense Fund. 1987. Summary of the Act for Better Child Care Services of (HR. 3660 and S. 1885) Washington, DC:

Children's Market. 1988 Winter. Canada:

Children's World Learning Centers. Information Packet. Philadelphia: ARA Services Inc.

Committee for Economic Development. 1987. Children in Need. Investment Strategies for the Educationally Disadvantaged. New York: Committee for Economic Development.

Consortium for Longitudinal Studies. 1979. Lasting Effects After School Final Report to Education Commission of the States. New Jersey: Lawrence Erlbaum Associates

Consumer Reports. 1989 February. p. 124

Elder J. 1988. The Super Baby Burnout Syndrome. Education Week

Edelman, Marian Wright. 1989 Spring. Economic Issues Related to Child Care and Early Education. Teachers College Record, vol 90, No. 3

Elkind, D. 1988 February 3. The "Miseducation" of Young Children. Education Week

Erikson Institute. 1987–1988. Annual Report. Chicago: Erickson Institute for Advanced Study in Child Development.

Evans, Sandra. (no date) United States Marine Corps Child Care Program. (5 page leaflet).

Farber, E.A., Egeland, B. 1982. Developmental Consequences of Out-Of-Home Care for Infants in a Low Income Population. In E. Zigler & E. Gordon (eds), Day Care. p. 102–125. Boston: Auburn

Garbarino, James. 1987. Preventing Childhood Injury: Developmental and Mental Health Issues. Chicago: Erickson Institute for Advanced Study in Child Development.

Haskins. R. 1985. Public School Aggression Among Children With Varying Day-Care Experiences. Child Development, 56, p. 689–700

Hutchinson, R.R. 1977. The By Products of Aversive Control. In Honig, W.K., Staddon, J.E.R. (Eds) Handbook of Operant Behavior. Englewood Cliffs, New Jersey: Prentice-Hall.

Howes, C., Stewart, P. 1987. Children's Play with Adults, Toys, and Peers. An Examination of Family and Child Care Influences. Developmental Psychology, 23, p. 423–430

Jacobson, Lauren. (no date) Children's Art Hazards. New York: The Natural Resources Defense Council, Inc.

Juvenile Products Manufacturers Association (JPMA). Brochure (no date). Be Sure It's Safe for Your Baby Pamphlet #984

Kagan, Sharon, L. February, 1989. Early Care and Education: Tackling the Tough Issues. Phi Delta Kappa. p. 433–439

Koek, Karin., Bayles, Susan. (Eds). 1988. Enclyclopedia of Associations. 22nd Edition. vol. 1. p. 7262–3. Detroit: Gale Research Company.

La Petite Academy. 1988. Annual Report. Kansas City

Learning About Labels. (no date) New York: Toy Manufacturer's of America, Inc.

Maeroff, Gene, L. 1985 October 2. Training Parents Helps Toddlers. New York Times.

Minneapolis Community Business Employment Alliance. 1985. Preventing Unemployment: A Case for Early Childhood Education. Minneapolis: Minneapolis Community Business Employment Alliance

NAEYC Brochure (no date). Washington DC: National Association for the Education of Young Children

NAEYC. 1988. Early Childhood Program Accreditation. Washington DC: National Association for the Education of Young Children.

National Center for Clinical Infant Programs. (no date) Washington DC: (1 page leaflet)

National Commission on Working Women of Wider Opportunities for Women: 1989 Spring–Summer. Women at Work Newsletter. Women Work and Child Care. Washington DC:

National Council of Jewish Women, 1988–89. Mothers in the Workplace. New York: National Council of Jewish Women

New York Times, 1988 Sunday June 26. Looking for Profits in Puppets and Play Doh. p. 10

Neifret, Marianne R., Seacat, Joy, M. A. 1986 July. Guide to Successful Breast-Feeding. Contemporary Pediatrics, vol 3. p. 1–1

Parents as Teachers. (no date) Facts About Missouri's Parents as Teachers (PAT) Program. Jefferson City: Missouri Department of Elementary & Secondary Education.

Phillips Deborah, McCartney Kathleen, Scarr Sandra. 1987. Child Care Quality and Children's Social Development. Developmental Psychology, vol. 23, No. 4, p. 537–543.

Porterfield, J., Herbert-Jackson, E., & Risely, T. 1987. Contingent Observation: An Effective and Acceptable Procedure for Reducing Disruptive Behavior of Young Children in a Group Setting. Journal of Applied Behavior Analysis. vol 9, no. 1, p. 55–56

Random House College Dictionary. 1982. Revised Edition. New York: Random House. p. 378

Reese, Hayne W., Lipsitt, Lewis P. Experimental Child Psychology Academic Press, New York: 1970

Sagan, Leonard, A., 1988. Family Ties: The Real Reason People are Living Longer. The Sciences. p. 28–29

Solomons, Hope C., Elardo, Richard. 1989. Bite Injuries in Day Care Centers. Early Childhood Research Quarterly, Vol. 4, p. 89–94

Stewart, Bernice. Analysis of Children's Reading Behavior As Controlled By Level of Difficulty of Reading Material and Reinforcement History. Unpublished Doctoral Dissertation. West Virginia, 1977.

Toy Manufacturers of America. (no date) The ABC's of Toys and Play. New York: Toy Manufacturers of America, Inc.

United States Air Force. 1987 November. Background Paper on Air Force Child Development Program (2 page leaflet)

United States Army. 1989 March. *Child Development Services (CDS)* Information Paper (4 page leaflet)

United States Navy. 1989 February. *Child Development Programs* Information Paper (3 page leaflet)

U.S. Consumer Products Safety Commission. (no date) Buyer's Guide. The Safe Nursery. Washington DC.

U.S. Department of Health Education and Welfare: Office of Child Development. (1971) Abstracts of State Day Care Licensing Requirements. Washington DC: DHEW Publication

U.S. Department of Health and Human Services: 1985. Model Child Care Standards Act—Guidance to States to Prevent Child Abuse in Day Care Facilities. Washington DC: U.S. Government Printing Office.

U.S. Department of Health and Human Services. 1986. A Report to the Congress: Joining Together to Fight Child Abuse. Washington DC: U.S. Government Printing Office.

U.S. Department of Labor. 1988. Report of the Secretary's Task Force. Child Care: A Workforce Issue. Washington DC: U.S. Government Printing Office.

Vargas, E. 1989. Verbal Behavior: Mediated and Mediating Relations in a Four Term Contingency Paradigm. Paper Presented at the Northern California Association for Behavior Analysis.

Wall Street Journal, July 19, 1988. p. 1

Working Mother Magazine. 1988. Reader Survey.

Weikart, David, P. 1981. Effects of Different Curricula in Early Childhood Intervention. Educational Evaluation and Policy Analysis, November–December, vol. 3, No. 6 p. 25–35

Weikart, David, P., et al. 1984. Changed Lives: The Effects of the Perry Preschool Program on Youth Age 19. Monographs of High/Scope Educational Research Foundation, No. 8. The High Scope Press.

White, Burton L., 1987. The Learning Experience How to be a Better Teacher to Your Child *American Baby*, p. 107–114

Williams Christopher, 1987, Dumping Diapers, Doula Magazine

Willier, Barbara, A. 1988. The Growing Crisis in Child Care: Quality. Compensation, and Affordability in Early Childhood Programs. Washington DC: National Association for the Education of Young Children.

Woolsey, Suzanne. 1977 Spring. Pied Piper Politics and the Child Care Debate. Daedalus, vol. 106, No. 2, p. 127–145.

Zero to Three Special Reprint. 1986. Infant Day Care: A Continuing Dialogue. Washington DC: NCCIP (16 page bulletin)

APPENDIX A:
NAMES OF LICENSING AUTHORITIES
AND LICENSING BOOKLETS

Alabama Department of Human Resources: Minimum Standards for Day Care Centers and Nighttime Centers Principles Regulations Procedures 1988; 1984.

Alaska Department of Health and Social Services: Division of Family and Youth Services. Article 2. Child Care Facilities. 1988; 1985.

Arizona Department of Health Services: Office of Child Day CareFacilities. Chapter Five Child Day Care Centers; 1988. Official Compilation of Administrative Rules And Regulations. 1980

Arkansas Department of Human Services: Division of Children and Family Service. Minimum Licensing Requirements for Child Care Centers; 1986.

California Department of Social Services: Community Care Licensing Division Children's Program and Support Branch. Manual of Policies and Procedures Child Day Care General Licensing Requirements Division 12, 1988. Manual of Policies and Procedures Day Care Centers Division 12 Chapter 2.; 1989.

Colorado Department of Social Services: Division of Child Welfare Services. Child Care Centers/Less Than 24-Hour Care (Draft) 1989. Minimum Rules and Regulations for Child Care Centers; 1975.

Connecticut Department of Health Services: Public Health Code Regulations for Child Day Care Centers and Group Day Care Homes. 1988. Public Health Code Regulations for Child Day Care Centers and Group Day Care Homes; 1982.

Delaware Department of Services for Children, Youth and Their Families Division of Program Support Licensing Service: Delacare Requirements for Day Care Centers. 1988. Delacare Requirements for Sick Day Care In A Day Care Center; 1986.

District of Columbia Department of Public Welfare: Chapter 3. Child Development Facilities; 1985.

Florida Department of Health and Rehabilitative Services: Child Day Care Standards Florida Administrative Code Chapter 10M-12, 1986; 1985.

Georgia Department of Human Resources: Rules and Regulations for Day Care Centers; 1983.

Guam Department of Public Health and Social Services: Division of Social Services Child Care Licensing Regulations.

Hawaii Department of Social Services & Housing: Subtitle 6 Public Welfare Division Rules Governing Licensing of Family Day Care Homes, 1985; 1982.

Idaho Department of Health and Welfare: Chapter 2 Basic Day Care License. 1988. Rules and Regulations for Implementation and Enforcement of Standards for Licensure; 1982.

Illinois Department of Children and Family Services: Licensing Standards For Day Care Centers; 1985.

Indiana Department of Public Welfare Child Welfare/Social Services Division: Regulations for Licensing Day Nurseries; 1985.

Iowa Department of Human Services: Child Day Care Centers and Preschools Licensing Standards and Procedures; 1988; 1984.

Kansas Department of Health and Environment: Regulations for Licensing Day Care Homes and Group Day Care Homes For Children. 1987. Regulations For Child Care Centers; 1985.

Kentucky Department for Social Services Cabinet for Human Resources Division of Licensing and Regulation: Standards for All Child Day Care Facilities (Informational Copy) 1988; 1983.

Louisiana Department of Health and Human Resources Division of Health Standards: Minimum Standards for Licensure of Child Day Care Centers; 1984. Guidelines & Enrichment Booklet.

Maine Department of Human Services Bureau of Social Services: Rules For The Licensing of Day Care Centers For Children. 1987. Rules and Regulation for the Licensing of Day Care Centers for Children (Draft); 1985.

Maryland Department of Human Resources: Child Care Center Regulations For Discussion at Public Meetings (Draft); 1988. Department of Health and Mental Hygiene Code of Maryland Regulations Group Day Care Centers; 1988.

Massachusetts Office for Children: Standards for the Licensure or Approval of Group Day Care Centers; 1987.

Michigan Department of Social Services: Licensing Rules for Child Care Centers; 1984.

Minnesota Department of Human Services: Child Care Centers; 1989.

Mississippi Department of Health Division of Child Care and Special Licensure: Regulation Governing Licensure of Child Care Facilities; 1988.

Missouri Department of Social Services Division of Family Services: Licensing Rules for Child Care Centers in Missouri; 1982.

Montana Department of Family Services Community Services Division Licensing Requirements For Child Day Care Centers; 1988. Supplemental Regulations For Infant Day Care; 1988; 1984 Department of Social and Rehabilitative Services Community Services Division Day Care Licensing Rules; 1981.

Nebraska Department of Social Services: Minimum Regulations For Day Care Centers; 1987.

Nevada Department of Human Resources Youth Services Division Bureau of Services For Child Care: Regulations and Standards for Child Care Facilities; 1989; 1984.

New Hampshire Department of Health and Human Services Child Care Agency: Day Care Licensing and Operating Standards (Draft); 1988.

New Jersey Department of Human Services. Division of Youth and Family Services

Bureau of Licensing: Manual of Requirements for Child Care Centers. 1989. Manual of Standards for Child Care Centers; 1985.

New Mexico Health and Environment Department. Public Health Division. Licensing and Certification Bureau: Regulations Governing Facilities Providing Day/Night Care To Children. 1987.

New York Department of Social Services: Day Care Center Licensing Regulations; 1989; 1980.

North Carolina Department of Human Resources Division of Facility Services: Child Day Care Requirements; 1988.

North Dakota Department of Human Services Children and Family Services: Child Care Center Early Childhood Services; 1987.

Ohio Department of Human Services: Rules for Licensing Child Day Care Centers; 1986.

Oklahoma Department of Human Services Licensing Services Unit: Requirements for Day Care Centers; 1988.

Oregon Department of Human Resources Children's Services Division: Rules for the Certification of Child Day Care Centers. 1988 Rules Governing Standards for Day Care Facilities; 1979.

Pennsylvania Department of Public Welfare Day Care Division Regulations for Child Day Care Centers; 1988; 1981.

Puerto Rico Department of Health Public Welfare Division Laws of Puerto Rico. 1955. Si Va A Cuidar Bebes; 1976.

Rhode Island Department of Children and Their Families Day Care Licensing: Day Care Centers and Day Nurseries; 1984.

South Carolina Department of Social Services: Regulations for Private and Public Child Care Centers; 1983.

South Dakota Department of Social Services Child Protective Services Office Program Management: Chapter 67: 42: 10. Day Care Centers. 1989; 1983 Environmental Health Standards. 1989 Provision and Scope of Services; 1989.

Tennessee Department of Human Services: ChildCare Handbook Licensure Requirements for Child Care Centers; 1987. Standards for Day Care Centers Serving Preschool Children; 1981.

Texas Department of Human Services: Minimum Standards for Day Care Centers; 1985.

United States Air Force Headquarters Air Force Military Personnel Center: AFR 215-27 Child Development Centers; 1983. AFP 215-37 Air Force Infant Care Guide; 1983.

United States Army Headquarters of the United States Army Army Regulation 608-10 Developmental Programming Child Development Services (Draft) 1988; 1983.

United States Marine Corp: Child Care Center Policy and Operational Guidelines; 1983.

United States Navy Department of the Navy: OPNAV Instruction 1700.90 Child Development Programs; 1983.

Utah Department of Social Services Division of Family Services: Child Day Care Center Standards; 1987; 1985.

Vermont Department of Social and Rehabilitative Services Division of Licensing and Regulation: Day Care Centers; 1989.

Virginia Department of Social Services Division of Licensing Programs: Minimum Standards for Licensed Child Care Centers; 1988; 1985.

Virgin Islands Department of Human Services: Rules and Regulations for Child Day Care Centers (no date).

Washington Department of Social and Health Services: Minimum Licensing Requirements for Day Care Centers for Children. 1987. Minimum Licensing Requirements for Mini-Day Care Programs for Children; 1983.

West Virginia Department of Human Services: Licensing Requirements for Day Care Centers; 1988; 1982.

Wisconsin Department of Health and Social Services Division of Community Services: Licensing Rules for Group Day Care Centers. 1984. Proposed Order of the Department of Health and Social Service. (Draft); 1988.

Wyoming Department of Health and Social Services Division of Public Assistance and Social Services: Child Care Certification Standards. 1985. Standards and Guidelines for Child Care Certification; 1980.

APPENDIX B:
DO YOU KNOW ABOUT . . . ? (DYK . . . ?)

DYK 1.1: Workforce Trends and the Lifestyle Revolution? Today most women work in order to support themselves and their families. (National Commission on Working Women. 1989) In 1988, 60% of all children, or 35 million children had working mothers. One in every four mothers in the work force maintains her own family. Of these working women 58% are either single (never married), divorced, separated or widowed, or have husbands who make less than $15,000 a year. It is estimated that 35% more families would be below the poverty line if both parents did not work. The most dramatic increase in the labor force has been the percentage of mothers with preschool children. By 1995, two out of three preschool children will have a working mother.

DYK 1.2: The National Center on Child Abuse and Neglect (NCCAN)? The Child Abuse Prevention and Treatment Act (Pl. 93-247) was passed by Congress in 1974, and established within the Children's Bureau. The aim is to identify, prevent, and treat child abuse and neglect, and follow a helping approach to the problem. Agencies are encouraged to try to rehabilitate families rather than punish them. Grants are provided to states to help them develop or improve their child abuse and neglect prevention and treatment programs. A National Clearinghouse on Child Abuse and Neglect operates a computerized data base that collects and makes available information on research, law and court decisions, programs, materials and bibliographies. (U.S. Dept. of Health & Human Services, 1986)

DYK 1.3: The Model Child Care Standards Act: Guidance to States to Prevent Child Abuse in Day Care Facilities? The United States Department of Health and Human Services (1985) was directed by Congress to make funds available to train child care providers, staff and licensing personnel. Model Child Care Standards were distributed and recommended: (1) staff employment history checks and intensive background screening (2) probation periods for new staff to allow further investigation and on-site evaluation (3) staff qualification requirements by job classification (4) an open door policy for parental visits (5) lower infant/staff ratios (6) training and supervision that focused on the prevention of sexual abuse. Further recommendation for state standards revision included community education about child abuse and neglect, parental involvement in the care of children in child care facilities, and written information for parents about their role in preventing and reporting child abuse and neglect.

239

DYK 1.4: The Child Welfare League of America (CWLA)? The league was formed in 1926, and is concerned with the care and protection of needy children. After World War 1, the CWLA, led the move to place abandoned or orphaned children with foster parents rather than in institutions. Then during World War 2, when women entered the work force, it played a role in setting standards for quality care. Currently the CWLA advocates services for teen parents and affordable quality care child care for working parents. (Child Welfare League of America, 1988)

DYK 1:5: The National Association for the Education of Young Children (NAEYC)? This is a non profit organization that was founded in 1926. Currently NAEYC has about 68,000 members. This association focuses on two general goals. One, the dissemination of research, resource and legislation information. Two, the improvement of child care and early childhood education. To accomplish these goals NAEYC publishes books, brochures, resource guides, posters, and a journal called Young Children. An annual conference is also held. (NAEYC Brochure, no date)

DYK 1:6: Military Child Development Services? The United States Army Child Development Services manual (Draft, 1988) states that Child Development Services are a basic community support services provided for soldiers and are not intended to be a revenue producing activity. This statement reflects the purpose of all child development programs offered by the United States Armed Services. **United States Air Force (1989):** As of April 1989, 129 bases world wide operated child development programs and served approximately 44,000 children. Center care is provided for children through the ages of 2 weeks to 10 years, and family home care is provided for children between the ages of 2 weeks and twelve years. **United States Army (1989):** In the Fiscal Year 1988 over 147,000 children were served at 174 Army locations around the world. Out of the total number of children served more than 100,000 were cared for in 300 centers (approximately 25,000 at any given time). The other 47,000 were cared for in 7,897 family care homes. **United States Marine Corp (Evans, 1988):** Child CareServices that include child development centers, preschools, drop-in care, and family day care homes are offered on 17 installations to over 10,000 children. In the Fiscal year 1989 all caregivers will participate in regular training and self paced instructional training packages will be available to center staff. The use of standardized training programs will make training transferable from base to base. **United States Navy (1989):** Child development services are provided world wide at most Navy installations supporting military families. Centers offer full day and drop-in/hourly care to children from 6 weeks to 12 years. Although programs provide care for about 20,000 children in centers and family homes there are 8,000 children on a waiting list.

DYK 1:7: The National Academy of Early Childhood Programs? The Academy is an independent accrediting system sponsored by the National Association for the Education of Young Children (NAEYC). It is designed to (1) help early childhood program personnel become involved in improving the quality of programs that serve young children (b) evaluate the quality of programs for the purpose of accrediting those that comply with the specified criteria. The validation criteria are based on components that address all aspects of the program. Each has a goal statement and rationale followed by goal achievement criteria. The components are: Administration, Curriculum, Evaluation, Food Service and Nutrition, Health and Safety, Physical Environment, Staff, Staff Interactions with Parents and Children, Staff Qualifications and Development. The term developmental appropriateness related to activities, materials and staff expectation of children's behavior is used throughout the process and is considered a critical indicator of quality care. (NAEYC, 1988)

DYK 2.1: Resource and Referral Services (R+R's)? These services developed during the eighties and are generally non profit agencies, funded by state or private organizations that help parents locate and select child care services. Brochures giving parents guidelines for observing centers and deciding on the type of child care they want are usually published. Some R+R's assist providers obtain insurance, help with licensing, publish newsletters, and run workshops to train family child care providers. (U.S. Dept of Labor, 1988)

DYK 2.2: Maternity and Paternity Leave? The United States is the only advanced industrialized nation that has no national maternity and paternity leave policy. About 60% of all working woman have no paid parental leave. Such leave is usually linked to disability insurance. The Pregnancy Disability Act of 1978 prohibits discrimination due to pregnancy. If the employer provides other kinds of short term disability coverage, insured wage compensation for a 6 to 8 weeks period is required. Women who have no coverage use a combination of sick days, or leave without pay. (National Commission on Working Women, 1989)

DYK 2.3: Mildly Ill or Get Well Care? Increasingly states are formulating regulations for mildly ill, get well or sick care. This is "care that is provided in a center or part of a center to children recovering from a short term illness or temporary disability. Such care can be a primary service or a component of other day care services. (Oregon, 1988 p. 3)

DYK 2.4: The Status and Salary of Child Care Workers? The three million men and women who work in child care facilities subside the real cost of child care by working for poverty level wages and few or no benefits. Only about half of all child care workers have health benefits and not even one in five has a retirement plan. Child care workers have been cited as the second most underpaid workers in the nation. Although they have an average education level of 14 years they have a median annual income of $9,724, which puts them in the bracket of dish washers, and zoo keepers. (National Commission on Working Women, 1989)

DYK 2.5: A Study Called Mothers in the Workplace? The National Council of Jewish Women (Fall 1988/Winter 1988–89) investigated the special needs of families of working mothers. The first stage surveyed over 2,000 businesses to gather information on health insurance coverage, alternative working conditions, temporary maternity and parental leave and employer assisted child care. The second stage surveyed working women in the third trimester of pregnancy to find out how they coped with parenting and work, work routines, health related fringe benefits, their own and husband's/companion's education and background. The third stage was a follow up survey, of the pregnant mothers four to seven months after childbirth. It documented child care arrangements and how they worked out, the roles husbands/companions play in homemaking and childrearing, and the effects of work/family conflicts on job performance. Bond and Lovejoy (1988) reported that "women who have understanding and helpful husbands and supervisors are much less stressed and much more satisfied with their lives than women who lack such support at home and at work." (p. 6)

DYK 3.1: Family Type Care and The California Child Care Initiative? In 1985, the state of California, the BankAmerica Foundation, (1987) and 23 corporations formed a partnership to fund a project called the California Child Care Initiative Project (BankAmerica, 1987). The project, which works through existing non profit community based child care resource and referral agencies (R+R's), helps train and recruit family day care providers, and bring unlicensed providers under state supervision. This project has shown that if local child care child needs are targeted properly, interested people can be trained to be professional child care providers.

DYK 3.2: The Alliance for Better Child Care (ABC)? The Children's Defense Fund (1988), played an active role in the formation of the Alliance which consists of almost 200 women's advocacy, business, civic, educational, religious, service, trade and union organizations. These groups joined together to support a major child care initiative and developed legislation for a bill known as the Act for Better Child Care. Although this bill was not passed child care advocacy groups are continuing with their lobbying. They hope to eventually make available, affordable and high quality child care for working parents.

DYK 3.3: The Child Care Employers Project (CCEP)? This project was formed in 1987 by child care workers (CCEP). It is a non profit advocacy organization that works to improve the status, wages, and working conditions of the child care worker. It sponsors the position that high quality child care depends on experienced and well trained staff. Lack of benefits, low professional status, poor pay, and stressful working conditions keep qualified people from entering and staying in the field. The project works with community organizations, employers, government agencies, policy makers, unions and the media on local and national issues that affect child care workers. (CCEP Brochure, no date)

DYK 3.4: Child Care Chains? Entrepreneurs have entered the $12 billion child care business. They are able to handle the increasing insurance and operating costs that small operators cannot meet. These large companies are rapidly expanding, for example: **La Petite Academy Inc.**, which began operation in 1970 is estimated to be the second largest provider of child care and preschool education in the United States (La Petite Academy Annual Report, 1988). At the end of the report year its 9,800 employees provided services to over 70,000 children from 6 weeks to 12 years, in 64 centers in 28 states. Revenues in 1988 increased 16.8 percent going up to $152 million. A variety of services are provided including Montessori programs. Corporate care services are rapidly expanding and most of the new centers opened are on site for large corporations. **Children's World Learning Centers** are a division of ARA Services and were organized in October, 1987 by a merger of Children's World, Daybridge Learning Centers, Learning Tree, and Teaching Centers. Children's

World is one of the largest child care providers with annual revenues of $170 million. Over 60,000 from the ages 6 weeks to 12 years are served. The 453 child care centers offer a developmentally-based curriculum which allows children to learn at their own pace. (Children's World Brochure, 1988)

DYK 3.5: The Child Development Associate Credential (CDA)? This program which was started in 1971 is administered by the Council for Early Childhood Professional Recognition provides a national system for training, assessing, and credentialing center based, and family child care providers as well as home visitors. (The CDA National Credentialing Program, 1989) Since that time nearly 30,000 credentials have been awarded. But that number comprises only a small fraction of the total number of individuals working in child care that are untrained and uncertified. (see DYK 9.4)

DYK 4.1: Employer Sponsored Child Care? An increasing number of employers are providing child care assistance to their employees. These include direct services such as on-site or near-site centers, consortium centers jointly funded by private and public sources, sick child care, and family day care networks which fund training for providers and approve and monitor family type care. They also include financial assistance such as subsidies and vouchers that employees can redeem at an arranged center or a center of their choice; flexible benefits where by employees select child care among other benefits; and spending accounts and salary reduction where by employees take reduction in income and pay for child care out of a non taxable account. Other options offered are job sharing, flexitime, part time and at home work. (Child Care Action Campaign, no date)

DYK 4.2: Missouri's Parents as Teachers Program (Pat)? (Booklet, no date) Promotes parent involvement in education and is a home and school partnership designed to help parents give their children the best possible start in life. An independent research study found that children of participating families regardless of their socioeconomic background were significantly more advanced in language skills than other 3 year olds. They were also further along in social development and problem solving than their peers, and scored significantly higher on all measures of intelligence and achievement.

DYK 4.3: Child Care Action Campaign (CCAC)? (Brochure no date) The Campaign is a coalition of leaders from various organizations, whose long term goal is to use existing private and public resources to set in place a national system of affordable, quality child care. The coalition participates in national discussion about child care issues, and works as a national voice for child care providers, interested citizens, parents and children.

DYK 5.1: Chemical and Disposal Problems Related to the Use of Disposable Diapers? Disposable diapers are made of several types of refined paper products. (Williams, 1987) As they are non-recyclable, non-biodegradable, bulky and infectious, they are a serious concern of the waste management industry. Health professionals are also concerned. (Children's Market, 1988) Viral and bacterial infections are becoming more common. It is believed that many infections result from higher skin temperature, lack of oxygen, and the increased length of exposure between diaper changes, that result from the use of disposable diapers.

DYK 5.2: Councils and Committes that Provide Safety Standards? Several organizations that provide safety standards for consumer products follow. (a) The U.S. Consumer Products Safety Commission (CPSC) (Brochure, no date) is charged with reducing unreasonable risks associated with consumer products. Toy manufactures follow the CPSC mandatory Federal safety regulations, which are also included in voluntary American manufacturers safety standards. (b) The Juvenile Products Manufacturer's Association (JPMA) (Brochure, no date) is an independent group which began its Safety Certification Seal Program in 1976 with safety standards for high chairs. Manufacturers seeking the JPMA Safety Seal for their products, voluntarily submit them for testing. The JPMA Safety Seal tells the consumer that the child's safety was considered when the product was designed and built. (c) The Toy Manufacturer's of America (TMA) (Brochure, no date) promote voluntary standards and it would be unusual for an American toy manufacturer not to follow them. (d) The Natural Resources Council (NRDC) is a non-profit organization of attorneys and scientists who are supported by 65,000 members. The Council acts as an advocate for an individual's right to a safe and healthy environment. It publishes a Children's Art Hazard Guide that lists materials such as paints, adhesives, modeling clay, and dyes; and states precautions to follow in their use; checks safe and unsafe products; and recommends materials that can be substituted for hazards products (Jacobson, no date).

DYK 6.1: Passivity in Babies? Many people consider a quiet baby a good baby. But passivity may be a sign that action needs to be taken. Some passive babies fail to thrive. The typical pattern of such a child is to sleep 4 to 5 hours between feedings, to fall asleep after a few minutes of sucking, and to accept a pacifier instead of food. Because of their passive, non-demanding approach to the world, their parents do not realize that they are getting inadequate nutrition. (Neifert and Seacat, 1986) Not only physical growth, but all other development suffers when a child is passive. Children need to be active for large muscle groups to grow properly. They must manipulate objects to develop finer motor control and eye-hand coordination. To learn about their world, children need to explore and investigate, and they must respond to what goes on about them. All of this requires activity on the part of the child.

DYK 6.2: Dangerous Child Behaviors? Children put themselves at risk for physical harm by their own dangerous behavior (Garbino, 1987). For infants, squirming and rolling over can lead to falls. For mobile children, finding things to place in their mouth or nose can lead to poisoning or choking. Babies particularly 9 to 12 months place themselves at risk by ingesting plants, mushrooms, household products, drugs, cosmetics, and other objects such as cigarettes. While we would not expect these substances to be within reach in a child care center, caregivers must keep alert to the fact that a parent or visitor may lay a purse or medication down temporarily, and walk off, leaving it within reach of a child.

DYK 6.3: Studies on the Effects of Center Care? Many studies have compared the behavior of children raised at home with those that spent their early days in a child care center. The results of these studies have varied. Some studies show the superiority of home care. (Belsky, 1986); Farber and Egeland (1982). Other studies show the superiority of center care. (Howes and Stewart, 1987; Haskins, 1985) More recently, researchers have looked at factors in day care environment which are correlated with positive ratings of children's behavior (Philips, McCartney and Scarr, 1987). Still conclusions vary. One reason that no clear-cut results have emerged from these studies is that no one has looked at the contingencies in effect in the centers investigated. Caregivers in one center may attend to children when they grab or push. In another center caregivers may follow the principles outlined in this book. Experience in the first center will make children more aggressive and non compliant, whereas in the second center children will learn to cooperate.

DYK 7.1: B.F. Skinner? Skinner is the founder of the science which investigates the relationship between behavior and environment. In the 1940's and 50's he conducted extensive research on the effect of different schedules of reinforcement on the behavior of individual animals such as rats and pigeons. Of course Skinner was no more interested in rats and pigeons than a geneticist is in fruit flies. The animals were simply convenient species to investigate relationships between behavior and environment, the same relationships that occur in human behavior. Skinner found that animals did not respond in a push-button way to stimuli. Instead, behavior changed as a result of selection by consequences. Skinner spent 40 years researching the selection process, clarifying the role of antecedents as well as reinforcers on behavior. He has been a consistent voice on the harmful effects of punishment in the schools. He and his colleagues and followers have developed methods of classroom management and motivation based on positive reinforcement instead of the traditional aversive techniques commonly found in the schools.

DYK 7.2: The Association for Behavior Analysts (ABA)? This association was formed in 1980 and grew out of a regional group known as the Mid-Western Association for Behavior Analysis. The original group formed in order to promote a more behavioral approach to their science than that provided by the regional psychological association. When their conferences attracted professionals nationwide, as well as overseas, they took their current name. Members come from many different professional areas including Psychology, Education, Social Work and Behaviorology. **International Behaviorology Association (TIBA)?** This group was formed by a small group of ABA members in 1987. Its founding members wanted a professional organization devoted to promoting the science founded by Skinner. (see DYK 7.2) They also wanted a name which would distinguish that science from approaches to the study of behavior which discussed mind or cognition rather than behavior.

DYK 8.1: Bite Injuries in Child Care Centers? Bites frequently occur in child care centers. Children not only bite each other they also bite their caregivers. In a study at the University of Iowa Childhood Education Center, 133 children were studied over a 42-month period. (Solomons and Elardo, 1988) During the three and a half years nearly half of the children received human bites. Discounting accidents during which children bit themselves, there were still 171 cases in which one child bit another. Few bites inflicted serious wounds. Of the total of 224 bites which included bites through falls and insects, only four bites actually broke the skin. Most biting, among toddlers aged 13 to 24 months of age, occurred in the middle of the morning. The biters usually went for the finger, hands and arms. Interestingly, the frequency of biting was highest in September, when most of the children were admitted to the center.

DYK: 8.2: The By Products of Punishment? Numerous studies have shown that "the delivery of an intense, aversive, noxious, or unpleasant stimuli, will produce in a variety of species movement toward, contact, and possibly destruction of animate or inanimate objects on the environment." (Hutchinson, 1977 p. 418) In applied studies the administration of strong punishers such as shock produces immediate escape and avoidance behaviors. But escape and avoidance behaviors are not limited to obviously painful punishers as shock. Over correction, point fine, and loud reprimands have been reported to result in escape and avoidance behaviors. (Axelerod and Apsche, 1983)

DYK 8.3: The National Center for Clinical Infant Programs (NCCIP)? The center was founded in 1977 by a group of professionals who had assembled for a series of meetings about ways to provide for the needs of infants and their families. They had a common belief that the care every child receives during infancy can have a critical influence on that child's future functioning. They agreed that their mission was to foster healthy development in infants. To achieve their aim they provide a forum for the exchange of information emanating form clinical infant and early childhood programs, stimulate and coordinate research, and encourage training of personnel. (NCCIP Leaflet, no date)

DYK 8.4: The National Center for the Study of Corporal Punishment and Alternatives in the Schools? This center is located at Temple University. It is a tax exempt organization that is interested in the study of the psychological and educational aspects of school discipline. (Koek and Bayles, 1988) Some activities of the center are: (1) conducting research related to discipline (2) administering the Delaware Discipline Clinic for diagnosis and remediation of discipline problems in homes, schools and institutions (3) maintaining a collection of news clippings and articles on corporal punishment and other methods of discipline (4) operating a Discipline Hot Line counseling service for teachers and parents (5) presenting workshops and speeches (6) providing inservice to teachers, social workers and psychologists (7) providing legal advocacy to protest the use of corporal punishment (8) publishing papers, articles and a journal on discipline.

DYK 9.1: Erikson Institute Community Child Safety Specialists Training Program? The Carnegie Corporation of New York provided a grant to the Erikson Institute to develop a national program to train and certify Community Child Safety Specialists. The program focuses on the prevention of risk of injury* to children from: (1) assaults by familiar persons (2) attacks by strangers (3) dangerous child behavior (4) environmental hazards (5) inappropriate parenting. (*Injuries have replaced illness as the major source of death and disability for children in the United States) (Erikson Institute, 1987–1988)

DYK 9.2: How a Manufacturer Age Grades a Toy and Age Labels its Package? Much research goes into age grading a toy and assigning an age label to its package.

Manufacturers consider 4 main criteria: (1) the ability of the child to manipulate and play with the features of a toy, for example a 4 month old may grasp or fumble a soft ball, while a 3 year old can also throw and catch it (2) the ability of the child to understand how to use a toy, for example a 7 month old enjoys banging single colorful blocks, while a 2 year old is more likely to stack them (3) the play needs and interests of children at various developmental levels (4) the safety* of a toy. (Toy Manufacturer's of America, no date) (*Despite councils and committees that oversea safety standards, unsafe and dangerous toys are on the market. The Consumer Reports (February, 1989) cites 8 recalls of unsafe toys. Five of these concerned possible choking on the small parts of baby rattles and toys.

DYK 9.3: Children's Defense Fund (CDF)? Brochure, no date) The CDF is a private organization that is supported by foundations, corporate grants and individual donations. The goal of the CDF is to educate the nation about the needs of children, especially the poor, minority and handicapped, as well as to encourage preventive investment in children before they get sick, drop out of school or get into trouble. The CDF is a strong and effective voice for the children of America who cannot vote, lobby and speak for themselves.

DYK 9.4: The Child Development Associate Professional Preparation Program (CDA PP) Geared for Implementation in 1990? Trends indicate that more working parents will select out-of-home child care. So to meet the needs of the future the Council is launching a nationwide network of this one year training course. The program is designed to provide uniform and accessible training for currently employed child care workers, or persons who have no experience and wish to be trained as a child care worker. (Competence, 1989)

DYK 9.5: The California Task Force to Promote Self-Esteem and Personal and Social Responsibility? This task force is looking into the relationship between low self-esteem and many of the problems documented in the state of California. As a part of the investigation task force members plan to identify policies, programs and environments that develop healthy self esteem and ones that are detrimental to its development. The following institutions and practices were targeted for investigation: (1) prenatal care and birthing (2) infant and child care (3) parenting and parent education (4) hunger and poverty (5) physical development (6) education (7) institutionalized religion (8) prejudice and discrimination (9) justice and the penal system (10) social service systems (11) media and advertising (12) dependency creating programs (13) family violence and spousal and child abuse. This task force was formed on the premise that the future success of our democratic society is dependent upon responsible citizenship; and that a function of government is to inform and educate citizens so that they can prevent behavioral and social problems. (California Task Force Leaflet, no date)

INDEX